POLLING TO GOVERN

POLLING TO GOVERN

Public Opinion and Presidential Leadership

Diane J. Heith

STANFORD LAW AND POLITICS
An Imprint of Stanford University Press
Stanford, California   2004

Stanford University Press
Stanford, California

Printed in the United States of America on acid-free, archival-quality paper

Library of Congress Cataloging-in-Publication Data

Heith, Diane J.
Polling to govern : public opinion and presidential leadership / Diane
J. Heith.
p. cm.
Includes bibliographical references and index.
ISBN 0-8047-4848-9 (alk. paper)—ISBN 0-8047-4849-7 (pbk. : alk.
paper)
1. Presidents—United States—Decision making. 2. Political
leadership—United States. 3. Public opinion—United States. I. Title.
JK516.H3663 2004
352.23'6'0973—dc21
2003007585

Typeset by Interactive Composition Corporation in Sabon 10/13.5

Original Printing 2003

Last figure below indicates year of this printing:
12 11 10 09 08 07 06 05 04 03

Contents

Figures

Tables

Preface

"I believe great decisions are made with care, made with conviction, not made with polls. I do not need to take your pulse before I know my own mind."

> *George W. Bush, Acceptance Speech, Republican National Convention, August 3, 2000*

"But the presidency is more than a popularity contest. It's a day-to-day fight for people. Sometimes you have to choose to do what's difficult or unpopular."

> *Al Gore, Acceptance Speech, Democratic National Convention, August 17, 2000*

In their first major addresses as candidates, Vice President Al Gore and Governor George W. Bush both repudiated the use of polls in presidential decision making. The White House traditionally shies away from acknowledging poll usage, because attention to surveys, from approval ratings to issue positions, potentially brands the user with the feared "lacking leadership" stain. Despite the public condemnations, the administrations of Presidents Nixon, Ford, Carter, Reagan, Bush, and Clinton each spent millions of dollars to develop the means to incorporate public opinion polling into the White House. The contradictions that emerged from the contrasts between the spin and the spending produced this book.

The presidential public opinion enterprise provides a unique insight into the operation of the modern White House and broader developments in American politics—especially the development of candidate-centered strategies and campaign-style leadership. This book ventures inside the White House to explain the value of public opinion to the president and the influence of polls on the presidency. My institutional focus explores the strategic value of public opinion as a tool within governing strategies, rather than in its traditional incarnation as a barometer of presidential performance.

While the White Houses of presidents from Nixon to Clinton were building polling operations, pundits and scholars accused these presidents of abandoning governing behavior in exchange for campaign-style leadership, dubbed the "permanent campaign." Outwardly, there was an increase in permanent campaign behavior as the plebiscitary and rhetorical presidents emerged. Presidents now routinely "go public" and make campaign appearances in support of policy options. Thus, exploring polls represents a unique opportunity to dissect these institutional changes to the presidency. The poll operation represents an opportunity to probe the institutional manifestation of the permanent campaign.

Exploring poll usage, I found that the White Houses of Richard Nixon, Gerald Ford, Jimmy Carter, Ronald Reagan, George Bush, and Bill Clinton employed former campaign workers and capitalized on their capabilities vis-à-vis public opinion. The White House poll operation influenced presidential messages and responses to events and crises. Moreover, the poll data enabled the production of a presidency-centered constituency strategy, which linked the president's initial electoral coalition to a viable reelection coalition. Thus, polling altered the target and framework of presidential persuasion toward an increasingly segmented and adversarial conception of the president's supporters. These changes are institutional and not related to an individual president's public relations skill level. However, the public's input waxed and waned, flourishing in the first two years, within crises, and languishing at other times and across a multitude of issues. Consequently, a model of leadership built upon the permanent campaign has not replaced traditionally styled governing behavior. Polling, and thus a campaign environment, exists in tandem with traditional governing strategies and approaches.

Presidents since Franklin Roosevelt have been interested in measuring public support and connecting those findings to the task of being president. However, presidents were unable to overcome the financial and technological hurdles that stymied consistent employment of public opinion polling within White House operations until the Nixon administration. Since the Nixon administration, millions of dollars have been devoted each year to purchasing polls and organizing focus groups that track the rise and fall of issues, attitudes, and popularity ratings.

FGs

Despite the dramatic rise of this polling infrastructure, little is known about how polls are used, and whether these weekly (sometimes daily) polls influence presidential leadership. Former staff members and presidents both insist public opinion is tangential to decision making. Nevertheless, the purchase of poll data and the ubiquity of popularity figures leads to hypotheses that presidents are subservient to the polls. Seemingly, the presence of public opinion data must promote presidential followership.

A unique relationship exists between the president and the public. In the American system of government, only the president can presume to articulate what the national public thinks and feels, because only the president purports to represent the entire nation. Not only does the president uniquely represent the nation, but the nature of this service also can be uniquely measured. Gallup, Harris, and other media cooperatives report on an almost daily basis what "the public" thinks about the president's job performance, the president's policies, the president's choices, and even the name of the presidential pet. Bombardment of the political sphere with poll data and the appearance of scientific certainty have furnished public opinion with a mythic quality. The net effect of this barrage is the belief that public opinion must be useful, and especially useful to the president.

However, no pollster, staffer, or president ever publicly acknowledges any influence for public opinion on presidential decision making. For the presidency, attention to public opinion seems to be an anathema to great leadership. If, as Bert Rockman claims, leadership is "the process of producing significant change," then to produce significant public leadership the president must, at the very least, change minds.[1] Polls, within this perspective, reveal change but do not factor into producing it. Winston Churchill encapsulated this view, claiming, "Nothing is more dangerous than to live in the temperamental atmosphere of a Gallup poll, always taking one's pulse and taking one's political temperature. . . . There is only one duty, only one safe course, and that is to try to be right and not to fear to do or to say what you believe to be right."[2] Even George Edwards, who argues that polling aids presidential leadership with Congress, contends that any assistance gleaned from polling affects leadership only at the margins.[3] Marginal leadership hardly represents great or even good leadership.

However, in an age of continuous poll taking and mediocre leaders, skeptics challenge this notion of poll taking only for awareness. Rightly so; it seems rather ridiculous that political parties would spend millions of dollars annually on behalf of their president merely to provide a monitoring mechanism. For the *National Journal* in 1981, Dom Bonafede highlighted the number of Reagan staffers who routinely had contact with the presidential pollster. Richard Wirthlin reeled off most of the key players in the administration: Baker, Meese, Deaver, Gergen, Nofziger, Rollins, Dole, Anderson, and Beal. Quoted in the article, these individuals articulated the party line: Polling does not drive or even influence decision making.[4] Presidents and their staffs who follow the polls are not leaders. In response, Bonafede slyly writes, "As this implies, the White House is heavily dependent on public opinion in its political and executive decisions."[5]

With subsequent administrations, questions vis-à-vis polling were repeated and repeatedly brushed aside. Are polls important to presidential decision making? If yes, is the presidency then a rudderless institution? However, with each subsequent administration since the 1960s, questions regarding presidential polling became more insistent. Thirty years later, journalists were calling the Clinton administration a "horse-race presidency" due to the incessant polling by the White House,[6] although it was acknowledged that times had changed. Kathleen Frankovic, director of surveys for CBS News, noted, "Our poll measurements have become so frequent and have received so much attention that they are accepted as reality—not only by political actors, but by many journalists who interpret polls for the public."[7] By 1993, those who asserted that polling must influence leadership and decision making offered a two-fold rationale: (1) The White House is purchasing the data; and (2) polling is now a part of the public dialogue about events and issues.

Spanning six presidents and more than thirty years, scholars and the media have questioned the role of public opinion for the presidency. And spanning six presidents and more than thirty years, presidents and their staffs have downplayed the significance of their attention to polls. This book goes beyond detailing merely the existence of the polling effort. Thus, it addresses the issue at the center of the debate: Does polling influence presidential leadership? I use the presence of polling operations to question the oft-cited, but rarely examined, presidential style of leadership—campaigning to govern, or the permanent campaign. Exploring the usage of public opinion polling demonstrates the prevalence of a campaign style of leadership within the White House, but not the triumph of the permanent campaign over more traditional governing styles.

I wrote this book for an audience interested in the presidency, public opinion, and the changing nature of leadership. In Chapter 1, I evaluate traditional conceptions of presidential leadership and the place for public opinion within that model. I then turn to the roots of polling within the presidency. Historically, public opinion intrigued presidents; the trick was to capture attitudes meaningfully and consistently. Chapter 1 concludes by establishing how White House polling can serve as a proxy for evaluating campaign leadership.

In Chapter 2, the substance of polling usage in the White House begins to emerge. In this chapter, I assess where public opinion fits into the White House organizational structure. Do policymakers or public relations staffers utilize polling? Does the president? What role does the pollster play? Who can access the information? Thus, Chapter 2 begins where most assessments end: Where does the poll information go after the pollster delivers the information to the White House? By tracking the paper trail, I found that access to public opinion covaried with White House staffing arrangements: Hierarchical staff structures produced similarly restrictive poll employment; collegial White Houses shared poll information. However, these staffing patterns did not affect usage of poll information. Despite differing staffing arrangements and patterns of data dissemination, I found that similar offices and individuals with similar responsibilities utilized polling data. Key members of the White House, including the president, routinely reviewed and employed public opinion.

Chapter 3 connects the staffers and the polls to presidential leadership. Here I categorize the White House usage of public opinion by considering the information within the exchange of memoranda described in Chapter 2. All private White House pollsters provided their respective presidents with reams of poll data on a wide variety of topics. From my coding, I determined quantitatively (1) the activities for which the White House employed poll data; (2) whether these activities changed across presidents; (3) on what issues the White House employed public opinion; and (4) the connection between issues, activities, and public opinion. I found that initially presidents were interested in their popularity ratings, but over time, that interest declined. Instead, presidents and their staffs turned to public policy attitudes and a range of detailed demographic information. The White House took the issue and demographic information and applied them to information gathering, public relations, and constituency-building efforts suggesting campaign leadership. With the exception of the Carter administration, the White House did not apply poll data to programmatic efforts.

Chapters 4, 5, 6, and 7 flesh out the findings of Chapter 3 and begin to explore the depth of the adoption of the permanent campaign with presidential processes. At the heart of any campaign is the need to determine who supports the candidate and who does not. Chapter 4 discloses how polling enables the president to define advocates and adversaries—the first step of any campaign. The White House used polls to create and track a presidency-centered constituency. The polls classified the mass citizenry first into traditional and then non-traditional categories. The classifications provided detailed definitions beyond party, age, gender, geography, and employment. More importantly, these administrations used polling to classify individuals by their support for the president and presidential issues. Over the course of six administrations, classifying supporters evolved from Nixon's approach (adding categorizations to the party base line) to Bill Clinton and Dick Morris' triangulation plan, which refashioned traditional coalitions.

Chapters 5 and 6 explore the presidential policymaking process from two distinct perspectives. Chapter 5 follows a traditional conception of presidential policymaking: from agenda formation to implementation. Chapter 6 uses a case study approach to explore four important agenda items. From both perspectives, campaigning is not the preferred form of presidential leadership. The use of polls was more prevalent across some stages of the presidential policy process than others, and was more relevant in some cases than in others. These two chapters clearly articulate that the tools of a campaign are present across multiple layers of White House action and activity. However, these two chapters also document the reluctance to adopt a truly adversarial approach, or an all-or-nothing definition of victory. Campaigns do not allow for compromise or bargaining. Despite the presence of campaign tools, these White Houses did not choose to obfuscate traditional presidential leadership styles of bargaining and coalition building.

Chapter 7 explores the cases of Watergate and Monica-gate. The presence of campaign leadership directly relates to the increase of institutional warfare between the president and Congress. A crisis of monumental proportions better suits the definition of campaign leadership than do ordinary agenda items. Chapter 8 concludes considering George W. Bush's use of polls, as well as what the presence of polling in the White House means for the presidency and for the public.

Acknowledgments

Several institutions and individuals provided the invaluable support necessary to complete this project. My trips to the presidential archives were funded by the Joan Shorenstein Center on the Press, Politics, and Public Policy at the John F. Kennedy School of Government, at Harvard University; the Howard and Jan Swearer Fellowship from Brown University; and a summer research grant from St. John's University. Brown University and St. John's University also funded several conference appearances from which this book took shape.

One conference, however, needs to be singled out for its important influence on this project: "Presidential Power: Forging the Presidency for the 21st Century," sponsored by the Presidency Research Division of the American Political Science Association and Columbia University, held on November 15–16, 1996. This conference, unique in its goals and design, endeavored to bring together new and established scholars to discuss the presidency, and also to foster mentoring. In my case, the conference was a wonderful experience and profoundly influenced my scholarship. In particular, I must thank Mark Peterson and Robert Y. Shapiro for their generous commentary, critiques, and their supportive e-mails. An earlier version of sections of Chapter 4 appeared in the conference volume as the chapter "Presidential Polling and the Potential for Leadership."[8]

Although I alone am responsible for the arguments made here, other scholars graciously provided their thoughts and insights on drafts of articles, conference papers, and early versions of this book: Jeffrey Cohen, Robert Eisinger, Lori Cox Han, Lawrence Jacobs, and Michael Genovese. Earlier versions of Chapter 2 and sections of Chapter 7 appeared in the articles "Staffing the White House Public Opinion Apparatus: 1969–1988" and "Polling for a Defense: The White House Public Opinion Apparatus and the Clinton Impeachment."

I am also indebted to those at Brown University who read and reread this work and my dissertation. Darrell West and Roger Cobb provided important assistance and support. However, it is Elmer E. Cornwell who has my eternal gratitude, as it is he who placed me on this path. Numerous conversations in his office eventually led to his generous suggestion that I should think about updating his important work, *Presidential Leadership of Public Opinion*. Without his advice and ceaseless support, I would not have questioned the implications of presidential polling.

I am most indebted, however, to my family and friends. My parents, Rosalyn and Elliott Heith, and my brother Eric J. Heith offered the encouragement and guidance necessary to complete a dissertation, graduate school, and this manuscript. Kenda Kroodsma, Kristin LeVeness, and Michell J. Wilson endured endless discussions and provided unflappable support.

Finally, I must dedicate this book to my husband, Stephen M. Kline. He deserves so much credit and thanks, for reading this manuscript in every incarnation and for providing such wonderfully loving shelter from the storm.

—Diane J. Heith

POLLING TO GOVERN

1   Public Opinion and Theories of Presidential Leadership

"President Roosevelt was, by all odds, together with Secretary Stimson the most alert responsible official I have ever known to be concerned about public opinion systematically. I never once saw him 'change his mind' because of what any survey showed. But he did base his strategy a great deal on these results."[1]

    Hadley Cantril, Franklin D. Roosevelt's pollster

"I don't think anybody can run a government, particularly the executive branch, by trying to rely on public opinion. That attempts to substitute followership for leadership."[2]

    Patrick Caddell, Jimmy Carter's pollster

"We used polling not to determine what positions he would take but to figure out which of the positions he had already taken were the most popular. I would always draw the distinction between deciding on policy and identifying certain issues for emphasis by telling Clinton, 'You print the menu of the things you want. Then I'll advise which dish to have for dinner tonight.'"[3]

    Dick Morris, Bill Clinton's polling consultant

These three presidential pollsters, speaking more than sixty years apart, essentially offer the same defense for their involvement in the White House: Public opinion polling is important for presidential leadership but is not a substitute for it. The fear that presidents are polling rather than leading pervades the presidential-pollster relationship. The fear stems from a sense that the office of the presidency has degenerated into a campaign: a campaign in support of an agenda, a campaign for personal popularity, a campaign for reelection, and a campaign for the history books. The president's calendar, travel plans, and network news coverage appear to document a shift to campaign-like behavior by the president. The frequency and quality of presidential rhetorical efforts and communications strategies further strengthen the notion that there is a qualitative difference in the governing style of the president since, if not the 1930s, then at least the 1960s.

There is little doubt presidents now "go public" to achieve that which traditional presidents never dreamed. Moreover, there seems little doubt that presidents are using polls to achieve their goals. However, using White House polling as an internal proxy for permanent campaign behavior demonstrates the presence of a campaign leadership style as well as its limitations. In this chapter, I develop a competing picture of presidential poll usage and an explanation for the patterns of institutionalization across six White House administrations.

My discussion is organized into three parts and considers the historical and theoretical relationships between the public, public opinion, the presidency, and leadership. The chapter begins with traditional conceptions of the presidency and its relationship with the public. Second, I present a picture of presidential polling prior to its consistent presence within the White House. Here are the seeds of a new style of presidential leadership. Finally, I describe the foundation of this book.

Polling and the Presidency: 1924–1968

Public attitudes have always been important to presidents. The White House has always received information about the public from a variety of sources: the media, the party, other elites, and of course, the presidential mail bag. Straw polls and canvassing have been commonplace with American officials since the 1700s.[4] Presidents as early as Hoover and Roosevelt sought quantitative representations of the public's attitudes. Hoover had his White House staff do, for its time, a relatively sophisticated content analysis of the editorial pages of newspapers.[5] Without the benefit of polls or statistics, Hoover effectively sampled opinion of the day.[6] It was in the 1930s that the modern presidential polling apparatus first emerged.[7]

President Franklin Delano Roosevelt was the first president to seek out public attitudes via public opinion polls.[8] The Democratic Party aided and abetted Roosevelt's efforts. "Emil Hurja's polls for the DNC and Hadley Cantril's polling for FDR signified the birth of presidential polling."[9] Hurja, according to Eisinger and Brown, served as a precursor to the modern-day links forged between pollsters and parties, for example, Oliver Quayle and the Democrats in the 1960s, and Robert Teeter and Richard Wirthlin with the Republicans from the mid-1970s through the 1990s.[10] Polling penetrated the executive branch, as the Department of Agriculture, the Works Progress Administration, and the Social Security Administration all sought public attitudes.[11] In addition to forging a connection between pollsters, the party, and the president, Roosevelt also established a secret polling operation. Eisinger and Brown argue that Roosevelt kept Hadley Cantril's work for the administration secret in order to receive politically valuable information independent of his party.[12]

Despite Hoover's and Roosevelt's efforts, public opinion remained tangential to the presidency until the 1960s. As Eisinger and Brown, Cornwell, Jacobs, and Ginsburg all note, the Truman and Eisenhower administrations continued querying the public, but substantially less frequently than had occurred in FDR's administration: "Many of its arrangements (including both the relationship with pollsters and the government's own polling operations) were abandoned under Presidents Truman and Eisenhower."[13] Polling was not institutionalized in the White House until after the high-level intelligence gathering exhibited during John F. Kennedy's 1960 run for the presidency.[14] The Kennedy and Johnson administrations vastly expanded presidential interest in and use of the presidential polling apparatus. According to Jacobs and Shapiro, the Kennedy and Johnson administrations dramatically increased interest in public and private administration polling, primarily for elections but also for governing.[15] However, none of the administrations from Roosevelt to Johnson received a continuous flow of public opinion data. The Kennedy and Johnson White Houses did place a greater emphasis on public opinion than their predecessors, but could only obtain partial, piggybacked control over their poll questions and surveys; subsequent presidents achieved complete control.[16] Marked by their infrequent poll usage, Jacobs and Shapiro argue that the Kennedy and Johnson administrations were quantifiably different from the institutionalized efforts evident in the post-Johnson presidencies.[17] In stark contrast, the administrations of Nixon, Ford, Carter, Reagan, Bush, and Clinton devoted substantial time, money, and attention to a White House public opinion apparatus.

Public Opinion and the Presidency: Barometer or Resource?

Due to the dearth of constitutional tools with which the president can pursue his legislative agenda, the modern president has endeavored to produce an informal collection of approaches. Neustadt, in his seminal work *Presidential Power,* presents the president's persuasive abilities as the preeminent tool in the presidential toolbox. The president seeks to persuade and bargain with other elites and officials. For Neustadt, the public remains a distant, indirect source of presidential power, as "public standing is a source of influence for him, another factor bearing on . . . [the] willingness to give him what he wants."[18] Public standing is prestige. It is not popular support, nor is it popularity. Prestige or standing is not the "job approval rating" found in most polls.[19] Prestige is the cumulative effect of the opinions of columnists, public opinion polls, and news reports. It includes the opinion on Capitol Hill that is determined by Washingtonians. Popularity influences prestige, but it is not a synonym for prestige. In Neustadt's conception, both public opinion and prestige are barometers of job performance. Public standing is a source of indirect influence, a factor in the background of the bargaining environment. Thus, presidents do not use the public in Neustadt's framework.

Subsequently, Elmer Cornwell agreed that popular support provided an indirect pressure on the lawmaking process, but he altered the Neustadtian perspective of the public by challenging Neustadt's picture of the public and the value of the public to the president.[20] "Since little is likely to be done constitutionally to strengthen the President's hand, his ability to lead and mold public opinion, for all its inherent limitations, must remain his prime reliance. . . . More than ever before in the history of the Republic, the strong President will be the skillful leader of public opinion."[21] Contrary to Neustadt's view of public standing, or prestige, Cornwell highlighted popular support manifest in the cumulative collection of attitudes and information, and included measures of popular support, such as public opinion polls, as a source of public influence for the president.[22] For Cornwell, the president's preeminent position is that of opinion leader, and as opinion leader the president enjoys the unique position of being able "to generate publicity and command public attention." As with Neustadt, Cornwell considers the public a fragile influence; however, Cornwell's conception of leadership success depends on the use of the public. Cornwell considers the public a powerful resource for the president, but also notes that presidents have not been "as effective as they ought to be" in using the public.[23] Cornwell considers the public an untapped source of power and rests the burden of appeal on the president; Neustadt considers the public less valuable because they are inattentive.

Following Neustadt's and Cornwell's work, scholars adopted the Cornwell focus on the skillful use of opinion. Significantly, the approval ratings became the preferred means for public support *and* leadership success. Kernell argued that recent presidents overturned Neustadt's traditional bargaining environment in favor of "going public," a strategy in which a president "promotes himself and his policies in Washington by appealing to the American public for support."[24] Support is measured by the survey question: Do you approve or disapprove of the job the president is doing? However, Bond and Fleisher's analysis of roll call voting found that "presidential popularity will have only a marginal impact on voting decisions of representatives in Congress," and going public has no impact.[25] Mark Peterson, using a "tandem-institutional" approach focusing on decision making, noted that the net effects of public approval on legislative outcomes were dubious at best.[26] Edwards found that presidents might want to use the public to pressure Congress, but are only successful "at the margins."[27]

However, the public continued to occupy a position of importance. Brace and Hinckley contend that the ability to measure public support produced a dependence on the polls, what they call a "follower presidency."[28] Due to the presence of polls, the White House's preeminent presidential goal is to achieve high approval ratings demonstrating public support.[29] The goal of popularity then infuses behavior. Highly ranked presidents' styles encompass efforts to be liked and follow external cues (polling) rather than internal cues. Moreover, Brace and Hinckley contend that all presidents are forced to accept tradeoffs between activity and success in their popularity ratings.[30] Thus, as Richard Brody notes, "the standing of the president with the American people has come to have a political life of its own. A president's 'popularity' is said to be a political resource that can help him achieve his program, keep challengers at bay and guide his and other political leaders' expectations about the president's party prospects in presidential and congressional elections."[31]

What began as recognition of the value of the public to presidential leadership (marshalling opinion as opinion leader) transformed into suggestions of dangerous behavior for leaders from attention to poll numbers. What all these understandings of elite behavior have in common is the public appeal, otherwise known as the rhetorical, plebiscitary, or public relations presidency.[32] In this framework, presidential success is dependent on public relations or communications efforts. Success is measured by evaluating presidential poll ratings (or the president's legislative agenda, or both).

In these conceptions, the approval rating variable provides the foundation for leadership that a trip to the voting booth supposedly provides. The approval rating variable is a mass number, a snapshot of the public as a whole. In a sense, approval ratings provide a daily mini-mandate check. Does the public support the president? Do they approve of the job he is doing? The constant evaluation of public ratings seemingly forces elite attentiveness and responsiveness on the public in lieu of actual public expression because no president wants his rating to decline. Presidential leadership in terms of attentiveness and responsiveness, then, is vague and undefined. The relationship to the polls, however, is clear. "Presidents who go public need pollsters."[33] They need pollsters to monitor "the pulse of opinion to warn of slippage and to identify opportunities for gain. Before adopting a policy course, they have assessed its costs in public support."[34] The "president's calculus" (as Kernell terms it) depends entirely on approval ratings for the public's presence.

However, the intense focus on approval ratings misses the relationship between the president and the public, as it ignores the origins of that relationship—the campaign trail. During any campaign, the media constantly inform a candidate who is ahead, who is behind, and who is showing improvement. Horse race information is clearly not enough information about public attitudes for candidates. Presidential candidates spend millions on public opinion polls in order to disaggregate supporters and opponents and explain why individuals support one candidate over another.[35] Attitudes toward candidates are morasses of opinions on issues, personality evaluations, partisanship, and other socioeconomic factors. These pieces of information are critical to successful campaigns. Presidents bring this interest and dependency to the White House.

As a result, this book encompasses and builds on the traditional plebiscitary conceptions of the presidency, but actually concerns presidential behavior that includes a "reelection imperative." Due to FDR and the Twenty-Third Amendment, modern presidents receive only one chance for reelection. As presidents are no longer legally eligible to run for more than two terms, presidents, scholars, the media, and Washingtonians all view the second term as the key to the presidential legacy. First-term presidents want that second term. However, in contrast to most congressional scholarship in which reelection and constituency factors drive congressional behavior, election imperatives are noticeably absent from analyses of the presidency.[36] The presidential reelection effort becomes a referendum on the presidency.[37]

Traditionally, the first presidential election connects to presidential governing via the transition and considerations of the president's electoral coalition. Seligman and Covington argue that presidential success depends on the stability of the president's governing coalition.[38] The governing coalition depends largely on electoral support, which propelled the candidate to the White House.[39] Seligman and Covington contend that groups and coalitions make up the core of the president's electoral coalition. Thus, the successful president must translate his electoral coalition into an effective governing coalition. In addition, the more of the electoral coalition the president retains, the more stable his governing coalition is. However, the modern presidential electoral coalition is better described as a conglomeration of party ideology; short-term, campaign-driven attitudes; and single-issue supporters, united only by the common act of voting for a single individual. Presidential candidates appeal to and hope to mobilize these blocs of voters based on political and socioeconomic factors derived from their sophisticated polling techniques.[40]

As a theory of presidential behavior, the permanent campaign contends that campaign behavior dominates White House behavior. The evidence for the permanent campaign, or campaigning to govern, stems from the decline of the political parties, the rise of open interest group politics, new communications technology, and new political technologies, and requires money.[41] The permanent campaign contains "the merger of power-as-persuasion inside Washington with power-as-public opinion manipulation outside Washington," according to Hugh Heclo.[42] The resulting merger produces a different form (a seemingly detrimental form) of behavior because campaigning is inherently different than governing. Campaigning depends on persuasive efforts, but also "is geared to one unambiguous decision point in time . . . [and] is necessarily adversarial."[43] Conceivably, then, the more the behavior of a campaign penetrates the process, the more the values of a campaign perspective will overrule governing.[44] The behavior and the values of a campaign have indeed penetrated the White House, but have not overwhelmed or subsumed the governing process.

Presidential Leadership via the Opinion Poll

The purpose of public opinion polling is to quantify public attitudes. As Susan Herbst argues, "public opinion has become a commodity: News organizations, politicians, pressure groups, and others with an interest in public opinion purchase data in hopes of gaining power, attention, or profits."[45] Herbst's analysis provides useful tools for conceptualizing public opinion and its relevance for leadership. She argues, in *Numbered Voices,* that public opinion has two functions: instrumental and symbolic. The instrumental function of the quantification of public opinion is relatively obvious. As Herbst articulates, "Pollsters collect a particular type of data and usually have concrete reasons for doing so."[46] But once the numbers are collected, instrumentality often merges with the symbolic uses of polling data. For Herbst, "it is only in the context of political discourse and ritual that the true rhetorical value of numbers becomes apparent."[47]

Herbst contends that polls are powerful numerical symbols, as they are often shortcuts for complex political beliefs.[48] Herbst uses the notion of symbolic communication to focus on the role of public opinion within debates. Others have adopted these concepts in order to capture the role of public opinion in the political sphere. Traditionally, these analyses have focused on the response to public opinion by elites. Amy Fried argues that during the Iran-Contra scandal, elected officials both responded to and influenced perceived public opinion.[49] Jacobs and Shapiro contend that politicians use public opinion to design "crafted talk." Crafted talk is the art of employing public opinion polls and focus groups to choose words and phrases that resonate with the public, even when the policy does not. Jacobs and Shapiro go on to say that "the influence of public opinion on government policy is less than it has been in the past and certainly less than commonly assumed by political pundits and some scholars."[50]

In this book, public opinion remains primarily an instrumental tool. The White House collects public opinion data in order to gather the public's attitudes for its own purposes. However, the use of public opinion by the White House is also a symbolic representation of a style of leadership. The campaigns of the modern era depend on the technology that evolved with it. "Three great technologies—electronic media, polling, and public relations—converged into immense and mutually supportive industries. For politicians and group activists, they opened the door of opportunity to orchestrate, amplify, and inject the presumptive voices of the American people . . . into the daily management of public affairs."[51] Without polls, the campaigns of the late twentieth century and early twenty-first century do not exist. Similarly, without a polling operation, presidential campaigning to govern does not exist. In this book, I employ the polling apparatus as a proxy for assessing the penetration of campaign-style leadership into the White House and the presidency.

Methods of Study

To understand the use of public opinion and cast light on presidential leadership, I investigate the employment of the polling apparatus in six consecutive presidencies. I capture the use of public opinion via archived White House memoranda. My data set includes material from the archives of Presidents Nixon, Ford, Carter, Reagan, and Bush. Because President Clinton's archives are not yet available, the Clinton administration's usage of public opinion will be based on the multitude of public accounts of his poll apparatus. Additionally, I examine public documents and memoirs from the six administrations.

The Data The archived material contains formal and informal memoranda, handwritten notes, pollster reports, and other written documentation. These memos provide firsthand accounts of polling usage and efforts to include public opinion in decision making. Archival records provide a glimpse into the inner workings of the executive branch in particular, illuminating how decisions are made.[52] Scholars generally consider archival records to be reliable sources of information on presidential processes. As my sample encompasses a wide continuum of issues and events (from the significant to the trivial), I minimize the dangers from "memo writers whose purposes run counter to those of the researcher" experienced when researching a narrow topic.[53]

The one danger in using archival documents stems from the inherent variability that exists in the number of memoranda available from each administration. Due to the volumes of data each White House turns over at the end of its tenure, it takes the archivists a long time to declassify the documents. As a result, all White House material is not immediately available to researchers. In a survey of the library's holdings, David Horrocks, chief archivist of the Ford Library, found that 71 percent of the Ford papers were open to research as of February 1999.[54] Moreover, Horrocks claims that the 71 percent underreports the openness of the holdings, as the backlog is of lesser research value. He estimates that 95 percent of the substantive domestic material is available for research.[55] The Carter Library approaches the level of openness found in the Ford archives. However, due to Watergate, the Presidential Records Act (1978), and the recent tenures of Reagan and Bush, there are varied levels of access and availability in the Nixon, Reagan, and Bush archives. Despite these limitations, there remains a wealth of "polling memos" to investigate.[56]

Some of the studies of presidential polling cited here relied on these same White House archives. Other scholars have investigated public opinion in the presidency using interviews and by following the money trail.[57] I chose to rely on empirical evidence of polling usage, and followed the paper trail in the presidential archives. All three methodologies are valid, and all three have flaws. Relying on interviews forces the researcher to depend on the memory of those interviewed. Following the money trail does not bring the researcher into the decision-making path of those in the White House. In addition, placing importance on how much money was spent on the presidential pollsters attempts to equate spending with usage. In effect, these research options, including my own, use a substitute for establishing not only the total number of polls conducted but also attention to those polls.

My analysis is unique, however, as I use the memoranda to produce a distinctive and comparable data set for each administration. Any memorandum, including any White House memo that referenced poll data, contains a few basic ingredients that categorize all memos. All memoranda include the date the memo was sent, the sender of the memo, the receiver of the memo, and the text, or information the document contained. These essential components reveal much about the employment of public opinion data in the White House. I used these components to code the memoranda from the Nixon, Ford, Carter, Reagan, and Bush archives at the sentence level of analysis for the type of poll data employed and the type of White House activities in which the data was employed.

Linking the flow of public opinion information to offices, to policies, and ultimately to patterns of behavior, reveals both the infiltration and limitation of the permanent campaign as a theory of governing. As I demonstrate in the forthcoming chapters, strategists emerged from the campaign and became White House leaders. These former campaign workers continued to rely heavily on polling, and assisted the top echelon of decision makers' reliance on polling. Moreover, the polling apparatus figured prominently in the design of persuasive campaigns selling the president's agenda. More significantly, and previously unseen, the White House used the poll apparatus to design behavior and track responses from a poll-identified constituency: an artificially created campaign-style adversary. However, the reach and range of these behaviors remained relatively localized to a small segment of the White House and to a small component of leadership.[58]

Conclusions

Conceptions of the presidency, which focus on presidential communications and public relations skills, include discussions of public opinion polling. In these models, polls provide the presidency with evaluations of performance. High ratings indicate presidential success and low ratings demand a change of style, approach, or policy. Campaigning-to-govern theories of the presidency subsume the public presidency and add the notion of winning. In this model, public opinion polls represent more than evaluation, providing a blueprint of behavior by identifying supporters and defectors, and appealing policy positions.

However, I argue that neither the evaluative role nor the blueprint model exists. Across six administrations, the White House polling apparatus neither thoroughly penetrated the policy process nor dominated the decision making. However, a campaign-like environment was evident.

The next chapter begins evaluating the connections between presidential campaigns and governing once in the White House. It examines who used public opinion in the White House. For public opinion polling, and thus a campaign environment, to penetrate the White House, the top echelon of the hierarchy—the decision makers—must be involved.

Bringing the Permanent Campaign to the White House: Staffing the Poll Apparatus

The spending by the winning presidential candidate has increased exponentially, from $25 million in 1968 to over $300 million in 2001.[1] The amount spent by presidential campaigns on public opinion polling has also increased over time, from $1.6 million by Richard Nixon in 1972 to almost $4 million in 1992. Similarly, Jacobs and Shapiro estimate that, while in the White House, President Nixon spent over $5 million (in 1995 inflation-adjusted dollars) on public opinion polling data.[2] Patrick Caddell received over $1.3 million between 1977 and 1979 polling for President Carter.[3] In 1981 alone, Richard Wirthlin received $820,000 polling for Ronald Reagan.[4] The Bush polling budget was $650,000 in 1989 for quarterly national surveys from Robert Teeter.[5] President Clinton spent over $15 million on public polls during his two terms in the White House.[6]

Campaigns spend so much money on poll data because during a run for the presidency, poll data pervades campaign decision making. Campaigns use poll data to decide where and when to push the candidate, to discover which issues to emphasize, and to determine which efforts worked, which did not, and why. Consequently, poll data is a crucial tool accessible to most members of the campaign staff. Interviews with presidents, White House staff, and presidential pollsters hint at the importance of poll data for governance, but the apparatus remains shrouded in ambiguity. As much a third rail as altering Social Security, no staffer, president, or pollster wants to admit to using polls to shape or influence leadership while in the White House. Nixon, Reagan, and Bush pollster Richard Wirthlin asserted, "The work we do may occasionally focus discussion in the White House on one topic or another. But it wouldn't be fair to typify what I do as getting involved in policy formation."[7] Moreover, no organizational chart of any White House highlights formal structures or guidelines that detail the use of public opinion in presidential activities.

This chapter will show the depth and breadth of the polling apparatus' (and thus, campaign-style leadership's) penetration of the White House. The Nixon, Ford, Carter, Reagan, Bush, and Clinton administrations routinized the incorporation of public opinion data and analysis into the office of the presidency. Unlike campaign organizations (and despite different presidential attitudes vis-à-vis the public), usage of public opinion was not widespread. However, as with campaign organizations, key White House strategists relied on polls. Moreover, skill and expertise affected the incorporation of public opinion, and thus campaign leadership, into the White House.

Following the Poll Data

The importance of the public for a democracy is obvious, regardless of whether the democracy is participatory or representative. In a democracy, citizens participate in decision making directly (for example, the town meeting) or participate by voting for representatives. The act of voting represents the core of the contract between those who govern and the governed. After all, as Ginsberg argues, the public will can either be expressed via a demonstration or even violently via riot, or be socialized and institutionalized via the voting booth.[8] In any case, the voice of the public draws the attention of those who govern.

The idea that citizens can and should participate beyond the minimal demands of a representative democracy persists, in what James Morone terms a "democratic wish."[9] Within the framework of the democratic wish, the distinctions between groups, classes, officials, and elites blur. "Even when social tensions are sharp, contending factions can converge on a set of symbols that appear to promote the interests of each."[10] The institutional nature of voting, however, tends to disaggregate citizens more than it combines.

The design of the American system of representative democracy disaggregates the citizenry beyond participant and nonparticipant. In the presidential election process, voters are separated by state as citizens' votes are translated into electoral college victories. To win the presidential election, a candidate must amass at least 270 state electoral votes. Therefore, a campaign for the presidency is at minimum a campaign for enough states to meet the electoral college magic number. To achieve state campaign success and national campaign success at the same time, the successful presidential candidate must motivate, activate, or convert voter opinion into a vote for the candidate. In this modern presidential campaign, polling is critical, as campaign polls reveal the short-term issues, attitudes, and agendas relevant to motivating, activating, or converting voter opinion into voter choice. If, as Ginsberg argues, voting is a mechanism to socialize, institutionalize, and channel public expression, then campaign polls represent the keys to that lock.

The importance of the public and polling for governing is much less obvious. Democratic theory promises that public opinion is significant for a properly functioning government but stops significantly short of advocating its incorporation into elite behavior. Dahl argues that "democracy cannot be justified merely as a system for translating the raw, uninformed will of a popular majority into public policy."[11]

Students of voting behavior have long disagreed over whether citizens have the intellectual capability and wherewithal to participate effectively in voting and governing.[12] In *Public Opinion*, Walter Lippmann argued that it would take too much effort and work by the citizen to remain informed enough to provide useful feedback to government.[13] For the public official, the debate can be framed in terms of behavior. A president or member of Congress can either respond to the will and whims of the people (act as a delegate) or rely on his or her own judgment (act as a trustee). Jacobs and Shapiro disagree with Dahl and those who frame the debate in terms of responsiveness (the delegate) or elite direction (the trustee). They present another pattern for elite behavior, termed responsive leadership, in which elites "exercise some degree of independence, discretion, and judgment as they respond to public preferences."[14] Responsive leadership sounds very similar to the flexibility engendered by a campaign environment, as circumstances force candidates to adjust to changes among the electorate. A campaign leadership style in the White

House would also require a response mechanism. In order to respond to public preferences, elites must be aware of those preferences and able to translate them into the governing arena. For a campaign style of leadership to flourish, the White House staff, as with a campaign organization, must use public opinion polls.

Setting the Tone

To understand any organization, the top of the power structure is usually a good place to start. Presidential management styles are so widely explored because of the influence that presidents have on their institution. The most influential member of the White House is clearly the president. The president sets the tone and the agenda for the White House. The case of presidential polling is no exception; all presidents since Nixon were aware of, interested in, and used the White House poll apparatus.

To quantify the underdefined "poll apparatus," I designed a simple assay. As I noted in Chapter 1, every memo written in the White House contains several ubiquitous features, most notably the names of the sender and recipient. Counting the number of individuals who exchanged memos that referenced public opinion provides the depth and breadth of the poll apparatus. This simple chore reveals the extent of polling usage throughout the White House. Not surprisingly, the president tends to receive more memos than he sends, as he is often flooded with information, although in the case of polling memos, the president was both sender and recipient.

Despite a successful campaign for the presidency, in which he trounced his opponent, portrayals of President George H. Bush generally did not include high marks for adroit public relations. Despite owning a reputation as lacking interest or awareness of the public, President Bush exchanged (that is, both sent and received) a greater percentage of public opinion memos than any other president (17 percent) (see Table 2.1). Another president lacking in performance skills, President Carter, received more memos about public opinion (over 10 percent of all memos his administration exchanged) than any other member of his administration or any other president. President Nixon generated more memos referencing public opinion than he received. Nixon actually sent more memos directing public opinion than most of his administrative staff.

TABLE **2.1** Exchangers of Poll Data

Staffer	Percentage of Memos Exchanged
Nixon Administration (N = 226)	
Haldeman, H. R., Chief of Staff	20.4%
Strachan, Gordon, Staff Assistant	9.7%
Higby, Larry, Staff Assistant	6.6%
Nixon, Richard, President	5.3%
Ehrlichman, John, Assistant to the President for Domestic Affairs	4.4%
50 other individuals	53.6%
Ford Administration (N = 84)	
Cheney, Richard, Assistant to the President	17.7%
Burch, Dean, Counselor to the President for Political Affairs	8.3%
Hartmann, Robert, Counselor to the President	8.2%
Ford, Gerald, President	4.5%
Jones, Jerry, Deputy Assistant to the President	4.5%
Gergen, David, Director, Communications	3.6%
29 other individuals	53.2%
Carter Administration (N = 238)	
Eizenstat, Stuart, Assistant to the President for Domestic Affairs and Policy	14.7%
Carter, Jimmy, President	11.0%
Rafshoon, Gerald, Assistant to the President, Communications	11.0%
Watson, Jack, Secretary to the Cabinet, Assistant to the President for Intergovernmental Affairs	4.6%
Powell, Jody, Press Secretary	4.6%
Jordan, Hamilton, Chief of Staff	3.8%
Mondale, Walter, Vice President	3.4%
50 other individuals	51.5%
Reagan Administration (N = 314)	
Beal, Richard, Director, Office of Planning and Evaluation	14.6%
Harper, Edwin, Assistant to the President, OPD	11.2%
Usaramoso, Frank, Assistant to the President, Communications	7.0%
Baker, James, Chief of Staff	6.4%
Gergen, David, Assistant to the President, Communications	4.8%
Darman, Richard, Deputy Chief of Staff	4.1%
Meese, Edwin, Counselor to the President	3.8%
Deaver, Michael, Deputy Chief of Staff	3.8%
Reagan, Ronald, President	0.6%
49 other individuals	43.7%
Bush Administration (N = 538)	
Bush, George, President	17.3%
Porter, Roger, Assistant to the President for Economic and Domestic Policy	9.5%

(continued)

TABLE **2.1** (*continued*)

Staffer	Percentage of Memos Exchanged
Carney, David, Deputy Director of the Office of Political Affairs	8.4%
Sununu, John, Chief of Staff	6.0%
Teeter, Robert, Pollster	5.2%
Goldstein, Edward, Senior Policy Analyst	4.8%
Rogers, Edward, Executive Assistant to the Chief of Staff	4.5%
67 other individuals	44.4%

Note: *N* represents the total number of memos sent and received.
Data sources: Nixon Presidential Materials; Historical Papers from the Gerald R. Ford Library; Historical Material from the Jimmy Carter Library; Historical Papers from the Ronald Reagan Library.

President Reagan's minuscule attention to public opinion memos appears to deviate from the presidential norm. However, Reagan's lack of involvement in the paper trail is not necessarily indicative of a lack of involvement in the polling apparatus. For all types of information, President Reagan preferred meetings to written "homework."[15] Poll meetings provided Reagan with visual accounts (for example, graphs and charts of sophisticated poll statistics) of the pollster reports and analysis rather than the copious volumes of data preferred by Nixon and Carter. In the Bush White House, poll meetings were the norm, but not for the president. Eschewing the larger poll meetings, Bush received poll data both formally and informally, verbally and via charts, graphs, pollster reports, and even newspaper accounts of public opinion.

President Clinton combined the involvement of prior presidents: relying on meetings and memos. Unlike his predecessors, Clinton was a thoroughly experienced poll user. While governor of Arkansas, Clinton three times read a detailed analysis and "personal manifesto of sorts" regarding the middle-class crisis and the Democrats of *The American Prospect*, written by Stan Greenberg.[16] Clinton's trusted consultant, Dick Morris, argued that Clinton approached the numbers like a consultant; he was familiar with public opinion and even enjoyed working with the polls.[17] Morris even told Clinton he was "better at reading polls than any pollster I know."[18]

Personal preferences did influence the presidential flow of polling data. The preference for "homework" and volumes of data fosters increased data exchanges. Thus, Presidents Nixon and Carter, who designed their White Houses around their high absorption rates of material, participated with greater frequency in the poll apparatus paper trail. As expected, Reagan preferred discussion and relied less on dense volumes of data, thereby almost eliminating his involvement in the nonverbal aspects of the poll apparatus. Ford's consumption rate appears surprising considering his noted preference for verbal exchanges and personal interaction rather than written material.[19] His open-door policy apparently encouraged an abundance of both written material and meetings.

These presidents, from Nixon to Clinton, had vastly different personal behavior patterns and vastly different styles of management. However, they all recognized the need for public opinion polling in the White House and devoted a portion of their time to using public opinion. Time is one of the more coveted, and protected, White House commodities.[20] The president's time is even more precious. Presidents would not devote the time required to actively participate and reference poll data if it were not relevant to White House goals. The involvement of the president also confers an importance to the public opinion network. Public opinion was important enough for these presidents to reflect on it and direct action about it, or at least send a memo about it.

An Institutional Approach

The growth of the White House staff is one of the enduring legacies of the institutionalized presidency. Despite the personal work habits of the individual presidents, much of the organizational structure and function of the White House has been institutionalized. Although vowing to cut the size of the executive branch, Presidents Nixon, Ford, Carter, Reagan, Bush, and Clinton all maintained, on average, 550 people within the White House staff.[21] Of the approximately 550 individuals, a remarkably similar number of staffers used public opinion within their daily activities.

As shown in Table 2.2, approximately 56 staffers, on average, utilized polling data in the Nixon, Ford, Carter, Reagan, and Bush administrations. Without any formal White House office for polling, these five different administrations had approximately the same number of individuals accessing poll information. However, Table 2.2 demonstrates

TABLE **2.2** Involvement in the Presidential Poll Apparatus

Administration	Total Staffers Involved	Sent More than One Memo	Received More than One Memo	Total Regularly Involved
Nixon	55	13	17	30
Ford	35	16	6	22
Carter	57	14	15	29
Reagan	58	14	23	37
Bush	74	26	27	29
Average	55.8			29.4

Data sources: Nixon Presidential Materials; Historical Papers from the Gerald R. Ford Library; Historical Material from the Jimmy Carter Library; Historical Papers from the Ronald Reagan Library.

the folly of relying on averages alone. In the Nixon, Carter, and Reagan White Houses, 57 individuals on average were involved in the poll apparatus. The Ford and Bush White Houses had over 1.5 standard deviations of difference in the number of individuals involved. Only 35 people exchanged poll data in the Ford White House; at the other extreme, over 70 sent and received memos under George Bush's watch. After removing infrequent poll users (individuals who sent or received only one memo), the number of individuals within the Nixon, Ford, Carter, Reagan, and Bush administrations who routinely included poll data in their communications remained functionally equivalent. In the five White Houses, approximately 30 staff members, 6 percent of the total White House staff population, routinely exchanged polling memos.

Access to Public Opinion

Organization and management styles matter for effective leadership. As John Burke asserts, "centralization of authority within a well-organized staff system can ensure clear lines of responsibility, well-demarcated duties, and orderly work methods. When presidents lack a centralized, organized staff system, the policy-making process suffers."[22] Richard Tanner Johnson, in an influential study of White House organization, found three patterns of staff organization: competitive, formalistic (hierarchical), and collegial systems.[23] Competitive systems feature overlapping areas of responsibility and are characterized by staff rivalries. Formalistic systems feature significant delegation and characteristically employ a complex hierarchy of authority. Collegial systems feature a team of colleagues who work together and ideally fuse the strongest elements of divergent points of view.[24] The exchange of data or information also follows these standards for interaction. Thus, a hierarchical polling arrangement would be characterized by limited access to polling data and a controlled distribution system. Conversely, a collegial apparatus could be identified from its fewer restrictions and wider distribution of poll data throughout the staff. A competitive polling apparatus is not likely to exist. FDR was the only president to establish competitive staffing arrangements. Without a competitive staff system, it is unlikely that a competitive polling system would emerge. Moreover, due to the features of a competitive system, it is hard to conceptualize how a polling distribution system could be competitive. A competitive poll apparatus would require multiple polling consultants and multiple exchanges of distinct polling data sets.

Despite similar levels of staff involvement in the poll apparatus, each administration disseminated their polling data according to their staffing systems. In the Nixon administration, "polling and public opinion analysis was incorporated into a hierarchical chain of command with H. R. Haldeman at the apex serving as gatekeeper to the president."[25] As shown in Table 2.1, Haldeman accounted for 20 percent of all memos sent and received in the Nixon administration. Haldeman ran the polling apparatus with the help of three aides,[26] Gordon Strachan, Larry Higby, and Bruce Kehrli, who together account for almost half of all memos exchanged. More than fifty staffers shared some access to polling data; however, half of all memos that referenced polling information were exchanged between the four men who disseminated the information. President Nixon preferred to keep poll data classified and instructed his top aides to hoard opinion information. In 1973, Nixon writes, "I do not want this . . . [poll information] copied and distributed but I would like for you [Ehrlichman] to discuss the matter with Bob Haldeman at your convenience."[27]

Even relatively trusted and highly placed members of the Nixon staff (for example, Bryce Harlow, Counselor to the President with Cabinet rank) received only minuscule amounts of public opinion information, and only when receiving the information served an outwardly political purpose. Furthermore, Cabinet members and other Republicans were uniformly excluded from the detailed, expert polling data, despite funding by the Republican party.[28] Poll data traveled outside a select few only to make a political point. The Nixon White House would routinely disseminate selected questions and the responses that were supportive of White House actions to various influential political figures. For example, in May 1972, the White House broadcast the positive poll, "7 out of 10 Americans Support Bombing of North Vietnam Military Targets," to everyone within shouting distance, including members of the Cabinet, members of the House and Senate, the White House staff, administration spokesmen, Nixon state chairmen, Friends of Richard Nixon Youth Spokesmen, state youth directors, Mayor Sam Yorty of Los Angeles, and Mayor Frank Rizzo of Philadelphia. Incidentally, this information was also distributed to "contacts at ABC, CBS, NBC, UPI, and AP."[29] In the Nixon administration, public opinion data were both tightly controlled and publicly displayed.

The Ford White House also shared information via the gatekeeper arrangement. The Operations Office, under Richard Cheney and his deputy Foster Chanock, ran the Ford White House polling operation, with Jerry Jones and Fred Slight providing staff support. Cheney controlled the dispersal of public opinion in much the same way Haldeman controlled the Nixon operation. Cheney and his staff dominated receipt and dispersal of polling information (see Tables 2.1 and 2.3). Cheney and his staff exchanged 30 percent of all Ford polling memos. Further supporting the notion of a hierarchical system design, the Ford White House distribution system was designed to limit access, believing that "security for the data will require that the coordinator provide the information on a need to know basis rather than providing blanket access."[30]

The Carter White House extended its open, "spokes of the wheel" staffing arrangement to the dissemination of polling data. Patrick Caddell, Carter's pollster, sent the poll data directly to the president. The president's secretary, Rick Hutcheson, often disseminated the poll data with little regard to restricting content. White House staff and Cabinet officials received poll data. The president only mildly restricted executive branch access. The Cabinet received "just issue material," but the entire White House staff had full access to the 300-page volume entitled *An Analysis of Political Attitudes in the United States of America,* which included political material as well as the raw data.[31] There was no Haldeman, or Cheney, controlling the dispersal of poll information in

TABLE **2.3** The Units Involved in Polling*

Administration	Unit	Percentage of Total Memos Exchanged
Nixon		
	Chief of Staff's Office	35%
	Political Liaison	13%
	Communications	12%
	Domestic Council	6%
	8 other offices	36%
Ford		
	Operations	32%
	Political Liaison	17%
	Public Liaison	5%
	9 other offices	46%
Carter		
	Domestic Policy Staff	29%
	Communications	14%
	Cabinet Secretary	5%
	Press	5%
	Chief of Staff's Office	4%
	7 other offices	43%
Reagan		
	Domestic Policy Office (OPD and OPE)	31%
	Chief of Staff's Office	16%
	Communications	16%
	Counsel	4%
	8 other offices	33%
Bush		
	Office of Economic and Domestic Policy	23%
	Chief of Staff	17%
	Political Affairs	12%
	Assorted Pollsters	8%
	Cabinet	6%
	Intergovernmental Affairs	4%
	8 other offices	31%

Data sources: Nixon Presidential Materials; Historical Papers from the Gerald R. Ford Library; Historical Material from the Jimmy Carter Library; Historical Papers from the Ronald Reagan Library.
*Units frequently involved in polling are those for which staffs both sent and received memoranda on polling.

Carter's administration. However, as Table 2.2 reveals, increased collegiality did not produce greater numbers of individual involvement. Table 2.1 demonstrates an increased variety in the nature and extent of the individuals and offices who used poll data in the Carter White House.[32]

Data sharing in the Reagan administration resembled both the gatekeeper arrangement and freely dispersed patterns found in the previous White Houses. In a somewhat apologetic memo to his superior, Edward Meese, Edwin Harper writes, "It may be useful to have some survey research to back up our judgments and opinions about the policy options facing the President. To make this happen, I understand you will need to raise this issue with Jim Baker, the coordinator of White House survey research" (as well as chief of staff for the Reagan administration).[33] Despite providing an official polling coordinator, more Reagan staff members shared polling information on a regular basis (see Tables 2.1 and 2.2). No staff member (high ranking or not) exchanged more than 15 percent of all memos. The far-flung Reagan polling apparatus mirrors the vast verbal communication structure Kessel found in his study of the Reagan White House.[34]

In comparison to the other administrations, the Bush White House was a mass of contradictions. Despite the large number of individuals involved in at least one poll memo exchange (74), the Bush administration had functionally the same-sized apparatus as the other White Houses. In Table 2.1, no staff member, other than George Bush, exchanged more than 10 percent of all memos. Thus, at first glance the Bush polling structure appears quite open with few restrictions to access. However, finding that the top users work for only three offices suggests the presence of a narrower environment than found in the Reagan and Carter White Houses. Part of the confusion might stem from the lack of a polling coordinator. The pollster, Robert Teeter, sent information personally to the president, although other staff members also received information from Teeter, as well as from the Republican National Committee (RNC). Ed Rogers, deputy chief of staff and the seventh most frequent exchanger of poll data, performed some coordinator, but not gatekeeper, functions. Rogers often directed poll data from both Teeter and Wirthlin to other staff members. However, nothing in the Bush archives suggests that access to poll information was restricted. There were poll meetings for the entire Office of Political Affairs, in addition to meetings for the top staffers such as Deputy Chief of Staff Andrew Card, Communications Director David Demarest, Press Secretary Marlin Fitzwater, Vice President's Chief of Staff William Kristol, Assistant for Economic and Domestic Policy Roger Porter, and Assistant for Public Events and Initiatives Sig Rogich.[35]

The Nixon and Ford White Houses deliberately restricted routine access to polling data. Conversely, the Carter, Reagan, and Bush systems for dissemination allowed widespread access to public opinion data. Normatively, Reagan's hybrid exchanges appear both efficient and encompassing. The Reagan system eliminated both the secrecy and hoarding of information characteristic of the Nixon apparatus. In addition, Reagan's less-restrictive gatekeeper system encouraged uniform access to poll data among its top staff, which a fully volunteer system, such as Carter's, could not achieve. The Bush system, on the surface, resembled the Carter system, with poll data widely shared; however, in practice the administration was closer to the Reagan model of uniform access among the upper echelons.

Despite different rules for access, a similar number of individuals communicated referencing poll data in the Nixon, Carter, Reagan, and Bush White Houses. The exchange of polling memos seemingly mimics the advisory networks found in these White Houses. The personal management style of these presidents did shape the routine dissemination of polling information. However, personal presidential preferences did not affect the scope of poll usage, because essentially the same number of individuals routinely utilized polling information in both Nixon's hierarchical and Reagan's collegial systems.[36] The basic elements of the poll apparatus (data dissemination and total individual involvement) were passed from one administration to another, despite the personal preferences of the individual president.

The Party Loses and the Strategists Triumph

As noted above, modern presidential campaigns rely heavily on public opinion polling. Campaign-style presidential leadership is similarly dependent on polling. Approximately thirty people (6 percent of the staff) in these five administrations exchanged memoranda referencing polls. From these findings, it would appear that neither polling nor a campaigning environment functionally exists within the White House. However, these numbers can be deceiving. Despite presidential involvement, the relative influence of public opinion data can best be understood by examining the staff that actively employed poll data (and those who did not), as well as their ability to influence White House output.

Removing the Party

The traditional patronage system, which had existed between the president and his party, died with FDR in 1932. According to Milkis, FDR sought supporters of his presidency rather than his party, in some cases appointing individuals who were not "Democrats in many instances, and in all instances were not organization Democrats."[37] FDR's New Deal programs diminished traditional partisan patronage in favor of "intellectual and ideological patronage."[38] Simultaneously, the expansion of civil service job protections eroded presidential sanctions and rewards for supporters.[39] Weko argues, "There is an inevitable tension between presidents and their parties over the handling of political appointments, a tension that is rooted in dissimilar incentives that guide presidents and party leaders."[40] "The loosening of the ties that bind"[41] the party and the president increased the likelihood that campaign-style approaches to governing would penetrate the White House.

The trend to diminish the appointments of political party loyalists continued through the Johnson administration, culminating in the Nixon administration's centralization of power and authority in the White House with staffers completely loyal to the president. Nixon desired to be above the party,[42] and his polling operation and usage reflect it. Virtually all of Nixon's trusted advisors were long-standing friends and associates. The Committee to Re-Elect the President (CREEP) worked in concert with the White House and not the party. The national and state party organizations increasingly were bypassed as the candidates for the presidency hired their own staff and raised their own funds.[43] Old-style patronage politics was dead.[44]

As the loss of party control over the nomination process eliminated obligatory appointments,[45] the number of campaign staffers turned White House staffers increased. The increased presence of former campaign workers resulted in the increased number of individuals comfortable with and aware of polling. In fact, these individuals, who can "campaign effectively for policy and political standing," are necessary to produce the new "campaign-oriented style of governing."[46] Consequently, "the reliance on presidential advisory system mechanisms has further minimized the role that party organizations have played as agenda setters and problem definers, not to mention problem solvers."[47]

Beyond encouraging a staff loyal to the president and capable of using tools to enhance that loyalty, the loosened ties between president and party produced an odd relationship regarding the polls. Jacobs and Shapiro note that Nixon relied on the Republican National Committee for $100,000 in 1971 to cover the cost of polling.[48] However, as noted above, the Nixon White House severely restricted access to the public opinion data, and this included the Republican Party. Few staffers outside this trusted core of poll users mentioned in Table 2.1 received even basic trend information. Not surprisingly, information this tightly controlled was not distributed to the party organizations, despite the fact that party funds purchased the polls.

Due to the abrupt manner in which Gerald Ford became president, the Ford White House retained many of the Nixon staffers. However, the reaction to Watergate forced the newly constituted Ford presidency to review many of the standard practices of the Nixon White House. In its assessment of the polling apparatus, the Ford administration did consider whether to rekindle a relationship with the party. In January 1974, Fred Slight updated Jerry Jones on the state of the Ford White House polling operation. Slight noted, "Decisions to continue, modify or terminate the previous [Nixon] program were deferred."[49] After deciding to continue operations, Slight provided three options for his superiors in describing how the Ford polling operation might run: (1) centralizing all polling functions within one office; (2) decentralizing the polling function to the RNC; and (3) compromising between centralization and decentralization.[50] The Ford administration's organization of polling data appeared remarkably similar to the Nixon administration's but did not completely shut out the party. In a halfhearted attempt aimed at conciliation, the Ford White House locked the party out of the administration of the poll apparatus but did share some of the data with the party.

For the Carter, Reagan, and Bush administrations, the separation from the party using the polling apparatus developed depth. These administrations devoted less time to actually maintaining their polling apparatus and distributed the data widely among the staff. These White Houses received poll information from their respective National Committees, but it is not apparent that the exchanges went both ways. Patrick Caddell bypassed the Democratic National Committee (DNC) to send information to Carter and his staff directly, although the DNC did send informational poll data they received from Caddell as well as other sources.[51] Caddell prepared his large volume, *An Analysis of Political Attitudes in the United States of America,* for both President Jimmy Carter *and* the DNC, but it's not clear who actually saw the material beyond the White House staff and the Cabinet.

The Reagan administration extended the connection between the White House and the Republican National Committee (RNC). Memos were transmitted from or to Richard Wirthlin and from or to the RNC. Wirthlin often prepared his large poll reports for the RNC. He also sent regular polling updates to Richard Richards of the RNC. These memos were in the White House archives and the public relations files, and are not the entirety of the polling Wirthlin did for the White House. The Reagan White House appears to have shared some poll data with the RNC, but by no means all. However, the involvement of the respective Democrat and Republican National Committees wanes once direction is added. Few memos exchanged between the National Committees linked poll data to any type of directed action. Moreover, none of these presidents appeared to have routinely shared the poll data with the members of their party in Congress.

The reticence of the White House to share the polling data with the party might have been augmented, initially, by Congress members' disinterest in national polling and opinion leadership. Herbst and Jacobs and Shapiro note that past Congresses and past congressional leaders did not identify opinion leadership and polling as significant.[52] Congress members and their staffs found polls to be easily manipulated; "they distrusted public opinion surveys and overvalued focus groups."[53] Even under the changing attitudes toward polling by the leadership, individual legislators were highly suspicious and even dismissive of public opinion polling data.[54]

Carter, Reagan, and Bush all extended the trend of employing campaign staff in their administrations. President Carter's pollster, Patrick Caddell, reminded the president-elect in a December 1976 memo that he was elected to remove the insiders and "clean house in Washington."[55] To appease the grumbling from party loyalists, Caddell further recommended that the separate inaugural party for the DNC include "a gathering of your state coordinators and other key political people." The president personally noted in the margin: "Ham [Hamilton Jordan] try to do this or equivalent."[56] By 1981, the Reagan White House was taking great pains to plant White House loyalists, not party loyalists, beyond the White House and into the departments and agencies.[57] President Bush's top-level staffers came directly from his campaign (Baker, Sununu, and Mosbacher), and he placed his campaign manager as chair of the RNC.[58] As with the Nixon administration, the combination of the loyal White House staff and the polling apparatus produced efforts to isolate support for the president separate from his party or other traditional governing coalitions.

Inner Office Usage

Neustadt argues that in "every administration [there existed] some three or four senior assistants, whose roles rivaled or outshone . . . those of even department heads."[59] I find frequent usage (more than 10 percent of all memos) written to or by Neustadt's "most influential members" from each administration. Haldeman, Cheney, Eizenstat, and Reagan's triumvirate (Meese, Baker, and Deaver) top their respective administration's list of poll users in these four administrations. The third most frequent user of public opinion in the Bush administration was Chief of Staff John Sununu. Although Sununu exchanged less than 10 percent of all memos, he was not chief for four years, and no Bush staffer exchanged more than 10 percent.

Influence beneath the top echelon is difficult to establish across presidencies despite the presence of formal titles, such as special assistant or assistant to the president, due to the inherent role of personalities on influence. Thus, rather than try to determine who was close to the center of power, I examined where those who used public opinion worked and focused on the importance of the office. Twelve units of the Executive Office of the President are directly responsible for creating, coordinating, and disseminating the president's domestic agenda. They are the Chief of Staff's Office (including the deputy chief), the Staff Secretary's Office, the Cabinet Secretary's Office, the Domestic Policy Office, Counsel, Legislative Affairs, Political Affairs, Intergovernmental Affairs, Communications, the Press Secretary's Office, Public Liaison, and Speechwriting and Research.

The chief of staff is arguably the most influential member of the White House staff after the president. "A chief of staff's power . . . derives from his ability to schedule the president's time, allocate access to him, and to shape his agenda."[60] Clearly, having the Chief of Staff's Office actively involved in the polling apparatus not only enhances the likelihood that polling information will reach the president, but also alludes to the importance of public opinion in the president's agenda. Table 2.1, which highlights active poll users, includes the chief of staff from all five White Houses. In four of the five administrations, it was the Chief of Staff's Office that dispersed and managed the polling data, much in the way it managed the White House (see Table 2.3).[61] Although most chiefs argue they are honest brokers between competing agendas and alternatives, Kernell and Popkin claim "observations of their actual performance . . . outline an entirely different story."[62] Thus, the delegation of the polling apparatus to the chief of staff and his office suggests that disseminating public opinion is congruous with the formal and informal roles of the Chief of Staff's Office: managing the White House and politically protecting and guiding the president's agenda.

Beneath the Chief of Staff's Office, the most frequent units utilizing polling are those predominately involved in the designing and selling of the president's agenda (see Table 2.3). Most poll exchanges took place within and between Communications, Public Liaison, Political Liaison, and the Domestic Policy Office (DPO).[63] With the exception of the DPO, the most frequent users of opinion were found within offices charged with what can be construed as "campaign-like" behavior. Communications, Public Liaison, and Political Liaison are designed to coordinate with and relate to "outsiders." Although the DPO is not mandated with maintaining relationships and coordinating connections, the office does have campaign-like functions.

In 1970, President Nixon's Ash Council on Executive Organization charged the Domestic Council (Nixon's DPO) with a large task: "to coordinate policy formation in the domestic area . . . [so that] to a considerable degree [it] would be a domestic counterpart to the National Security Council."[64] Thus, the domestic coordinating body's objective was both large in scope and vague in design. However, coordinating policy formation includes considerations of the public's agenda, and attempts to monitor that agenda for changes in much the same way that campaigns must bend with changing public attitudes. In contrast, the Congressional Liaison is not among the frequent polling units. The Congressional Liaison relates not to the public or to groups, but to other elites—members of the House of Representatives, the Senate, and their staffs—over policy in the congressional pipeline.

Finding a high exchange of public opinion in the DPO but not within the Liaison's Office begins to define the extent of a campaign style of leadership in the presidency. The dearth of polling data utilized in the Liaison's Office implies that public opinion information was not a useful tool for persuading individual congressional members to support the president's agenda. Bargaining remained the preferred form of contact. During these administrations, individual congressional members did not rely heavily on poll data for strategic planning and did not often react to changes in opinion data.[65] However, congressional leaders were more attentive over time. After the critical 1994 elections, the incentives for the congressional leadership to rely on polling were greater than for rank-and-file members.[66] However, finding public opinion in the DPO suggests that poll data were useful for policy formation.

For twenty-five years, the exchange of poll data remained within a narrow locus of power. In these five White Houses, the political strategists dominated the polling apparatus. As in any good political campaign, those staffers who designed the message and kept the president on his agenda were the dominant poll users. A glance at Table 2.1 reveals that three of the five administrations did have policy specialists among the top poll users (Ehrlichman, Eizenstat, and Porter).[67] More significantly, although some White Houses (namely Carter's) shared information with the Cabinet secretaries, few memoranda containing poll data passed between the White House staff and the Cabinet.[68] The majority of poll users were political generalists focused on the success of the presidency, and not particular policies.

The Importance of Skill

Leadership directly correlates with the successful wielding of information. Information management affects all four dimensions of presidential activity (advisory processes and decision making, administrative strategies, public leadership, and congressional leadership).[69] The circumstances in which a particular president finds himself also influence leadership. Context (also termed "political time," or "opportunity levels") always matters, as presidents must play the political hand they are dealt.[70] "What determines whether presidents achieve the political results their opportunity levels permit? Skill."[71]

Campaigns are often won or lost due to the skillful mastery of information. Successful penetration of a campaign style of leadership is directly dependent on the ability to use campaign-quality information. Jacobs and Shapiro emphasize staff training in public opinion analysis as one of several features that can significantly improve the quality of polling usage.[72] "The Nixon administration introduced . . . changes that enhanced the White House's specialization . . . it qualitatively improved the training and professional experience of White House aides and consultants who analyzed public opinion."[73] Not only is specialization a measure of the breadth and depth of the institutional development that Jacobs and Shapiro outline, but staff specialization also captures the ability of White House staff members to realistically incorporate public opinion into their goals and plans. Logically, individuals skilled in public opinion analysis and more comfortable assessing poll data are more likely to do a better job incorporating public opinion into daily tasks.

Sophisticated Users

The Nixon administration was quite hard on the pollster who offered information that was not up to its exacting standards. Haldeman indicated his displeasure and expectations by angrily scrawling on the top of one memo: "Useless—I can read the statistics myself—what we need is analysis, not highlights." As a result, Haldeman's aide, Larry Higby, sent one of Nixon's polling consultants, Professor David Derge, a memo tactfully stating, "As you can see by Bob's comments written on the attached, this is not what he is looking for in terms of analysis. What he is looking for is the conclusions that can be drawn if the results change in trend and possible reasons why trend shifts are changing and other types of analysis that you would feel would be appropriate."[74] The Nixon White House set the standard for the pollster's services: Raw polling data was expected, and direction, duration, and scope of public opinion was required.

The Ford administration did not expressly follow the rigorous example set by the Nixon administration. Ford utilized pollsters Teeter and Wirthlin (as did Nixon and Bush), who provided detailed analysis and suggestions for presidential action.[75] Contrary to the Nixon aides taking control of the apparatus and directing its needs, the Ford White House followed Wirthlin's lead. In his proposal to the Ford White House, it is Wirthlin who notes that the White House needs a "continuous measurement of the nature, direction and depth" of public opinion.[76] Although the Ford White House retained individuals skilled in opinion analysis (for example, Dick Cheney, David Gergen), the Ford White House relied mainly on univariate, percentage measurement of responses, although they did utilize some trend data and cross-tab analysis.[77]

The Reagan polling apparatus employed many of the same pollsters and staffers as the previous Republican administrations and, as a result, improved on the Nixon and Ford White Houses in both style and understanding. The continued usage of the same pollsters and staff members provided continuity and increasing specialization in applying opinion analysis to White House decision making. As with the Nixon administration, the Reagan White House staffers possessed sophisticated knowledge of public opinion analysis. The most frequent user of poll data, Richard Beal, worked for Wirthlin's polling firm prior to White House employment. The Reagan White House employed individuals extremely skilled in public opinion analysis. By the time of the Bush administration, the Republicans were quite skilled and accustomed to incorporating public opinion into the White House structure. Public opinion usage was habitual and expert.

Sophisticated polling knowledge provided the Republican White Houses (although to a lesser degree in the Ford White House) with a check on the pollster. The poll data was clearly read and the pollsters' reports digested, but always with a healthy understanding and respect, not awe or blind followership. The information was challenged, and the sources and limits of public opinion were understood. There were some noticeable changes in the presentation of data, no doubt in response to the change in presidential style between the three Republican presidents. The information that went to the Reagan senior staff and President Reagan came with beautifully color-coded charts, simple to read and interpret, even by the uninitiated.[78] However, the raw data, univariate and multivariate analysis, as well as pollster reports, were still available. By the time of the Bush administration, Republican pollsters were skilled in working with both the sophisticated and the untrained user of poll data.

Poll analysis skills were not the sole purview of the Republican Party. The Clinton White House staffers were awash in public opinion data. The Clinton White House received reams of detailed attitudinal data and poll analysis from outside consultants and pollsters. President Clinton's primary pollsters and consultants were Stanley Greenberg and Dick Morris, both of whom date back to the president's Arkansas gubernatorial days. Greenberg and Morris provided the public opinion data and analysis to the president and the White House in written and verbal form. In sharp contrast to the monthly or even haphazard polling efforts of the previous administrations, President Clinton and his staff received information and updates weekly.[79] Greenberg, as with the Republican pollsters, was "analytical and nuanced" but, according to other White House staffers, did not "make definitive recommendations."[80] According to Morris, Clinton often lamented that "Greenberg never told me what to do."[81] Clinton, as with Nixon and Carter, wanted his pollsters to provide clear prescriptions. George Stephanopoulos argued that Dick Morris "spoke to the part of Clinton that wanted to be told what to do."[82]

During President Clinton's first term, the top layer of the White House staff consisted of the central players from the successful presidential campaign, to the consternation of many loyal Washington Democrats.[83] Like the Republican administrations, the Clinton White House employed former campaign workers familiar with public opinion techniques. The poll users in the Clinton staff came almost entirely from the campaign organization and consisted of individuals skilled in the usage of public opinion polls.[84]

Scheduling memos and meetings cited in "insider" tales reveal that the topmost layer of the Clinton White House staff was extremely attentive to public opinion.[85] In the Clinton administration, Secretary of Commerce Ron Brown, United States Trade Representative and Secretary of Commerce Mickey Kantor, and Secretary of Housing and Urban Development Henry Cisneros were even included in the weekly poll meetings.[86] However, these Cabinet inclusions reflected the closeness of these individuals to the president rather than an increased reliance on policy staff. Despite these Cabinet inclusions, the White House staff dominated the poll apparatus. The positions and offices cited above are well represented in the Clinton strategy meetings, which included the president, the vice president, the Chief of Staff's Office, Counsel, Communications, Legislative Affairs, the Press Office, and Political Affairs.[87]

Novice Opinion Users

In contrast to the Republican polling dynasty and the Clinton administration, fewer staffers acquainted with public opinion polling techniques inhabited the Carter White House. Patrick Caddell and his firm
Cambridge Survey Research (CSR) provided the Carter White House
with "detailed poll data a minimum of four times a year for four years.
These analyses (generally six to eight chapters, and well over 300 pages)
contained questions and analyses of public opinion on all the significant
issues and attitudes pertaining to the Carter presidency." As in the Republican White Houses, Caddell provided raw data, univariate and multivariate analyses, and detailed reports suggesting how the data related to
White House activities. Although a large number of staff members and
Cabinet members had easy access to Caddell's polling data, that access
did not necessarily imply sophisticated understanding of public opinion
techniques or limitations.

Top Carter administration staff members, as well as less influential members of the Domestic Policy Staff (DPS), communicated directly
with the pollster and his firm, in sharp contrast to the Nixon and Ford
administrations, which privileged few staffers with direct access to the
pollster.[88] Access to Caddell and his poll data was virtually unrestricted.

The weaknesses in the Carter staff are first evident in the exchanges with the pollsters. White House involvement in designing the
presidential surveys began with the Nixon administration.[89] Pollster
David Derge "spent much of his time working with Haldeman and his
aides to design question wordings," often the "exact question that the
President asked to be included in the next poll."[90] Similar practices can be
found in the Ford and Reagan administrations. The Carter administration had a close working relationship with Caddell and CSR, but with
subtle restrictions. In a memo between DPO staffers, Steve Simmons
notes that Dotty Lynch of CSR claims, "Generally it is helpful to give us
[CSR] a list of topics (in order of priority) and let us [CSR] write the questions. However, if you have some specific questions in mind, we will *try*
to incorporate them."[91] Teeter and Wirthlin did not offer similar guidelines, although they did refine staff questions in order to remove bias.

The events leading to the infamous Carter "Crisis of Confidence,"
or "Malaise," speech underscore the devastating consequences of novice
opinion users relying on polls and pollsters. Beginning in late 1978 and

early 1979, Patrick Caddell began submitting a series of alarming memos to President Carter on "the state of America." In January 1979, Caddell writes that the survey "we have most recently received may well be the most significant and disturbing survey I have looked at in the ten years I have been conducting polls. Not because of your political situation, which while relatively stable is still disturbing."[92] Caddell littered his later reports with alarmist rhetoric unequaled by any of the Republican pollsters' reports. His rhetoric was often far beyond the scope of relating presidential activity to public opinion. More importantly, there was no one in the Carter administration capable of challenging Caddell's dogmatic assessments, such as: "One can only conclude from these figures . . . that all the legislative initiatives, programs, foreign policy efforts while being good and important governmental actions are essentially irrelevant to solving this deeper, more fundamental, and more demanding problem."[93] Haldeman may have wanted analysis rather than highlighting statistics, but what is a president supposed to do with Caddell's assertion that no program or government effort could possibly alter the dismal malaise affecting the country? It took Caddell only six months to convince Carter to give his "Crisis of Confidence" speech.

Caddell urged the president to respond to the historically high public pessimism about the future of the nation, the role of government, and the leadership provided by Jimmy Carter, with a pep talk. Unable to convince the staff and the president to rewrite the 1979 State of the Union, Caddell persisted and approached First Lady Rosalynn Carter in April 1979. After a meeting with Press Secretary Jody Powell and Caddell, Rosalynn Carter agreed to present Caddell's message to the president. Caddell's harangue (widely referred to as the "*Apocalypse Now* memo") urged the president to connect to "the broader public sentiments which constituted the real mandate of 1976."[94] Carter gave the speech July 15, 1979. Initial response to the speech was favorable.[95] But negative media reactions to both the speech and the administration caused Carter's popularity to plummet, never to recover amid the Cabinet resignations and the Iran hostage crisis. The "Crisis of Confidence" speech intended to inspire and unite instead "did not produce any long-lasting change in the public perceptions of the Carter administration, and may have even made matters worse with the malaise legacy it left behind."[96]

How did Jimmy Carter deliver a message to the public that his top advisors opposed? Stuart Eizenstat's and Walter Mondale's opposition to Caddell's findings did not stem from a lack of faith or trust in poll data. In fact, Eizenstat was the most frequent user of poll data (see Table 2.1). Eizenstat and Mondale mistrusted Caddell's interpretation of the data but not the data itself, calling Caddell's "social psychology a dry hole." Strong contends Eizenstat and Mondale believed the energy plan was the top priority, not the "mood" of the nation.[97] How could Caddell convince first Jody Powell, then Rosalynn Carter, and ultimately the president to override other trusted advisors' opinions? By 1979, crucial members of the White House staff devotedly supported Caddell and believed in both his advice and his interpretation of public opinion. Internal memos between staff members of the DPS highlight the administration's dedication to Caddell and his analysis.

Peter Bourne began the debate noting:

"In addition to whatever Pat Caddell may have to offer us, Roper can also offer a most useful service. . . . By the way Roper was the only pollster who was still predicting Carter as a sure winner by 4 points November 2nd [1976]."

Steve Travis claimed:

"If you are looking for the *most accurate* poll, you need expert opinion, like Caddell's. I would like a series of these reports, i.e., Gallup, Harris, Roper etc., coming to us, but costs are high and I need clearer lines for communication to those who need this information."

David Rubenstein firmly concluded the discussion:

"I strongly believe that this would be a waste of money—Caddell already provides us with as much detail as we need; no one will really need these [other reports]."[98]

Needless to say, the DPS did not purchase outside poll data. The devotion to Caddell and his data was unmatched in the Republican administrations. Nixon relied on three separate polling consultants, Derge,

this is a good quote for Chap 8

Teeter, and Wirthlin, and also monitored commercial poll information. Ford relied on both Teeter and Wirthlin until the end of 1975. The Reagan administration primarily employed Wirthlin, but Wirthlin himself offered the Reagan administration other sources of poll data. Wirthlin created a databank of all polling questions on particular issues, which included Wirthlin's surveys as well as commercial surveys on all pertinent issues. On any issue, Wirthlin's firm, Decision Management Information (DMI), could provide all DMI's survey data and any questions publicly released by Gallup, Harris, or any other firm. The Bush administration abandoned the databank system, realizing that it was more cost effective to simply track public opinion in the media. The four Republican administrations used various sources of competing survey data to compare results, and to control for question wording, bias, and comprehension.[99] The Carter administration used only Caddell.

Arguably, Dick Morris was as influential (and as controlling) in the Clinton administration as Caddell was in the Carter White House. However, the Carter staffers employing public opinion lacked the public relations and the opinion analysis skills found in the Clinton White House, or in the other administrations. Neophyte opinion knowledge appears as a potential flaw for the incorporation of public opinion into Carter's leadership strategies. The Republican administrations' polling users were people capable of understanding multivariate analysis and employing raw data in their own work. Essentially, the differences between the Republican (and Clinton) and Carter staff members remained the ability to question pollster recommendations and analyses. Recognizing the flaw in single poll or single pollster reliance, the Republican administrations employed several sources of poll data. No significant challenge emerged to Caddell's and CSR's data gathering or survey interpretation, either from sophisticated staff understanding or from additional pollster interpretation. Rather than provide a source of information and analysis, Caddell provided information, analysis, and an agenda. Morris also provided information, analysis, and an agenda, but other skilled users (such as George Stephanopoulos) could contravene Morris' expertise and polling analysis coating. The "Crisis of Confidence" speech debacle dramatically demonstrates the danger from the lack of polling acumen across the White House.

Conclusions

This book seeks to consider whether a campaign style of leadership rather than traditional governing exists in the presidency. To explore the penetration of a campaign style, I use the public opinion polling apparatus as a proxy representing this leadership. Thus, the presence, penetration, and importance of campaigning to govern are predicated on the presence, penetration, and importance of public opinion polls to the presidency. In this chapter, I began with basic questions. Does the White House use polls? Yes, they do. Who in the White House relies on public opinion and how significant are they to the operation of the presidency? The president, the chief of staff, and other key figures in the White House all were part of the exchange of polling information. However, as Lammers and Genovese articulate, context and circumstance matter for leadership. Some figures in some White Houses were more attentive to polls than others: Patrick Caddell and Bill Clinton, for example.

Campaigns have a defined beginning and ending. The goal of any campaign is simple: to win office. The key to any campaign is convincing 51 percent of the voting population to vote for the candidate. Polls reveal who's ahead, who's behind, and more importantly, why. Thus, campaigns, particularly presidential campaigns that must run both statewide and nationally, are dependent on public opinion for decision making.

In contrast, governing between elections lacks defined endpoints beyond artificial creations such as the first 100 days or the midterm elections. As a result, identifying that the top echelon of the White House staff, including the president, was immersed in the polling apparatus provides only the first step toward evaluating the presence of campaign leadership. The offices charged with behavior similar to a campaign, such as outreach and coordination with various publics, all actively participated in the exchange of public opinion. The next chapter explores what the users of the polling apparatus did with the information once they had it.

In the new millennium, the centrality of public opinion polling for presidential politics pervaded even popular culture. On *The West Wing*, the enormously popular NBC television show about a fictional White House, the presidential pollster, the polling operation, and the status of the presidential approval rating was the focus of one highly charged episode. Titled "Lies, Damn Lies, and Statistics," the episode follows one character, the press secretary, who gamely contends in the face of pressure that the president's approval rating will rise significantly. The episode ends triumphantly with the staff and the president savoring the bounce and moving on to the difficult business at hand.

Aided by its consultant, President Carter's former pollster Patrick Caddell, *The West Wing* trumpets the approval rating mythos: Presidents spend millions of dollars on a polling operation to ascertain the public's perception of the president's job performance. Popular culture underscores the scholarly and media interpretations of the value of public opinion for the presidency—as a mechanism for evaluating campaign-like behavior in the absence of a trip to the voting booth. The behavior requiring evaluation is the president's persuasive efforts, as campaigning is inherently about persuasion—persuading an individual or group of individuals to vote.

The permanent campaign is a leadership approach defined by the use of campaign techniques to sell individuals, agendas, and issues, according to Burdett Loomis.[1] However, traditional conceptions of governing also include persuasive components. In "going public," Samuel Kernell's widely cited presidential leadership approach, presidents reach out to the public to pressure other elites.[2] Charles O. Jones argues that presidential performance and persuasion also include efforts to "maintain status and credibility."[3] Poll data in these conceptions provide evaluation of the approach, via the approval rating.

Persuasion for the candidate (or the president) is dependent on effective definitions of who supports the candidate and why. Candidates must form a connection to individuals in order to overcome the myriad reasons for not voting. Presidents must understand their audience in order to produce the desired reaction among other elites and the media. Thus, public opinion data gathering and the persuasive presidency naturally fit together. Nevertheless, presidential governing and leadership includes more than rhetorical efforts. Presidential governing consists of information gathering; administrative tasks; defining, selecting, and fighting for policies; as well as implementation.

Chapter 2 connected the poll apparatus, and thus the permanent campaign, to the White House and its staff members. This chapter explores the penetration of presidential tasks and decisions by the permanent campaign. The White House used campaign techniques in governing—but not as conceived by traditional formulations. The poll apparatus provided the White House with more than the tracking of popularity ratings; the White House queried the public across agendas and issues. The poll apparatus was present in generic public relations decision making as well as constituency relations. However, the poll apparatus was not present in program design, policy development, or implementation. Campaign tools did not penetrate completely into areas traditionally defined as governing, but the skills, technology, and behavior of a campaign did worm their way into the White House.

Defining Public Opinion Data

The presidential poll apparatus contains public opinion data derived from any correctly performed survey. Specifically, information received from polls includes the questions asked, the answers received, and the statistically achieved cross-tabulations providing relationships between questions, answers, and demographics. Polls are distinctive in terms of their sample size, the questions asked, the answers, and the analysis performed. However, my analysis absorbs and accounts for these differences.

I coded memoranda from the Nixon, Ford, Carter, Reagan, and Bush archives at the sentence level of analysis for the type of poll data employed and for the type of White House activities in which the data was employed.[4] By structuring my presidential analysis by distribution and applications of public opinion, I can generalize across presidencies. I coded for three distinct types of poll questions that could be referenced by the White House: (1) Popularity; (2) Policy; and (3) Personal. I then coded the memos for four distinct White House activities: (1) Information Gathering; (2) Program Development; (3) Public Relations; and (4) Constituency Building. From my content analysis, I can determine what kind of public opinion the White House employed, as well as how and where it was used.

From inspections of standard survey question techniques, I created a mechanism for comparing public opinion itself. For example, the question "Do you approve of the job the president is doing?" asks the respondent to evaluate the president generally. A question such as "Do you want universal health care?" asks the respondent to make a policy choice. Consequently, I was able to code White House poll memoranda without including the respondent's answer.[5]

Presidential references to public opinion response types were cataloged into three broad categories: Popularity, Policy, and Personal (Policy was further subdivided into issue subcategories). I also coded White House memoranda at the sentence level of analysis for classification of presidential activities: Information Gathering, Programs, Constituency, and Public Relations. Thus, there are two levels of analysis: the *type* of public opinion questions asked, and their incorporation into White House processes, or *activity*. I first examine the type of opinion questions asked by the Nixon, Ford, Carter, Reagan, and Bush administrations. I then discuss both the application of poll data by activity, and the interaction of type and activity.

Classifying Polls

The type of response a question seeks from respondents can classify any survey question included in any public opinion poll. Questions coded Personal ask the respondent for any individual information, typically: party identification, political philosophy, and socioeconomic status (SES) data. Questions coded Popularity require the respondent to gauge the performance of the president, in general and in specific areas (for example, the economy). Questions coded Policy ask the respondent to choose between policies, to rate policies, or otherwise indicate knowledge of policies. The questions do not ask for opinions of presidential performance or success regarding those policies. A Policy question requests a choice, such as "Do you favor or oppose continuing the social security program?" Because the Policy category could include a vast array of domestic policy issues, I subdivided the category. Table 3.1 lists the major and minor categories.[6] "A total of 12 Policy subcategories were developed for coding, and each reference to a particular policy" in a polling memo was counted.[7] The coded subcategories include: Domestic Fiscal, Monetary, and Tax Policy, and Inflation; Unemployment, Job Creation, and Industrial Policy; Defense Spending, Conversion, and

TABLE **3.1** Polling Categories by Type

	Popularity
Popularity	Do you approve or disapprove of the job the president is doing?
Specific Job Performance Evaluation	Do you approve or disapprove of the president's handling of the economy?
General Congressional Job Performance Evaluation	Do you approve or disapprove of the job the Congress is doing?
Specific Congressional Job Performance Evaluation	Do you approve or disapprove of how Congress is handling the impeachment of the president?
	Policy
General Policy	What do you feel should be done to avoid the crisis in the social security system? *(Refers to a policy but does not give the respondent a choice between policies.)*
Specific Policy	Do you favor or oppose switching school vacations to wintertime so that schools can be closed in the winter to conserve fuel as a method of dealing with natural gas shortages? *(Refers to a policy and asks the respondent to make a choice between options.)*
	Personal
Party Identification	Do you consider yourself a Democrat, Republican, or Independent?
SES Data	Gender, Income, Region *(Refers to personal information only.)*

Personnel; Political and Government Reform; Crime; Entitlements (including welfare, insurance, social security, Medicare, and Medicaid); Education; Environment and Land Management; Energy; Science, Technology, and Transportation; Economic Affairs; and Social Issues (for example, abortion, separation of church and state).[8]

The poll questions employed by these five administrations varied both by type and in usage. In the aggregate, Policy questions were referenced in White House memoranda more than either Popularity questions or Personal questions (see Table 3.2). Studies linking approval ratings with presidential actions account for only 36 percent of presidential use of public opinion.[9] Combining all five presidents' polling references suggests that perhaps popularity data were not as useful or as important to presidents as policy information.[10] However, considering individual presidential data grouped over time by category produces a significantly more productive tool for assessing trends in type of opinion usage across presidencies. Table 3.3 provides each administration's usage of public opinion by the type of question.

Figure 3.1 more effectively demonstrates the patterns of poll question usage across the five administrations.[11] As this figure reveals, there

TABLE **3.2** Total Poll Question Usage by Type ($N = 431$)

Popularity	Policy	Personal
36.5%	41.1%	22.4%

Data sources: Nixon Presidential Materials; Historical Papers from the Gerald R. Ford Library; Historical Material from the Jimmy Carter Library; Historical Papers from the Ronald Reagan Library.

TABLE **3.3** Specific Presidential Poll Question Usage by Type

	Popularity	Policy	Personal
Nixon	44.7%	26.8%	28.5%
Ford	45.1%	38.5%	16.5%
Carter	34.7%	48.4%	16.8%
Reagan	25.4%	48.5%	26.0%
Bush	15.7%	61.2%	23.1%

Data sources: Nixon Presidential Materials; Historical Papers from the Gerald R. Ford Library; Historical Material from the Jimmy Carter Library; Historical Papers from the Ronald Reagan Library.

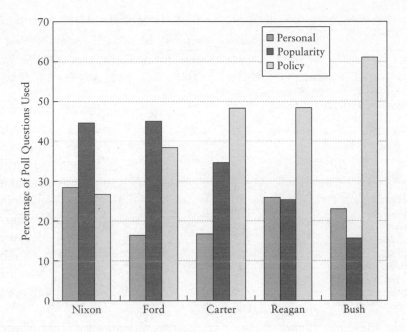

FIGURE **3.1** Poll Question Usage by Type

are two significant patterns of usage: Policy usage increases over time and Popularity usage declines. Of course, a visually perceived trend does not ensure the existence of statistically significant trends over time. To confirm the presence of a trend in poll question usage, I performed the Mann-Kendall test for trends on all three sets of data. A nonparametric test, Mann-Kendall distinguishes between fluctuations due to random (unassignable) causes and cycles that indicate long-term change.[12] With alpha set at .05, I found Popularity and Policy significant. I can be 95 percent confident that Popularity usage decreased; Policy usage increased. Moreover, I can be 95 percent confident that both cycles are trends and not the result of random vacillations in administration usage. Personal exhibited no statistically significant trends; the question type usage remained unchanged over time.[13]

The Policy Category   Policy questions ask the respondent to comment on specific aspects of the president's agenda. Policy questions attempt to account for the complexities of individual attitudes as well as

TABLE **3.4** Polled Policy Issues Referenced in White House Memoranda

	Nixon	Ford	Carter	Reagan	Bush	Avg.
	N=82	N=66	N=114	N=130	N=158	N=110
Domestic Fiscal, Monetary, and Tax Policy, and Inflation	28.1%	29.8%	17.5%	42.3%	23.4%	28.2%
Unemployment, Job Creation, and Industrial Policy	8.5%	10.6%	7.9%	6.9%	0.6%	6.9%
Defense Spending, Conversion, and Personnel	3.7%	3.0%	0.0%	3.9%	0.0%	2.1%
Political and Government Reform	3.7%	18.2%	14.9%	4.6%	2.5%	8.8%
Crime	26.8%	9.1%	0.0%	2.3%	3.8%	8.4%
Entitlements	11.0%	6.1%	15.8%	13.9%	6.3%	10.6%
Education	1.2%	4.6%	0.0%	15.4%	7.0%	5.6%
Environment and Land Management	12.2%	0.0%	1.8%	0.0%	43.0%	11.4%
Energy	0.0%	13.6%	30.7%	3.3%	0.6%	9.7%
Science, Technology, and Transportation	1.2%	0.0%	8.8%	3.1%	1.9%	3.0%
Economic Affairs	3.7%	6.1%	2.6%	3.9%	3.2%	3.9%
Social Issues	0.0%	0.0%	0.0%	1.5%	7.6%	1.8%

Data sources: Nixon Presidential Materials; Historical Papers from the Gerald R. Ford Library; Historical Material from the Jimmy Carter Library; Historical Papers from the Ronald Reagan Library.

the complexities of the political system.[14] Thus, the Policy category provides a wide variety of information about public attitudes. Coding questions as Policy reveals that presidents are interested in the public's position on issues—but which issues? In Table 3.4, I assembled all the references to issues and public opinion in the archived memoranda across the Nixon, Ford, Carter, Reagan, and Bush administrations. Categorizing the frequency of references to opinion across all domestic issues revealed some interesting institutional patterns. Economic issues dominated presidential public opinion references in all five administrations. Three issue subcategories accounted for almost half the opinion references: Domestic Fiscal, Monetary, and Tax Policy, and Inflation (which primarily includes the issues of tax policy and inflation); Unemployment, Job Creation, and Industrial Policy; and Entitlements (which includes Medicare, Medicaid, social security, and references to health care, health insurance, and welfare). Domestic Fiscal, Monetary, and Tax Policy, and Inflation was the most frequently referenced issue by far, accounting for, on average,

28 percent of all presidential memo references to public opinion. The Carter and Reagan administrations represented the extremes on this issue, with the Carter administration referring to tax and inflation policy only 18 percent of the time, and the Reagan administration referring to tax and inflation policy 42 percent of the time.

The other half of the apparatus belonged to only four issue subcategories: Political and Government Reform, Crime, Environment and Land Management, and Energy. Unlike the economic categories, Political and Government Reform, Crime, Environment and Land Management, and Energy are not uniformly referenced by all five administrations. As Table 3.4 demonstrates, Nixon, Reagan, and Bush did not reference Energy or Political and Government Reform issues more than 5 percent of the time. Contrarily, the Ford and Carter White Houses referenced Energy over 13 percent of the time, with the Carter administration utilizing Energy poll information 31 percent of the time. Energy was the Carter administration's most frequently mentioned issue. Similarly, on the Political and Government Reform issue, both the Carter and Ford administrations referenced it approximately 16 percent of the time. In fact, both issues combined represent the bulk of their opinion usage, after the economic issues. For the Ford administration, Energy and Political and Government Reform account for over 30 percent of its usage, and Energy and Political and Government Reform account for almost 45 percent of the Carter administration's usage. Instead of Energy and Political and Government Reform, the Nixon administration's attention shifted to the Crime issue, and to a lesser degree, the Environment and Land Management. The Nixon administration referenced Crime opinion approximately 27 percent of the time, second only to Domestic Fiscal, Monetary, and Tax Policy, and Inflation. The Bush administration catapults the Environment and Land Management issue on to the list of most frequently referenced issues. The Bush White House referenced Environment and Land Management issues, 43 percent of the time, almost twice as often as economic issues. In the context of the polling apparatus, at least, Bush was the environmental president. Interestingly, the Bush administration was the only White House to reference Social Issues (7.6 percent). It was interested in public opinion about the social issues of abortion, school prayer, gun control, a balanced budget, and tuition tax credits. Thus, seven issue subcategories represent virtually the entirety of presidentially polled topics.

Lit Review

Role of
Pres Popularity
+ governing

Exploring which type of public opinion the White House utilized revealed some interesting, and unexpected, findings. Approval ratings have a mixed record as a direct, strategic resource. On one hand, scholars consider presidential popularity a political resource because it is a performance rating.[15] Similarly, Brace and Hinckley assert that popularity functions "as a kind of continuing referendum" on the job the president is doing, to which presidents must respond.[16] Kernell takes this argument a step further, asserting that if a president's popular support declines, so too does his ability to govern.[17] However, Bond and Fleisher, in their analysis of roll call voting, and George Edwards, in *At the Margins,* find that "presidential popularity will have only a marginal impact on voting decisions of representatives in Congress."[18] Mark Peterson, using a tandem-institutional approach focusing on decision making, notes that the net effects of public approval on legislative outcomes are dubious at best.[19] The focus on approval ratings restricted the public to post-policymaking input either through ongoing public efforts targeted at moving Congress or commentary for the next election.[20] Moreover, Paul Light and John Kingdon dismiss the value of public opinion poll data for the policymaking process.[21]

Therefore, the assumption that popularity is useful presumes that it evaluates past performance and influences the environment for future action. Despite the increased attention to approval ratings, the cottage industry surrounding the approval rating variable continues to find evidence of only an indirect resource, confirming the argument originally articulated by Neustadt in 1960. The findings in Chapter 2 provide further evidence against the approval rating argument. Presidents are spending millions of dollars each year to purchase public opinion data and pollster analysis. Rationally speaking, there is no logical reason to spend so much of a scarce resource for information that cannot directly help a president achieve his goals. The poll apparatus must offer something more tangible to the White House. Poll data must offer more than opportunities to evaluate past job performance or compare performance to past presidents.

The findings in this chapter further separate the White House polling operation from conventional wisdom and the reams of scholarship concerning the approval rating variable. Popularity ratings did not dominate discussions in White House memoranda. Popularity was not a significant source of information for the White House, and its use declined over time. Information on issues, rather than performance, represented the bulk of exchanges. The preference for issue data rather than popularity ratings and personal information suggests that presidents and their staffs are looking for proactive planning information rather than reactive evaluations. Clearly, presidents want information to help with where they are going and not simply evaluate where they have been.

Polling and the Practicalities of Leadership

For centuries, across all positions of power, people have investigated what it means to lead. Why are some individuals effective leaders, but others appear doomed to failure? Richard Neustadt asks on page 1 of *Presidential Power* what are we measuring, what are we calling presidential leadership? What do presidents need in order to lead? The heart of leadership is decision making, deciding what to do and when. Leading with the permanent campaign outside the White House requires "shifting the weights on the scales of the public's business from . . . deliberation and teaching to persuasion and selling."[22] Leading in the White House requires management of individuals and information. Reams of data routinely flow through the White House, often without rhyme or reason. The White House suffers from what Paul Light describes as a problem of too much raw data and too little analysis.[23]

Poll data provide information—information about the public and their attitudes. In their memos to each other, White House staff were attentive to the public's opinion in seven distinct issue areas other than presidential approval. This information was in memoranda exchanged by staff in the offices highlighted in Chapter 2, the Chief of Staff's Office, Communications, Political and Public Liaison, and the Domestic Policy Office. However, these memos tell us more. Not only do they reveal who used poll data, when they used them, and what type of information the staffers referenced, they also indicate where polling was utilized. Thus, the memos also reveal whether the permanent campaign exists.

Classifying White House Tasks

My first category, Information Gathering, honed in on the most basic of staff behavior: gathering data. The key to this classification was the absence of a directional referent. I classified phrases or groups of phrases, and usually the entire memo, as Information Gathering when no subsequent action was mentioned. All Information Gathering memos provided only poll data without referencing anything else. For example, in a memo to President George Bush, Bob Teeter, Bush's pollster, writes, "Attached are the results of a poll done last night. . . . Overall, very good results for the U.S. and you."[24] Thus, the poll data exchange is for informational purposes only. The memo includes several different types of Policy data as well as some Popularity data. I called this category Information Gathering because so many of these memos read, quite simply, "FYI" (for your information) or "I thought you would be interested in this." No other action is discussed.

My second category, Program Development, isolated all phrases or groups of phrases referring to program development, from implementation to the selection of policy alternatives. The category Program Development captured sentences discussing the designing of, creating of, implementing of, and options involved in presidential policy. A memo from several of President Carter's Domestic Policy Staff effectively illustrates the Program Development category. Public opinion poll questions on privacy were cited "in order to help us decide how to handle the follow-on implementation actions."[25]

For my category Public Relations, I followed Kernell's definition of "going public" to isolate activities, actions, or references concerning the selling to; educating of; impressing; and urging or garnering support from the public by the White House.[26] Contrary to Kernell's outward focus on the message and the targets of the message, I concentrated on

TABLE **3.5** White House Tasks by Activity

	Tasks			
	Information Gathering	Program Development	Public Relations	Constituency Building
Memo Contents	Poll data only	Design, creation, and implementation of policy	Design and creation of rhetoric to nationally sell the president and his policies	Creation and identification of electoral and policy coalitions

the internal creation of public relations strategies. I coded as Public Relations phrases that designed, critiqued, or concerned speeches and other statements for the public arena. I also classified as Public Relations any phrase or group of phrases referring to the national selling of policy or national public relations regarding the presidency. For example, a Nixon administration memo identified attitudes regarding the president's environmental program and then identified "short-term initiatives." The memo urged President Nixon to "visit a new park or pollution facility for which he can take credit. . . . Criticize Congress for dragging its feet on his environmental proposals."[27]

My final category was created to account for reelection efforts by the election and reelection committees. The category Constituency Building included and was restricted to the building, creating, or identifying of the president's constituency. A careful line was drawn between the categories Public Relations and Constituency Building. The distinction between the two rested on whether the particular White House action was delineated in terms of constituent or group support. Nationally directed activities I always considered Public Relations. Actions directed at, or based on the identification of, subgroups fell into the classification Constituency Building. After completing the coding of all memoranda, the data were tabulated by activity and president, and then cross-tabulated with poll question type. These four categories broadly define the type of White House activities to which poll data can be applied.

Unlike examining the type of poll question, simply coding all memoranda for four different White House activities produced no immediately identifiable trends or patterns (see Table 3.6). With the exceptions of

TABLE **3.6** Allocation of Poll Questions by Activity

	Information Gathering	Program Development	Public Relations	Constituency Building
Nixon	20.7%	11.8%	44.1%	23.5%
Ford	17.6%	15.4%	38.5%	28.6%
Carter	20.5%	30.5%	29.5%	19.5%
Reagan	26.7%	13.7%	36.1%	23.7%
Bush	53.8%	19.2%	23.9%	3.0%

Data sources: Nixon Presidential Materials; Historical Papers from the Gerald R. Ford Library; Historical Material from the Jimmy Carter Library; Historical Papers from the Ronald Reagan Library.

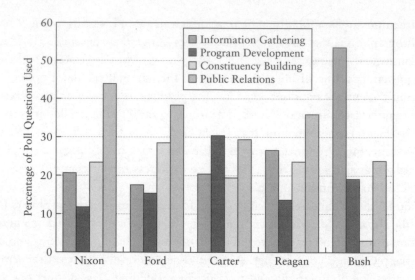

FIGURE **3.2** Poll Question Usage by Activity

Carter and Program Development as well as Bush and Information Gathering, there is remarkable uniformity in each category as to how much of the poll apparatus resources the White House devoted to each activity. Figure 3.2 puts a graphical face to this data. As indicated, Nixon, Ford, Carter, and Reagan devoted most of their poll apparatus to public relations, which averaged 37 percent of poll applications. Program Development functions received the opposite of Public Relations usage; Nixon, Ford, and Reagan devoted few poll resources to Program Development. Removing Carter drops the average usage to 13.63 percent. Carter, however, devoted more poll attention to Program Development than did any other president, equivalent to Public Relations, and more than both Information Gathering and Constituency Building. Constituency Building and Information Gathering for the four presidents fell equally between Program Development and Public Relations, representing a combined 45 percent of all apparatus usage.

Factoring in the Bush administration, however, changes this pattern slightly. As Table 3.6 demonstrates, the Bush administration allocated the poll apparatus overwhelmingly to Information Gathering, with 53.7 percent of all references occurring in that category. Public

Relations follows the Information Gathering category, and is trailed by Program Development. The Bush Constituency Building category languishes far behind the other three categories, with only 3 percent of all poll applications. Adding the Bush percentages changes the aforementioned averages significantly. With the Bush figures, the Public Relations category drops from a dominant 37 percent to 30 percent. The Information Gathering category increases, not surprisingly, from 21 percent to 27 percent. The Program Development and Constituency Building averages are not as significantly influenced by the Bush administration.

Examining Figure 3.2, however, presents difficulties for determining meaningful comparisons of poll usage across time or within categories. It's not clear whether Nixon employed significantly more poll questions in Public Relations than did Reagan, or even how fast the usage is increasing or decreasing across activities. To determine if any patterns existed over time, I again utilized the Mann-Kendall statistical test for trends. With the test statistic set at .01, no White House activity was significant for any of the five administrations.[28] With this test, I am 99 percent confident there are no trends, upward or downward, in any White House activity category over time. Despite the fluctuations apparent to the naked eye, over time and across presidents, there is no significant increase or decrease in the use of poll data among White House activities. All five presidents statistically devoted their poll apparatus resources primarily to Public Relations, followed closely by Constituency Building, Information Gathering, and Program Development applications.

Quantitatively speaking, the use of the poll apparatus remained the same over time. Nevertheless, the information in the apparatus was refined. The activities to which public opinion was applied may have remained constant, but the type of information used in those categories did not, as discussed earlier. Table 3.7 delineates these fluctuations by disaggregating poll question usage for each White House category. In the category Information Gathering, poll question usage was relatively uniform across all types of questions and administrations, with the exception of the Bush administration. Policy questions dominate the Information Gathering category, but the Popularity and Personal question types are also quite strong. In the Program Development category, there are greater fluctuations about the mean, as Policy opinion polls dominate the later

TABLE **3.7** Poll Question Type by Activity

Category	Nixon	Ford	Carter	Reagan	Bush
Information Gathering					
Popularity	7.3%	5.5%	5.8%	8.3%	16.0%
Policy	7.3%	6.6%	12.6%	8.9%	25.7%
Personal	6.1%	5.5%	2.1%	9.5%	11.9%
		Average—9.3%			
Program Development					
Popularity	4.5%	3.3%	7.4%	1.2%	0.0%
Policy	3.9%	8.8%	16.8%	10.1%	19.4%
Personal	3.4%	3.3%	6.3%	2.4%	0.0%
		Average—6.0%			
Constituency Building					
Popularity	8.4%	12.1%	9.5%	5.9%	1.9%
Policy	5.0%	9.9%	5.8%	10.7%	0.4%
Personal	10.1%	6.6%	4.2%	7.1%	0.7%
		Average—6.6%			
Public Relations					
Popularity	24.6%	24.2%	12.1%	10.1%	3.0%
Policy	10.6%	13.2%	13.2%	18.9%	15.7%
Personal	8.9%	1.1%	4.2%	7.1%	5.2%
		Average—11.47%			

Data sources: Nixon Presidential Materials; Historical Papers from the Gerald R. Ford Library; Historical Material from the Jimmy Carter Library; Historical Papers from the Ronald Reagan Library.

presidents' usage. The change over time to Policy questions is most obvious in the category with the greatest allocation of resources, Public Relations. In Table 3.7, it can be seen that Policy question usage is increasing and Popularity questions are decreasing across these administrations. Interestingly, in the Public Relations and Constituency Building categories, Nixon and Reagan utilized more Personal information than did the Ford, Carter, or Bush administrations. Because Ford, Carter, and Bush were not reelected, this finding suggests an interesting connection between the governing poll apparatus and reelection. Moreover, the Bush Constituency Building category is considerably small in comparison to the other administrations (3 percent versus an average of 23 percent). I discuss the connection between the Constituency Building category and reelection efforts in subsequent chapters.

Apparatus Influence

The previous discussion provided a quantitative picture of the disbursal of public opinion in White House activities across four general, but parsimonious, classifications. Approval ratings clearly are not the determinant of any presidential decision making (not at 36 percent of usage). Moreover, Popularity questions do not dominate any of the specific categories across all administrations. But consider that Popularity questions were more relevant across all categories to the Nixon and Ford administrations than to the Carter, Reagan, and Bush administrations. Those findings, however, could have been related to my coding. For example, Policy questions might be used more in Program Development and Popularity questions might be used more frequently in Public Relations, because specific question types lend themselves to usage in specific White House activities. Alternatively, the type of White House activity in which staffers wish to employ data potentially influences the type of opinion on which staffers choose to rely. Thus, the type of White House activity might influence poll question usage and vice versa. The trends I discovered in this and previous sections, and Chapter 2 (increasing policy usage and continuity in poll application), might simply be related to each other and not to any outside, systemic phenomenon. In effect, these trends may be an artifact of my coding and not related to the political environment in which presidents function.

To test the interrelatedness of the two dependent variables, I created a cross-tabulation of question type and White House activity for each president. The chi-square test results presented in Table 3.8 suggest that I can reject the null hypothesis that there *is* a relationship between question type and White House activity. As Table 3.8 indicates, all five presidents have a Pearson's χ^2 greater than the expected value, at varying degrees of significance. It is possible to reject the hypothesis of independence at an observed likelihood ratio of less than .05. Thus the existence of independence can be clearly rejected for all administrations except Nixon's. Although the χ^2 for the Nixon administration surpasses the critical value, the significance level for both the Pearson's χ^2 and the likelihood ratio equals only .10. Neither statistic presents an overwhelming case for the rejection of the null hypothesis.

A strong case was found for accepting the interrelatedness of poll question type and White House activity among administrations: The data

TABLE **3.8** Chi-Square Test Results[1]

Administration	χ^2	Significance	Likelihood Ratio	Significance	*Lambda*
Nixon	10.77	.10	10.47	.10	.025
Ford[2]	13.40	.04	15.02	.02	.10
Carter	12.06	.06	12.45	.05	.069
Reagan	12.15	.06	12.89	.04	.025
Bush	53.40	<.001	70.94	<.01	.02

Data sources: Nixon Presidential Materials; Historical Papers from the Gerald R. Ford Library; Historical Material from the Jimmy Carter Library; Historical Papers from the Ronald Reagan Library.

[1] The congressional job ratings, presidential character, and national mood were not included in the overall tabulation of presidential popularity. So few references made the omissions insignificant.

[2] The Ford cross-tabulation has three cells with frequencies less than 5. Although it is recommended that "all expected frequencies be at least five, studies indicate that this is probably too stringent and can be relaxed" (Norusis, 1993, p. 208).

for four out of the five administrations allows me to reject the null hypothesis. The next step requires quantifying the association between the variables. The statistical measures of association for the chi-square test cannot indicate direction or the nature of the relationship, but can quantify levels of interaction. *Lambda* reveals the error when predicting the value of one variable using another, and thus indicates the strength of association between the two variables. *Lambda* ranges from 0 to 1. "A value of 0 means the independent variable is of no help in predicting the dependent variable. A value of 1 means that the independent variable perfectly specifies the categories of the dependent variable."[29] However, since my independent and dependent variables cannot be clearly distinguished, I used a symmetric version of *lambda* that predicts row and column variables with equal frequency.[30] The *lambda* values in Table 3.8 demonstrate little reduction in error when using either question type or White House activity to predict the other as the outcome. Nixon's *lambda,* which equals .025, means that using either variable, question type or White House activity, reduces the error of prediction to 2.5 percent. Only Ford achieves a reduction of error of at least 10 percent. Variables that predict each other well would exhibit reductions for over 50 percent; clearly none of these variables predict each other well.

Other measures of association, such as *phi,* Cramer's *V,* and Kendall's *tau-b,* produce similar results. For all five presidents, neither question type nor White House activity is a strong predictor of the other. Question types and White House activities are not entirely independent of each other, but are only weakly interrelated. Therefore, although these two variables are not independent, neither variable is the causal explanation for either variable outcome. Because the two variables are indirectly interrelated, an outside variable or set of variables must be acting on the poll apparatus and producing the decrease of popularity question and increase of policy questions, as well as the continuity of poll usage.

Conclusions

Building on the concepts introduced in Chapter 2, this chapter further illustrates the depth and breadth of the polling operation. With the exception of the Clinton White House, the memos from which cannot yet be coded, these administrations directed their polling apparatuses toward elements reminiscent of a campaign, but not as presidential scholars articulate. Approval ratings were not the presidential public opinion data of choice. These administrations sought more detailed and more sophisticated information from the public. Clearly, the White House wanted to use the public for more than mere leadership evaluations. As expected, the White House employed the polling apparatus primarily within Public Relations tasks, followed by Constituency Building, Information Gathering, and Program Development.

However, both campaign and leadership efforts (even in governing models) revolve around selling and persuasion. The findings here and in Chapter 2 are thus suggestive but not conclusive evidence of a campaign environment in the White House.

The next three chapters explore the use of polls in public relations, coalition monitoring, and the policy cycle, and also investigate the core of the permanent campaign theory. Chapter 4 articulates how the White House uses the poll apparatus to define its audience and bring an "us versus them" approach to governing. Chapters 5 and 6 investigate policymaking, and Chapter 7 explores crisis response. These chapters connect my coding to the political sphere, and explore how the permanent campaign limitedly penetrates policymaking and thoroughly dominates crisis response.

4 The Adversarial Presidency: Using the Polls to Define "Us and Them"

An election is a zero-sum game. There is a winner and a loser, and the prize cannot be shared. The political campaign is the contest to achieve victory over one's opponent. Campaigns are, by definition, adversarial. Governing, in contrast, is defined as primarily collaborative rather than adversarial.[1] "In that sense, campaigning is self-centered, and governing is group-centered."[2] The lessons learned from a presidential campaign are many, but primary among them is the candidate-centered principal. To win over their adversaries, presidential candidates seek to discover who their supporters are, who their opponents are, and who languishes in the middle from their unique perspective. The candidate must define the election as well as his candidacy with his persona, and stand on the issues as the central theme. Voters respond first to the candidate and second (if at all) to the party.

Polling aided candidate-centered campaign development. Prior to the 1960s, polls played a secondary role in campaign strategy. Kessel contends that older candidates did not trust the data and that the surveys and analysis were relatively simple.[3] By 1976, however, pollsters and surveys were crucial to campaign structure and strategy, as politicians, the media, and even the general public grew to trust and rely on the "scientific" certitude of poll data. Polling consultants increased their expertise to produce sophisticated levels of analysis, moving from "simple cross-tabulations to multidimensional scaling and simulation."[4] The net effect of the increased trust and reliance on polls has been a dependence on a fragmented picture of society.

Since Nixon, all presidents have internalized the lessons learned on the campaign trail. Successful presidential candidates bring their knowledge and dependence on the polls from the campaign trenches to the White House. Does the incorporation of polling produce permanent campaign leadership? The triumph of campaigning over governing in the presidency must begin with a switch from governing or group-centered coalition building to self-centered strategizing. Self-centered strategizing during campaigns is completely dependent on poll-produced relationships. Therefore, evidence of the presidential permanent campaign begins with the retention of campaign techniques, to maintain, expand, and utilize presidency-defined supporters. Using the presidential public opinion apparatus to define who is for and who is against the president is the most obvious, outward indicator of the permanent campaign. Instead of defining likely voters, presidents seek to define a base of support for the presidency as well as the presidential agenda.

The Nixon, Ford, Carter, Reagan, Bush, and Clinton administrations all employed the poll apparatus to define and monitor a presidency-centered coalition. These administrations, on average, devoted a quarter of the entire polling apparatus to constituency efforts. The Nixon and Ford administrations used the polls to define additional traditional descriptors of support. The Carter White House continued this evolution of the presidential coalition, and defined members of the coalition by support for certain issues. The Reagan and Bush administrations redefined the presidential constituency, reincorporating party ideologies and other identifiers. By the time of the Clinton administration, the president, his consultants, and his staff were quite sophisticated in defining advocates and adversaries. Triangulation, the Clinton administration's constituency-based strategy, represents the epitome of an adversarial approach.

Partisanship Loses Its Centrality

The gradual separation of party identification from the focal point of the presidential polling apparatus mirrored and extended the rise of candidate-centered behavior on the campaign trail. As partisanship declined in relevance for the voter, it also declined in relevance for the

Q 8
Chap 8

candidate. [The lessening value of party identification shifted focus from the parties to short-term issues and personal, politician-specific factors for both the presidential candidate and the president.] Candidate-centered issues "can be broadly categorized into either policy decisions (what the candidates will do or have done) or performance judgments (the results expected or produced)."[5] Nixon and Ford took the candidate-centered approach and translated it to the White House.

The Nixon White House devoted 23 percent of its apparatus usage to tracking, monitoring, and searching for the keys to support for Nixon (see Table 3.7). Despite trying to deny members of the Republican party access to poll data, the Nixon administration initially relied on traditional party identifiers for survey analysis. Nixon's polling advisors cautioned that tracking narrower measures of group support and desires might not be sensible. For example, "farmers always constitute such a tiny part of a national sample that results which are extrapolated from a national sample are often misleading."[6] Typical socioeconomic variables such as religion, race, and geography were common distinctions employed to identify current and future support for Nixon's policies and his reelection. Age became a key identifier as the passage of the Twenty-Sixth Amendment (which reduced the voting age from twenty-one to eighteen) created either potential allies or potential threats. Because young people had never voted, the Nixon administration did not "really know anything about the voting probabilities of kids who are now 17 or 19. But there are a great many of them and it behooves us to find out whatever we can."[7] The Nixon White House also closely followed the liberal-to-conservative spectrum, believing that a vast bastion of conservative support existed and endorsed Republican presidents.[8] This segmentation of support once prompted President Nixon to direct H. R. Haldeman to cease all national polls "because he doesn't feel they will be meaningful—RNC may have some argument with this."[9]

President Nixon became aware of the declining efficacy of the party for voters, as well as for politicians, from their own experiences as candidates, and also from political scientists. On September 17, 1975, political scientist Robert Goldwin, a member of President Ford's Chief of Staff's Office, had a conversation with Norman Nie. In a four-page summary of that conversation, Goldwin informed Donald Rumsfeld and Richard Cheney of Nie's views on the declining potency of parties and the

*Norman
Nie*

increased potency of issues.[10] Moreover, Goldman, in summarizing Nie's statements, notes, "There seem to be tendencies toward greater ethnic awareness, the general ties of ethnic groups to party identification and to issues seem to be breaking down."[11] The Nixon, Carter, Reagan, and Bush administrations were similarly attentive to scholarly observations from political scientists identifying a breakdown in traditional categorizations.

Over the course of the Nixon administration, the classification and tracking of the American public gradually became more detailed. Former Bureau of the Census Director Richard Scammon informed the Nixon administration that in the 1970s "political power will shift to the suburbs. . . . The constituency is relatively affluent, essentially middle-aged. . . . These people are less committed to parties as an electorate. They are drawing their knowledge from television, and can be reached much more so than 25 years ago."[12] Following Scammon's advice, the Nixon White House began to track supporters using traditional identifiers sparingly, and began to hunt for better demographic descriptions.

The first significant nontraditional support terminology was from the phrase the "Silent Majority." Although the White House received letters and telegrams from self-identifiers, the Nixon administration went to great lengths to capture the Silent Majority in surveys. The administration used its poll apparatus to identify supporters, not by party or group affiliation, but by identification of attitudes contrary to those of the students protesting against the Vietnam War. As an extension of the Silent Majority, the Nixon administration also undertook a serious campaign to identify the "forgotten American." The staff wanted to develop a profile in order to assess "the impact of existing Federal programs on the forgotten American. . . . Careful definitions, followed up by this kind of analysis, must be obtained before the forgotten American can become a serious subject for governmental programming."[13]

Using Scammon's terms, the Nixon White House closely examined its suburban supporters, but not simply by geographic locale. Nixon noted to John Ehrlichman that from poll results "people who live in homes that they own tend to take a much more conservative view on public issues than people who rent. I think this has significant consequences as far as our own programs are concerned. . . . I would like you to follow through in any way that you think would be appropriate to reach our homeowner constituency."[14] Thus, Nixon's staff disaggregated support not only by urban, suburban, and rural areas but also by lifestyle, with home ownership as the prized, constituency-defining attribute.

The premise behind the development of the permanent campaign is that the methodology of campaigning is so pervasive and compelling that it comes to dominate governing. President Ford entered office with no presidential campaign experience and thus no permanent campaign to import. As noted in Chapter 3, polling for constituent efforts represented approximately 20 percent of the polling apparatus for the Nixon, Ford, Carter, Reagan, and Bush administrations (see Table 3.7). Ironically, the Ford administration had the highest percentage in the Constituency Building category, 28.6 percent (see Table 3.7). Due to President Ford's appointment to the vice presidency, and then his elevation to the presidency with Richard Nixon's resignation, he was never elected. President Ford did not have an electoral constituency. However, the lack of a personal constituency produced the greatest attention to constituent efforts because President Ford and his staff tried to both construct a constituency and retain Nixon's.

Because Ford did not enter office with an electorally produced constituency, he could not trace support for himself to the behavior of voters in the last presidential election. The lack of an electoral coalition resulted in the absence of a constituency that was attached to Ford personally. To overcome the appointment problem, Ford's staff attempted to create a base line for comparison by employing a standard, almost stereotypical, measure for comparison.

The Ford administration's constituency data follow the approach of the Nixon administration, hardly surprising as it retained the same pollsters. As with the Nixon White House, the Ford White House monitored traditional SES data. However, the monitoring revealed problems for Ford. National and regional responses to Ford were tracked monthly, although there were few regional differences in Ford's approval rating (it ranged from a low of 43 percent in the Pacific region to a high of 64 percent in the Mountain region in February 1975).[15] Frustratingly across all traditional SES categories, Teeter continued to find that "the President has not created any Ford constituency unique from that of any Republican President."[16] Age, however, offered hope: "The one exception to this is that he does show unique strength with young voters for a Republican."[17]

In search for a "unique constituency," the Ford pollsters began employing the more segmented view of society favored by the end of Nixon's tenure. The Ford White House tracked those it defined as "major sub groups": northern and southern WASPs, Roman Catholics, Jews, and Blacks. The WASPs and Roman Catholics were further divided by age and education.[18] As with the Nixon administration, the nontraditional categories appear to be directly related to certain issue areas. For example, on energy issues, "total Americans who work outside the home" was a separate category. For questions concerning college education, individuals were asked if they had children, producing a "no children" category. However, the Ford approach appeared more haphazard than Nixon's, as it became more like a "search and rescue" mission than an effort to define constituent support.

The Horse You Rode in On

Under Patrick Caddell's tutelage, the Carter administration immediately refashioned traditional SES and party tracking beyond the Nixon and Ford efforts. According to Caddell, "Jimmy Carter managed to garner the 'traditional' majorities from a number of 'New Deal Coalition' groups. Unfortunately, the size of many of those groups is shrinking in the general populace. . . . To make up the difference—and to win the election—Jimmy Carter did far better than is 'traditional' among a number of groups that did not participate in the old coalition."[19] Carter won traditional Democratic support from Catholics, Jews, Blacks, labor, the poor, and traditionally Democratic geographic areas, such as Chicago. It was "clear that while Carter benefited from their support, he may owe his election more to the non-traditional groups that helped him to do better in unexpected places."[20] Those supporters were white Protestants, the better-educated, white-collar, and rural, small-town voters. Poll data also revealed problem constituencies for Carter on entering the White House, including voters aged twenty-five to thirty-five, in particular nonworking housewives and those from the west.[21]

The Carter White House believed it owed its campaign success and future presidential success to independent issue voters and segmented selections of the population. Other explanations for Carter's narrow victory, such as Nixon and Watergate, and Ford's debate gaffe in which he claimed Eastern Europe was not under Soviet control, did not factor into Caddell's poll-produced constituency assessments. Instead, the administration tracked the support (or lack thereof) flowing from the nontraditional Carter constituency during the administration's four-year tenure because "relatively small changes in the popular vote totals [in the 1976 election] could have changed the Electoral College outcome dramatically."[22]

The Carter administration continued to disaggregate presidential support by lifestyle choices, and extended the linkages of new categories to new issues. On energy policy, on which the administration polled extensively, in addition to traditional socioeconomic factors, the White House investigated the opinions of individuals based on the type of heating used in their homes. Caddell cross-tabulated answers to questions on Carter's energy policy with traditional respondent characteristics and also the type of home heating used by the respondent. The White House believed that there was a correlation between the type of home heating that was used and support for various energy programs and options for conservation.[23] However, no significant levels of support for the president's energy program were discovered in the public as a whole or in any segment of home heating users. No "home heating" constituency was discovered when the opinions of homeowners were compared by their oil, gas, coal, or electricity usage and their answers to questions such as "How serious do you think the problem of real shortages of natural fuels—such as oil and gas—is?" and "Do you favor or oppose a tariff (tax) on imported oil that would raise the price of gasoline 10 to 15 cents per gallon if it would end our dependence on foreign oil?"[24] The extra classification simply revealed more of the same—that the public did not believe the oil shortage was a crisis requiring sacrifice.

The Bull's-Eye Approach

The process of identifying and tracking a personal, presidentially defined constituency continued to evolve. Nixon began and Carter continued a process designed to assess the depth of support across numerous unnatural demographics alongside presidential policies. The Reagan and Bush administrations continued this approach but added their own refinement to the Nixon approach. The Reagan and Bush administrations used polling to define, identify, and track supporters in terms of their strength of support for the president, which they defined as core and peripheral support. Peripheral support required the constant monitoring that only public opinion polling can provide, because support from weak identifiers is transitory. "Peripheral supporters can be appealed to only on the issues of concern to them, and their demands may constrain a president's option and even conflict with the preferences of the president's core coalition."[25]

Reagan's strategists not only identified the Reagan constituency, but also used polls to gauge the intensity of the connection between Reagan and his supporters. The Reagan White House returned the party to the mix, but retained the presidency-centered focus. The White House analysts divided Reagan supporters into the core and periphery of both American society and Reagan's reliable base of support. The strong support group, they found, "represents the core of American society and . . . support for the President weakens as one moves away from this core."[26] The White House staff's characterization of the Reagan constituency is presented in Table 4.1.

The Reagan staff tracked this new constituency arrangement religiously, receiving monthly updates on the distribution of Reagan's

TABLE **4.1 Reagan Supporters**

Strong Support Group	Mixed Support Group	Low Support Group
35–54 years old	55–64 years old, 25–34 years old	65+ years old and nonaffluent, 24 years old and under
College educated	Post-graduates, high school graduates	Less than high school graduates
$20,000+ income earners	$10,000–20,000 income earners	Less than $10,000 income earners
Nonunion workers, professionals, managers, owners, farmers, and white-collar (clerical and sales) workers	Blue-collar workers	Union members
White, Anglo-Saxon Protestants (Teutonic and Scandinavian)	Some ethnics: Hispanics and Anglo Catholics	Ethnics: southern and eastern Europeans, Jews, non-Anglo Catholics, Blacks Women

Data source: Memo to the Senior Staff from Beal, 12/21/81, in PR 15 050001-056000 doc # 0533818, Ronald Reagan Library.

supporters. As with those in the Carter administration, the Reagan strategists were very concerned with the fringe of Reagan's support. Substantial time and effort were also devoted to watching the newly identified "gender gap." Polling revealed that Reagan suffered on the "war issue . . . RR's personal style . . . [and the] economic issue among working women."[27] The Reagan White House was very concerned about the creation and persistence of this gap, and therefore monitored it regularly.

The Reagan White House extended the effort to segment and identify further which factors affected support for the president and his policies. Both Jack Burgess, deputy director and special assistant to the president, and Elizabeth Dole, assistant to the president in Public Liaison, worked on a coalition-building program targeted at ethnics. Dole and Burgess wanted to break down ethnicity further in a way "which would enable us to track the opinions of Italian-, Polish-, Lithuanian-Americans, etc."[28]

The Reagan administration also tracked more detailed religious categories than any other administration, distinguishing among Presbyterians, Methodists, Lutherans, Baptists, other Protestants, Catholics, Jews, and agnostics; there was no direct reference to Islam, but a follow-up question inquired into born-again status.[29] These categories were used frequently to classify supporters on the social issues of abortion, school prayer, gun control, a balanced budget, and tuition tax credits. Interestingly, the Reagan administration believed that "even when we are on the 'wrong' side of some of these issues from a [general] public opinion standpoint, they still may be politically positive. For example, there is little doubt that the Democrats are suffering greatly among urban Catholics because they have been associated with abortion on demand. They [sic] President ran extremely well among this group in 1980."[30] As with Nixon's and Carter's strategists, Reagan's advisors clearly distinguished between general and segmented levels of public support. Moreover, the Reagan strategists recognized the value of specific single issues to certain supporters regardless of party affiliation. Information about public opinion empowered presidents to reframe their actions and decisions based on the possibly shifting constituent support found in survey data.

As noted earlier and in Table 4.1, the Reagan White House classified the president's supporters in order to monitor that support over time. The importance of an electoral or constituency strategy was outlined in some detail in "Strategic Planning Memorandum #3," which contained twenty-four recommendations for the president's 1982 State of the Union Address from Richard Beal to Reagan's troika. Meese, Baker, and Deaver were informed that "electoral coalitions deserve credit for the President winning the office."[31] Beal argued that "Eleanor and Joe Q. Public . . . are the ultimate members of the coalitions the President will need to accomplish his goals and visions."[32] Polling was central to encapsulating these individuals because "these coalitions must be thought of in terms of geography as well as individual and group identity."[33] Only polling reveals the level of detail necessary to track these classifications. Unlike traditional public identifying assertions, such as voting or party affiliation, polling allows presidents and their staffs to monitor private affiliations such as age, income, religion, and home ownership.

Using the Reagan base line aided efforts surrounding the 1982 budget efforts. Reagan staffers closely monitored reactions to the Reagan proposals, but not simply for public relations purposes. "Support for continuing to cut domestic spending as a means to balance the budget and improve the economy centers in the core of Reagan support group: Republicans, westerners, southerners, upper income earners, high church Protestants, and men. The problem is, these alone do not constitute an electoral majority. The group that took Reagan over the top in 1980 is the group that has begun to shift toward defense cuts. These include the old voters (45–64 years of age), those with some college experience, middle to upper income earners, Midwesterners, some high church Protestants, those who are ideologically somewhat conservative or moderate, and weak Democrats."[34] Richard Beal highlights the strength of the presidential reelection imperative, and achieving that goal was tied directly to the initial Reagan base line.

To underscore this point, the Reagan White House even wanted to know which columnists, newscasters, anchors, and networks their supporters preferred. As of February 2, 1982, the public preferred CBS by a narrow margin (26 percent, compared to ABC with 25 percent and NBC with 23 percent). Interestingly, "Jack Anderson and William Buckley have close to the same visibility and the same thermometer ratings despite significant differences on the ideological backgrounds of the two columnists."[35] The administration broke down support for the networks and columnists by the Reagan coalition categories (see Table 4.2 for this

TABLE **4.2** Coalitions' Network Preferences

Network	Supporters
CBS	Best educated
	Blacks
	Registered Independents
	Residents of southern states
NBC	Senior citizens
	Lower-income individuals
	Registered Republicans
ABC	Youngest viewers
	High school graduates
	Blue-collar workers
	Blacks
	Democrats

Data source: Memo to Meese, Baker, Deaver from Wirthlin, 2/2/82, in PR 15 doc. # 061990, Ronald Reagan Library.

breakdown). Comparing Tables 4.1 and 4.2 demonstrates that individuals in the mixed and low support groups primarily watched NBC and ABC. Responsiveness and attention to constituent attitudes was pervasive. Moreover, as indicated by the dissection of media approval, any type of targeting was possible once the administration established the baseline. Without the understanding of an electoral coalition, in this case Reagan's, any information that categorizes by groups becomes less significant.

The Bush campaign and administration borrowed significantly from the Reagan method of classifying supporters, despite utilizing less constituency tracking. The Bush staff further subdivided the conception of the core and periphery model of constituents. The Bush administration subdivided the core (which it called the "base") into four base groups: political, ethnic and demographic, geographic, and issue oriented. The Bush staff used these divisions to contrast its base with target groups in the same categories (Table 4.3 contains the base and target breakdown). Conservative Democrats represented a political target group; Blacks, Hispanics, and seniors fell into the ethnic and demographic group.[36] Pollster Robert Teeter termed Bush's constituency "the expected Republican coalition: putting together large majorities of Northern white Protestants and Southern whites with a smaller majority of Catholics and over 40 percent of union families. Blacks, Jews, and Hispanics again

TABLE **4.3** Assessing the Bush Constituency

	Political	Ethnic and Demographic	Geographic	Issue Oriented

Base groups	Republicans
	Conservatives
	Republican office
	  holders
	Bush supporters
		Asians
		European first through
		  fourth generation
		Northern Catholics
		Younger voters
			California, Texas,
			  southern states
			Rocky Mountain states
			New England (not
			  including Rhode Island)
				Law enforcement
				Veterans, national defense
				  groups
				Teamsters, conservative union
				  members
				Social value groups
				Small-business owners,
				  entrepreneurs
				Corporate trade associations
				Conservationists
				Evangelicals
				Anti-tax organizations

Target groups	Conservative
	  Democrats
		Blacks, Hispanics, seniors	Industrial Midwest	Parents, students, teachers,
				  education reformers
				Service organizations, Points of
				  Light groups, celebrities
				Farm organizations
				Sports, fitness, health groups

Data source: Memo to Sununu from Demarest, 12/2/90, in Sununu Box 3 Persian Gulf Working Groups OA/ID CF 00472, George Bush Library.

went overwhelmingly Democratic."[37] These traditional social divisions dominated, as Teeter argued that baby boomers and "Reagan Democrats" were not useful constructs in 1988.[38]

The similarity to Reagan constituency classification efforts ends here. As noted in Chapter 3, constituent efforts represented the smallest component of the Bush White House polling apparatus. Consequently, the Bush classification system was more general. For example, the Bush administration was also interested in religion, but dropped Reagan's classification system in favor of a more religiously generic one (including the categories Active Protestant, Inactive Protestant, Active Catholic, Inactive Catholic, Jewish, and Non-Religious).[39] Although the Bush staff tracked ticket splitters, conservative Republicans, and conservative Democrats,[40] unlike Carter and Reagan, the Bush administration rarely employed innovative or distinctive subgroup terminology.

Triangulation

President Clinton's electoral coalition was a mix of the traditional and nontraditional. President Clinton's core support came from traditional Democratic sources: party identifiers, liberals, non-Whites, those with lower incomes, women, and easterners (there were no linkages to age or education).[41] Clinton, according to Edwards, "polarized the public along partisan lines."[42] Moreover, in the 1992 election, Democrats turned out and Republicans stayed home.[43] Clinton's appeal to independents and moderates, as well as the siphoning created by the Perot vote, produced the Clinton victory. In addition, Clinton received the youth vote (eighteen- to twenty-nine-year-olds). The only demographics Clinton could not include in his conglomeration of support were the wealthy, white Protestants, born-again Christians, and homemakers.[44] "Thus . . . [Clinton] took office with a very weak governing coalition and a campaign commitment to a dramatic first hundred days."[45]

The Clinton administration polled continually throughout its first term, tracking his personal mix of individuals. The Morris memoranda in *Behind the Oval Office* demonstrate an intensive, detailed tracking of supporters, nonsupporters, and those on the fence. For example, the Clinton pollsters used polls and focus groups to identify "swing Democrats" and Independent voters in San Francisco, Louisiana, Minneapolis,

New York, and Florida.[46] The Clinton administration was extremely attentive to the "20 percent of [the] vote that is up for grabs."[47] The White House used the poll data to "focus on expanding [the] base, not just strengthening it."[48] However, the high point of polling for constituency purposes in the Clinton administration clearly came during the Dick Morris era with efforts to "triangulate" the public.

Triangulation has received a lot of coverage, due in part to its emphasis on capturing the middle rather than the traditional method of building out from the party core. According to Dick Morris, "triangulation demanded that Clinton abandon 'Democratic class-warfare dogma,' rise above his partisan roots, and inhabit the political center 'above and between' the two parties. . . . That meant Clinton had to deliberately distance himself from his Democratic allies, use them as a foil, pick fights with them."[49] As presidential strategy, triangulation caused dissention in the White House ranks and produced murky results, as the public's issue positions suggested action, but Clinton received no corresponding upward movement of his popularity ratings.[50]

Triangulation represents the ultimate extension of a campaign approach because it embodies the defining of supporters with an acknowledgment of single point-in-time goals. According to Morris, Clinton's use of polls did not identify "What should I be for? What should I do?" Clinton knew what he wanted to do; he wanted to know how to get there. The poll data lit the path—similar to a presidential campaign. Rather than focus on traditional Democrats and their traditional goals, the Clinton White House targeted the goals that overlapped. From the polls, Morris and Clinton determined that "massive majorities consistently rejected the doctrinaire views of both the left and the right and embraced an amalgam of conservative and liberal positions."[51] The president and Morris' strategy resembled a "'median voter' strategy of adopting positions on salient issues that were closest to the midpoint of public opinion in order to show most voters that they would benefit from his reelection."[52]

Triangulation demanded an expansive polling effort, which was entirely presidency centered. Support from the center is not instinctively identifiable, as are core party supporters. Traditional governing coalitions stem from their relationship to ideas and interests, such as the Christian Right and the Republicans, or Labor and the Democrats. The middle represents those individuals who fall between other clear identifiers—the middle-of-the-road opinion is not apparent without those traditional endpoints. Clinton and Morris built a triangulated constituency that centered on trumping Clinton's opponents. Traditional issues, policy, and even the 1996 election were secondary steps.

Classifications and Coalitions

These six administrations classified and categorized individuals via public opinion polling. The component at the heart of the presidential classification effort was not voter mobilization, but rather support for the president and his policies. Using the poll apparatus, these administrations attempted to define their unique presidential constituency. The hunt for the presidential coalition began with the traditional demographic divisions: party identification and socioeconomic variables. Over time, the White House increasingly segmented the presidential constituency by issues, and ultimately by nontraditional socioeconomic factors.

Creating coalitions that place the president as the fulcrum are nothing new. In a traditional typology, the common, constituent, and partisan approach, the president's potential audiences exist apart from definitions as presidential supporters. These audiences exist and the president seeks their support. For example, the common audience refers to the president's unique relationship with the entire country but is not predicated on the entire country liking the president.[53] Constituent patrons are "specific groups within the broader national community," such as the American Association for Retired Persons, who might or might not support the administration. Partisan audiences by definition stem from the president's party and are thus more likely to be placed in the president's corner.[54] Analysis of public appearances reveals that presidents are more attentive to their common and constituent audiences than partisan audiences, with the exception of during election years (see Table 4.4).[55] Presidents make 4.5 times more appearances in front of partisan audiences in election years than in nonelection years.[56] Presidents consistently have to work to garner common and constituent support, but courting of partisan support is only necessary during election years.

Poll-defined constituencies, however, do not exist in the political sphere outside of the pollster's reports, charts, tables, and memoranda. Homeowners, home heating constituencies, and soccer moms never

TABLE **4.4** Presidential Public Activities

Type of Appearance*	Nixon	Ford	Carter	Reagan	Bush
	N = 425	N = 829	N = 646	N = 680	N = 781
Common (major speeches, news conferences)	12.5%	6.4%	11.8%	6.3%	19.0%
Constituent (minor speeches, nonpolitical appearances)	63.5%	44.3%	52.0%	63.5%	35.2%
Partisan (political appearances)	24.0%	49.3%	36.2%	30.2%	45.8%

Data source: Gary King and Lyn Ragsdale, *The Elusive Executive: Discovering Statistical Patterns in the Presidency* (Washington, DC: Congressional Quarterly Press, 1988), pp. 262–275.
*From first terms only.

mobilize on their own—there are no marches on Washington to vocalize demands. Thus, via the polling apparatus, these administrations meet the first criteria for a permanent campaign leadership strategy. The polling apparatus, which could disaggregate individuals only by the questions asked, permitted a continuation of the leadership strategy that presidents learned on the campaign trail: Connect individuals to the president based, not on party affiliation, but on disconnected affiliations ranging from individual attributes, to lifestyle choices, to presidential policy positions.

Conclusions

Polling stands at the heart of the modern, candidate-centered presidential campaign, thus making it a fitting proxy for evaluating the presence of a permanent campaign environment in the White House. In an era of declining party identification and loyalty, public opinion polls and the polling consultant represent a critical component for the successful campaign. Careful identification of supporters and nonsupporters depends on the ability to discern who supports the candidate and why. As Chapters 2 and 3 indicated, Presidents Nixon, Carter, Reagan, Bush, and Clinton clearly transferred their campaign polling apparatus to the White House. This chapter demonstrates that the White House also imported the first step of any campaign: defining your adversaries and advocates. However, the key connection has not been established. Are these artificial coalitions translated into policy, rhetoric, and legislative desires? Chapter 5 will explore this question by looking at the policymaking process.

5　The Policy Cycle Meets the Permanent Campaign

The presidential agenda and policymaking process is a difficult path to quantify. In a rational model of policymaking, "policy is created in a fairly orderly sequence of stages."[1] An issue is placed on the agenda and is defined. Then the issue moves through government, where alternatives are considered. A solution is implemented, challenged, revised, and ultimately evaluated, at which point the process could start all over again. The model, however, fails to include the "struggle over ideas," according to Deborah Stone.[2] Moreover, political realities blur the lines of any carefully drawn flowchart. Paul Light resequences the model to account for the real world, and thus argues that the presidential agenda has a political component, as "every agenda item (1) addresses an issue; (2) involves a specific alternative; and (3) has some priority in the domestic queue."[3] As Light's focus is presidency centered, he begins with what the president wants to do, and then considers what the president can do. Lammers and Genovese similarly reconceived the policy marketplace by addressing challenges and opportunities, the public mood, public support, the legislative setting, promising issues, economic conditions, and foreign policy influences.[4] Stone and the presidency scholars agree that a merging of ideas and opportunity must occur for a policy item to move through the traditional cycle of public policy.

Combining these approaches suggests that there are four areas in which presidents exercise leadership skills and choices. (1) Light argues that presidents have the greatest influence on the process in their first two years. (2) Stone, Light, and Lammers and Genovese (as well as others) all agree that issues must get on the public, congressional, and presidential agendas. Once on these agendas, issues, problems, and alternatives interact to produce solutions. (3) The solution must move through government institutions, traditionally through Congress' legislative labyrinth. (4) Ultimately, the Executive branch must implement the policy outcome.

The lament regarding the presence of a permanent campaign and a leaderless presidency arises from the intense focus on public relations, which occurs as solutions move through government institutions. However, campaign-style leadership is not simply the admittedly increased presidential reliance on public persuasion. The permanent campaign is not simply new terminology for public relations. The campaign-to-govern approach to leadership subsumes traditional governing techniques in favor of techniques that connect to the identified wants of the president's constituency (detailed in Chapter 4), with decisions made throughout the policy process. Polling for the campaign-to-govern approach is the "essential guide for the distribution of a politician's financial and political resources."[5] This chapter tests the depth of the presence of permanent campaign leadership by exploring the presence of poll usage in all stages of the policy process. Presidents do poll during their best opportunity for success with Congress (the first two years of tenure); however, the public's desires only tangentially penetrate presidential policymaking.

Timing

Time and timing are critical commodities for the president and his staff. As Paul Light notes, there is a rhythm to domestic policy process. During the first two years of an administration, the president and his advisors focus on the president's agenda. "The rise in congressional competition and the coinciding increase in complexity have led to a scramble for scarce agenda space. Presidents cannot afford to waste the few opportunities they have . . . [and thus] set their domestic agendas early and repeat them often."[6] If polling is going to influence the leadership strategies invested in the president's agenda, then polling usage must be present throughout the first two years of presidential tenure.

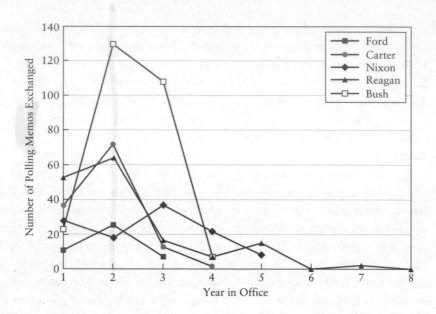

FIGURE **5.1** Timing of Poll Usage

Graphing the exchanges of White House memos by date produced a pattern of increasing and decreasing public opinion usage over time (see Figure 5.1).[7] The curves peak with high levels of White House polling usage in year two of the first term, and exhibit a significant decline in staff polling usage as the reelection campaign approaches. This pattern of high early usage followed by declining usage correlates with Light's conception of "the problem of policy cycles."[8] "If the first two years are for learning, they are also the most important focus for agenda activity."[9] Polling usage, as with agenda activity, peaks in the second year of the administration.[10]

The declines after year three also match the change in focus after the congressional midterm elections. In years three and four of a first term, presidents and their staffs tend to focus on reelection, and polling is a central part of any modern campaign organization. The "White House pollsters" and the "reelection pollsters" are generally one and the same, and during years three and four the pollsters primarily focus on election polling. Thus, most of the poll data generated are supplied to the reelection committee and not the White House, leading to the apparent decline in White House polling. Furthermore, the nature of the poll data shifts to the campaign, as questions turn to choices among candidates rather than policy options.[11] As presidential focus and strategy shift to reelection efforts, White House usage of poll data overwhelmingly declines, suggesting the new focus on campaign material is not as useful to the White House staffers. The decline of poll usage conforms to research, suggesting that a campaign focus dominates White House leadership during years three and four, as they vet everything through reelection scenarios.[12]

Although presidents highly prize reelection, second-term presidents invariably attempt less and accomplish less. Second-term presidents do not begin with a clean slate and a new mission. Instead, presidents sell the second term as a continuation of the mission rather than an opportunity for change. As Figure 5.1 reveals, poll usage severely declines during a second term. Second-term administrations not only incorporate public opinion less frequently, but also actually purchase less data from the pollsters.[13] The dearth of poll exchanges during the second terms of the Nixon and Reagan presidencies emphasizes the connection between constituency pressures and presidential polling.

Issues, Ideas, Problems, and Solutions

Timing is critical to the presidency. Scholars urge incoming presidents to "hit the ground running."[14] However, policy outcomes depend more on how the agenda was set and how an issue was framed. The president is thought to have the advantage in agenda setting, as he alone commands the national stage. Since the 1930s, presidents have had the advantage over Congress in setting the national agenda, but even presidents are at the mercy of the political environment. "You can't just change the subject as President. You can't wish Bosnia away. You can't wish [Branch Davidian] David Koresh away. You just can't ignore them and change the subject."[15]

In Chapter 3, I demonstrated that the president's approval rating is simply not relevant to the White House effort to utilize the public. Instead, these administrations were attentive to demographics and issue attitudes (84 percent of the apparatus—see Table 3.4). Disaggregating the Policy category revealed that of the twelve different issue types, only seven figured into the White House's interest in public opinion. In order of importance, these five administrations sought the public's opinion regarding Domestic Fiscal, Monetary, and Tax Policy, and Inflation; Unemployment, Job Creation, and Industrial Policy; Entitlements; Political and Government Reform; Crime; Environment and Land Management; and Energy.

Traditionally, scholars deemed the public useful for agenda setting and not choosing among alternatives. Both Light and Kingdon suggest that public attitudes matter for agenda setting or prioritizing, and not for program development.[16] "Public opinion is generally too ambiguous to be of help in framing specific programs."[17] Kingdon furthers this contention by separating the public from the policymakers in the potentially intersecting streams of his garbage can model. The current scholarly observations restrict the public to post-policymaking input through public relations efforts targeted at moving Congress, efforts outside the White House walls, or commentary in the next election.

In contrast to the scholarship, the White House interest in issue attitudes evolved over time. Using the poll apparatus, the White House focused on agenda issues, but also used the polls to determine how they wanted the public involved. The White House asked poll questions that enabled Americans to prioritize issues as well as to choose among issue alternatives. For prioritizing, respondents would answer the open-ended "most important problem" question. For choosing, respondents would indicate support for a proposed response to a policy problem, or would select among options.

Table 5.1 reveals some remarkable institutional patterns regarding choice versus prioritizing. There is change over time from 1969 to 1992. The Nixon administration typically sought and utilized information that

TABLE **5.1** Polled Issue Types

Administration	N	Agenda Issues	Alternative Issues
Nixon	82	90.24%	9.76%
Ford	66	75.76%	24.24%
Carter	114	24.46%	75.44%
Reagan	130	36.15%	63.85%
Bush	158	29.70%	70.30%
Average	110	51.26%	48.72%

Data sources: Nixon Presidential Materials; Historical Papers from the Gerald R. Ford Library; Historical Material from the Jimmy Carter Library; Historical Papers from the Ronald Reagan Library.

TABLE **5.2** Distribution of Alternative Issues

Issue	Nixon	Ford	Carter	Reagan	Bush
N	8	16	86	83	111
Domestic Fiscal, Monetary, and Tax Policy, and Inflation	17.39%	36.84%	85.00%	56.36%	54.10%
Unemployment, Job Creation, and Industrial Policy	14.28%	0.00%	55.56%	44.44%	0.00%
Defense Spending, Conversion, and Personnel	0.00%	50.00%	0.00%	100.00%	0.00%
Political and Government Reform	0.00%	8.33%	64.71%	33.33%	75.00%
Crime	9.09%	16.67%	0.00%	66.67%	66.70%
Entitlements	11.11%	25.00%	88.89%	77.78%	40.00%
Education	0.00%	0.00%	0.00%	95.00%	81.80%
Environment and Land Management	0.00%	0.00%	100.00%	0.00%	85.30%
Energy	0.00%	44.44%	68.57%	66.67%	100.00%
Science, Technology, and Transportation	0.00%	0.00%	90.00%	0.00%	66.70%
Economic Affairs	0.00%	25.00%	66.67%	40.00%	0.00%
Social Issues	0.00%	0.00%	0.00%	100.00%	83.30%
All alternative issues	9.76%	24.24%	75.44%	63.85%	70.30%

Data sources: Nixon Presidential Materials; Historical Papers from the Gerald R. Ford Library; Historical Material from the Jimmy Carter Library; Historical Papers from the Ronald Reagan Library.

emphasized the public's "most important problems" and the job the president did in handling those issues. Contrarily, the Carter, Reagan, and Bush staff primarily employed alternative information in their memoranda when referencing poll data. Moreover, Carter, Reagan, and Bush referenced more opinion items, making the increased percentage actually more dramatic. As Table 5.2 demonstrates, the increased use of respondent's alternatives in White House memos is not issue specific. In the categories that all administrations polled, the Carter, Reagan, and Bush administrations relied on alternative suggestions more than 50 percent of the time in all cases[18]; the Nixon and Ford administrations showed considerably less attention to respondents' choices.

The Presidential Issue Agenda

Using poll data to identify the public's priorities suggests the White House wanted to determine if their top agenda items dovetailed with the public's top agenda items. The Nixon, Ford, Carter, Reagan, and

Bush administrations included the public's identification of problems and solutions because it helped solve a fundamental problem for the White House. Presidents need "a great deal of information on a wide range of topics . . . information on the problem itself and on potential solutions; information on the political setting, public support, congressional acceptance, and bureaucratic resistance . . . information is the key to good policy. Without information, careful planning is an elusive goal. . . . Yet, despite the pressing need, information is a scarce resource."[19]

In Chapter 3, my coding category Information Gathering accounted for the singular act of gathering the public's agenda items. These "for your information" (FYI) references to public opinion contained issues from the "most important problem facing the nation today" list. This question by virtue of its open-ended nature seeks personal knowledge, not prompted responses. Open-ended questions require real understanding by the respondent because the respondent is not simply asked to choose among stated options, but to remember content without prompting or specific cues. This question captures agenda relevance by virtue of its open-ended nature; the public responds based on personal knowledge, not prompted responses.

The public opinion found in these informational memos reads like a top-ten list for each administration's agenda. For the Nixon administration, inflation was the most frequently mentioned item. The Ford staff also tracked economic issues closely, as their particular agenda included such issues as inflation, gasoline rationing, and wage and price controls. The Carter administration tracked issues ranging from those directly connected to the presidents' agenda to seemingly irrelevant issues. In December 1978, the Carter White House tracked awareness among the public for California's Proposition 13, along with poll data revealing areas in which "people would like to see government spending reduced."[20] Privacy, information about deregulation of AT&T, and attitudes about energy dominated informational memos. The presence of so many topics so far from the president's agenda was surprising. Seemingly, polling resources would be dedicated to presidential priorities. The Carter administration exchanged polling for informational purposes beyond anticipated topics, because as one Carter aide claimed:

> "I'm not sure whether we would have been so concerned about the tax-cutters if Proposition 13 hadn't been so popular. Normally, the tax-cutters would have been considered part of the fringe. But when the

issue started to spread, there was no way to get out from under. Christ, even Jerry Brown reacted. Imagine a balanced-budget amendment under Brown. That's how strong the public opinion was."[21]

The Reagan administration explicitly connected constituency breakdowns to collected information on its agenda items by cross-tabulating that information by subgroup. Although both Nixon and Ford employed party identification and philosophical information ("Are you liberal or conservative?") for agenda items, Reagan's staff was more interested in the socioeconomic data than any other administration. Traditional divisions into subgroups included gender, race, age, area of country, and specifics depending on the question.

The Bush White House took identifying information using the poll apparatus to an entirely new level. As noted in Table 3.7, the Bush administration devoted 54 percent of its poll apparatus to informational activities, more than twice the 21 percent averaged by the other four administrations. The bulk of the exchanged public opinion information stemmed from memos beginning with "FYI." These informational memos did cover Bush agenda items such as education, the environment, and the budget. However, the variety of public opinion referenced ranged across some topics few would have imagined residing in the White House archives. In August 1991, EPA Administrator William Reilly sent President Bush a memo of "what's in."[22] The memo's contents and George Bush's penned comments can be found in Table 5.3. Apparently, President Bush did not watch much television.

TABLE **5.3** What's "In" in 1991

Topic	"In" Score	George Bush's Comments
Environmentalism	85%	↑ good
Safe sex	83%	For it
Patriotism	75%	For it
The Simpsons	74%	Don't care
Short skirts for women	72%	For it
Marriage	68%	Yeah!
Having children	66%	Too late
The Cosby Show	58%	Don't care
Bowling	41%	Marginally good news
Men's double-breasted suits	32%	Sig Rogich will be pleased

Data source: Memo to Holiday from Bush, 8/5/91, in PR 15 Box 157 26668855-2999372, George Bush Library.

Alternative Selection

This section tends to contradict much of J+S

As important as is collecting information on issues, it is the link between problems and solutions that shapes outcomes and leadership opportunities. "A problem is linked to a solution; a problem is a problem only if something can be done about it."[23] Paul Light asserts that "selecting alternatives is perhaps the single most important step in the presidential policy process. It is the point where the programmatic content is framed, where the political benefits are set."[24] Contrary to Light's assertions, the public is significantly involved at this stage for three of the five administrations, and somewhat involved for the other two.

Although all five of these administrations used the poll apparatus to track the public's top agenda items, the Nixon and Ford administrations were not as interested in the public's choices for solutions. The Nixon and Ford administrations were attentive instead to themes and goals. A Nixon memo entitled "Administration Impact On Public Opinion" extensively discussed the "positive themes that have come through in the first year," as well as the "positive themes that have not come through," by citing poll data.[25] As with the Nixon administration's interest in economic themes, the Ford administration also polled for thematic information. "More than half the people still regard Inflation as Public Enemy No. 1, as against 20% who list unemployment or depression as their principal personal concern."[26] In the Ford administration, polling was used to focus issues for the State of the Union, which, according to Jeffrey Cohen, is an agenda-setting activity, but not an alternative-selection activity.[27] On December 24, 1975, Robert Teeter informed Richard Cheney that, based on national polling results, "over half the people mention one of these two issues as their leading issue concern. They are obviously the cause of the strong negativity and pessimism in the data. A large majority of people in the country are or think they are hurting financially and want the government to do something now. Interestingly, only 7% of them think that the Ford Administration is the leading cause of the inflation but an overwhelming majority think the administration is not doing anything or enough to solve the problem."[28] In the Nixon and Ford memos, the standard foci were on identifying issues moving on and off the public agenda, and assessing credit and blame allocation.

using polls for self amusement

The Nixon administration connected their focus on themes in their agenda to the details of their programs, but did not use the public to determine the alternatives. The Nixon and Ford administrations were more likely to connect performance or job approval responses to their preferred alternatives. One memo noted that of the 48 percent of the individuals who had seen President Nixon's environmental program, "26% said he was handling the environment poorly. The environmental poll data were included on a memo that stated that the objective on the environment was to "maintain and expand lead on pollution issue."[29] To accomplish this objective, the White House staff recommended attacking the "major hurdle . . . air and water pollution caused by industry" with several options, including continuing on the present course, new environmental taxes, and research and monitoring, but did not often reference poll information for those options.[30] Moreover, when the Nixon White House used alternative questions, it was for factual information explaining the public's reasoning rather than delineating a choice. For example, on welfare, President Nixon himself designed several poll questions seeking "the basic point as to whether the American people want people who work but who don't receive incomes that equal that of welfare recipients to receive a federal subsidy, or in other words a guaranteed income of $2,600 a year."[31] Thus, the public evaluated performance and options, but that choice was only theoretically meaningful.

Occasionally, in the early White House memoranda, staffers hinted that public opinion was more meaningful for decision making. For example, the Ford administration commissioned a survey to "find out what kinds of complaints people may have as a result of their experiences in the marketplace with over 200 individual products and service[s] . . . and what they do about their complaints."[32] Although Virginia Knauer, President Ford's special assistant for consumer affairs, did not specifically relate these findings to a course of action, she believed surveys delving into the problems facing citizens could be of valuable assistance to the government. "The results of the survey should have broad implications for government policy makers, industry and the consumer behavior research community."[33] However, more often than not, the Nixon and Ford administrations did not employ public attitudes for selecting among options.

The Carter, Reagan, and Bush administrations were more likely to seek support for solutions and options from the public. In a Reagan

White House "Strategic Evaluation Memorandum" designed to assess the "support, opposition, reaction and alternatives to the President's Economic Program," Richard Beal connects the "significant drop in the public approval ratings on the President's handling of the economy, inflation and unemployment" to confusion among the public over specific alternatives to the president's plan.[34] The Reagan staffers were very attentive to attitudes regarding the specifics of the economic plan. "Polls have consistently shown high support. For example . . . . his spending cuts were favored 72–21% and his tax cuts by 73–22% . . . by a margin of 70–25%, the public thought the economic program fair and equitable . . . 61% backed the President's budget cuts and 71% favored his tax plan."[35] In fact, much of the Reagan administration's referencing of Domestic Fiscal, Monetary, and Tax Policy, and Inflation opinion (see Table 3.4) stemmed from the focal point of his first two years in office: the Economic Recovery Program. In 1982, Reagan's Office of Policy Development (OPD) staff sought the public's opinion on the least-hated method of tax increase in order to reduce the deficit. Interestingly, much of the discussion of Americans' tax preferences centered around the validity of the information and whether commercial polling sources were valid, because they did not take into account "the recent acceleration in the increase in the average level of unemployment, the recent increase in gasoline prices, and the recent fall in the average price of natural gas sold." In this instance, the memo's author, OPD staff member Velma Montoya, used the poll results, not to recommend choosing the public's preferred policy alternative, but rather to recommend that the administration commission a new poll!

The level of detail pollsters can achieve in their alternative issue questions often allows for several alternatives to be considered at a time. The Ford and Carter administrations often lamented the connection between energy issues and economic issues. "Only 43% favor imposing a special tax on gas guzzling cars 'if this creates unemployment in the auto industry.'"[36] "Gasoline rationing is hateful to most people. Standing alone, sentiment is still nearly 2 to 1 against coupon rationing. But when compared to your [Ford's] tariff increasing the price by 10 c. a gallon, rationing comes out 48 to 46% ahead (statistically 50–50)."[37]

In most instances, the Carter administration was more likely to use polling alternatives and take those views seriously than any other administration. On many levels, President Carter believed in a role for the public in government.[38] Responding in part to the legacy of Watergate, President Carter sought public input for his administration on several levels: mail, phone calls, public opinion polls, and his People's Program.[39] The president's strong belief in supporting the public's role in government encouraged the Carter administration to utilize the public as a legitimate voice for selecting among alternatives. This is evident in Table 5.2—no domestic issue falls below 55 percent of alternative usage.

On almost all domestic topics, Nixon and Ford relied on polling information that demonstrated general levels of support. The Carter, Reagan, and Bush administrations preferred detailed information on the public's policy choices. For the Carter, Reagan, and Bush administrations, alternative questions were a frequent source of "causes and solutions." Stuart Eizenstat, assistant to the president for domestic policy, passed along a memo on health care to President Carter, who, as was his habit, underlined sections of the memo. The section that caught Carter's interest specified "alternatives for making health care more affordable."[40] Carter's highlighted alternatives included government price controls, federal aid to help the poor buy insurance, and even higher taxes.[41] The Reagan administration tested options for social security, and even queried the public as to what plan to choose: "design an initial solvency package," work with Congress, or provide a "menu of solvency proposals from which the Congress can select."[42] The Bush administration even utilized open-ended questions, which are "in some ways, the most valid survey data" to inquire into preferred methods for reducing the deficit, in which the issue of "fairness" dominated the public's solutions.[43]

Using public opinion information that identifies the public's preferences invites the public into the presidential agenda process. However, involving the public often yielded mixed results and mixed signals for leadership strategies. The following is a question asked to ordinary Americans by Patrick Caddell's polling firm for the Carter administration:

> "Some of our country's larger oil companies have acquired coal reserves in order to compete in the coal fuel supply business and have developed uranium mines to supply fuel to the nuclear power industry. Do you think having the oil companies expand their activities into other energy areas is good for America, or would you prefer to see the large oil companies prevented by the government from doing this? On a scale from one to seven, where would you be with regard to this question if 'one'

represents strong support for letting oil companies get involved in other areas of the energy business besides oil and gas and 'seven' represents strong opposition to letting oil companies get involved in other areas."[44]

Not surprisingly, the answers to that question were decidedly mixed, averaging 14.28 percent across the scale, and with no category receiving more than 24 percent. The category receiving 24 percent was four, approximately the middle answer to a complex question. Few other administrations actually asked that complicated a question, but the Carter polling question is illustrative of a problem with using public opinion in the policymaking process. Yankelovich argues that polling cannot be useful for any policy debate because the responses that polling reveals are not the type of opinions that produce change or even an appropriate manner of dialogue.[45] Polls reveal public opinion; solutions or transformations require public judgment. Public judgment is "a particular form of public opinion that exhibits: (1) more thoughtfulness . . . than ordinary opinion as measured in opinion polls; and (2) more emphasis on the normative, valuing, ethical side of questions."[46]

In 1982, Associate Director of OMB for Human Resources and Labor Ken Clarkson elucidated why poll data is not always useful for designing policy: "The poll data compiled by Dick Wirthlin demonstrates some of the pitfalls in trying to gauge how citizens feel about extremely complex and emotional issues like social security. On their face, many of the responses appear inconsistent: respondents generally indicate support for the status quo, but provide seemingly contradictory answers."[47] Despite the caveat, however, Clarkson still recommended that the Reagan administration utilize poll data to determine whether or not the president should get involved in social security, "design an initial solvency package," work with Congress, or provide a "menu of solvency proposals from which the Congress can select."[48] White House poll usage across these five administrations essentially supports Clarkson's argument, but provides mixed support for the domination of campaign leadership behavior. Poll data are exceptionally useful for designing the general direction of presidential policy choices, particularly the presidential agenda. Three of the five administrations did query the public for its options and referenced those preferences. However, even those administrations were wary of the information, and only cautiously relied on it for choosing among alternatives.

Moving Through the Institutional Maze

A permanent campaign presidency is one that extends continuous solicitations of support for policy initiatives. Kernell argues that "the strategic prescriptions of going public" require campaign activities such as "political travel, numerous appearances before organized constituencies, and extensive use of television—even paid commercials during non-election periods."[49] The strategy of public relations and the permanent campaign is to work with and from the people—rather than with Washington.[50] Thus, the permanent campaign, according to Sidney Blumenthal, produces its own behaviors and language, which mirror a true campaign. "Reagan's men converse about 'open windows' (the relative openness of public opinion to Presidential initiatives), 'targets of opportunity' (events or issues than can be quickly taken advantage of), 'sequencing' (the timing and order of a series of actions), 'resistance ratios' (the degree to which the public accepts [what the president] is doing and the need to be proactive rather than reactive."[51] An administration plans, persuades, and evaluates itself steeped in the polling apparatus. This stage of activity encompasses, on average, 35 percent of White House polling usage.

Planning the Fight

Preparing, limiting priorities, and controlling the agenda are the tools of the "strategic presidency."[52] Moreover, successful articulation of "the policy direction of the administration" can maximize the strategic president's time.[53] The "most important problem facing the nation today" list is an excellent source of what issues matter to the public. This top-ten list of issues most certainly will be on the president's agenda—but are these issues a priority? Paul Light defines presidential priorities as "the president's must list." "From the staff viewpoint, the must list constitutes a shortened version of the legislative agenda and contains the critical priorities, the items considered crucial to the presidential program."[54] From Light's perspective, this list is dependent on resources and capital—can the issue and its alternative be acted upon in Congress? Thus, the must list is shaped by phenomena outside the president's control, for example, Congress, impending crises, and costs. Seemingly, the public opinion apparatus would not play much of a role in prioritizing the president's agenda for institutional warfare. However, public opinion does affect this must list. The president's long-term priorities originate with the campaign, the party, and the president's personal goals. Moreover, the White House must frequently adjust that list due to the vagaries of the political environment. The poll apparatus factors into two planning avenues: assessing the political environment and the issue environment.

The Political Environment　The most common way in which presidents take the political temperature is by using approval ratings—the president's and Congress'. Low institutional job performance ratings give the president ammunition with which to urge congressional action. Professor Derge found that, for the Nixon administration, the public was divided on its rating of Congress. "Thirty-eight percent of the public approve of the job done by Congress, while 37% disapprove. When the performance of Republican and Democratic members of Congress is evaluated separately, the division of opinion is again evident. . . . These ratings, as might be expected, tend to be highly partisan."[55]

Ammunition can be found not just in general institutional job ratings, but on specific issue ratings as well. In the Nixon surveys, Congress is frequently the bad guy. For example: "During the coming months, President Nixon says he will try to hold down government spending and taxes. Many congressmen, on the other hand, say Congress should pass social programs that would give more money to the poor, the aged and to schools and the like. Which position do you agree with?"[56] The Bush administration took these ratings to another level, assessing not just past performance but also future. "Who will do a better job of providing leadership in the months ahead: Dems in Congress, Reps in White House." Bush pollsters followed up, asking, "Who will do a better job, Dems in Congress, Reps in White House, on Combating drugs, Federal Budget Deficit, Achieving balance between domestic and defense spending, Dealing with problems facing the middle class, Strengthening the Economy." Democrats led all categories on the issues in August 1989.[57] With this information, the president and his staff distinguished between issues worth pressing the presidential advantage on and those that should be avoided.

The challenge of dealing with Congress encouraged Presidents Nixon and Reagan to display the institutional evaluations in an effort to procure an advantage. President Nixon released poll information that

Negotiator vs congress

warned Congress about taking unpopular steps on a preferred presidential program. In a press release from Market Opinion Research (MOR), the Nixon administration gleefully pointed out that "should the President veto spending proposals that go beyond his budget, only three-in-ten Americans would favor a Congressional override of these Presidential vetoes."[58] Reagan and his staff also wanted to warn Congress; unfortunately in their case, public opinion did not support the preferred action. On October 7, 1981, the Reagan administration was informed that "the public overwhelmingly rejects the idea of returning impoundment powers to the President . . . fully two-thirds."[59] The polls revealed that the political environment did not support the president's preferred option.

The Issue Environment   Poll results helped determine the timing and necessity of speeches by providing evidence of what the public wanted or needed to hear. The troubling political aftermath of the Nixon administration represented a unique problem for President Ford's effort to go public. In November 1975, Ford's staff concluded that a major address to unite "legislative, diplomatic and executive initiatives" was necessary. From their data, Ford's pollsters detected anomalous support from the public: "Almost like jilted lovers, the American public seem reticent to give their whole-hearted support to the President. . . . The President has a high rating on foreign policy and personality, and a low one on domestic policy and strength of decisiveness needed to achieve results."[60] To reconcile these conflicting findings, the staff decided President Ford needed a speech to demonstrate how his policies tied together.

In December 1975, Teeter gave the administration a laundry list of poll results that begged for attention in the State of the Union Address. For the upcoming election year address, Teeter recommended specifically dealing with the following issues: inflation and unemployment, crime, energy, health care, increased aid to the elderly, and education. Every item appeared in the January 19, 1976, State of the Union Address to the nation.[61] However, despite the State of the Union Address's traditional emphasis on programs, Teeter also recommended a message based on the worrisome results on the national mood.[62] He emphasized, "Our most important job is to repair the President's perception so that he is seen as a decisive, forceful leader with a plan for the country."[63] Perhaps the most infamous use of poll data to determine the timing and content of a major presidential address was President Carter's "Crisis of Confidence" speech. Caddell urged First Lady Rosalynn Carter and Press Secretary Jody Powell that the alarming state of the national mood, discovered in the poll data, demanded a presidential address.[64] Caddell informed Carter's White House staff that "on a broad front of social, political, and economic issues we find a deep, significant, and accelerating decline . . . we find a unison of negative movement at a velocity that raises doubts not only of political survival but of national cohesion. . . . If this process continues at the current rate and direction, you . . . inadvertently run the risk of being identified as the President who presided over the dissolution of the American political society."[65] Carter was clearly seduced by Caddell's seemingly overwhelming information.

Public opinion findings also helped these administrations plan legislatively significant rhetorical efforts. Planning the president's "Moral Equivalent of War" strategy for energy legislation before Congress, President Carter and his staff used polls to determine the reception for particular themes and strategies. "The public will probably not be receptive to the argument that we need energy legislation because we are running out of fuel. . . . Pat's [Caddell] figures show 'real energy shortages' running a poor third (38%) to 'the way oil companies act' (58%) and 'high fuel prices' (65%)."[66] However, Caddell's figures did show that the public was concerned with inflation, so the staff tried to tie energy to inflation by using the trade deficit and energy price arguments.[67] Carter's staff employed a strategy designed, not to convince the public the president was right because he was a "leader," but rather to convince them that the administration presented the "real" version of the energy crisis. A poll commissioned to evaluate the public's energy knowledge and concerns found that "the public is preoccupied with the economy, particularly high prices, while the energy crisis is remote and unreal."[68] Moreover, polling identified for the administration how education was required to improve the prospects for a successful policy outcome of Carter's energy bill: "One viewpoint is that as energy prices continue to increase, consumers will engage in self-help. [Thus] . . . government-funded public education efforts are a waste of money, and perhaps even counter-productive. . . . The other viewpoint is that a concerted public education campaign must be developed to overcome these barriers. . . . Once that new ethic is widely adopted, people will eschew gas guzzling autos, needless driving, overheated and overcooled homes, etc."[69]

Similarly, the Reagan staff utilized poll data to define the terms of debate prior to the legislative discussion of an issue. For example, they commissioned polls on the 1981 social security proposals in order to "draw out those conclusions which you think are most relevant and important to the emerging [1982] debate on social security."[70] In addition to the questions on policy alternatives, such as tax increases to pay for the cuts and support for eliminating the earnings test on the elderly, staffers examined issues of trust in the administration. The Bush administration went the next step in agenda setting through debate control by not only polling on the issues but also polling on the circumstances surrounding a potential debate. In June 1990, Ed Rogers sent his boss, Chief of Staff John Sununu, detailed poll data on the political environment, which included observations about policy initiation: "58% believe Congress has the responsibility to make the first concrete proposal to reduce the deficit. 37% believe the President has this responsibility. By 69% to 24% the public prefers that Congress and the President reach a deficit reduction plan that increases taxes and cuts spending vs. reaching no agreement at all."[71] The public's attitudes toward what to do remained significant, but the Bush staff added a new wrinkle. Unlike the Nixon and Ford administrations, which tracked blame allocation after events had occurred, the Bush staff used polling in order to *prevent* blame allocation.

Making the Pitch

Presidential staffs honed presidential rhetoric by testing phrases for unwanted reactions. Nixon, for example, wanted to be recognized for containing the lawlessness feared during the 1960s, but he did not want to appear racist. Thus, the administration tested phrases for heightened constituent responses. "When asked whether the phrase 'law and order' is nothing more that a code word for racism, 70.5% of the persons polled disagreed and only 20% agreed with that statement."[72] The poll data reassured the administration that they could use the phrase "law and order" in speeches without fear of seeming derogatory.

In addition to testing for inflamed rhetoric, presidents have also polled for understanding and clarifying terminology. In a briefing to the National Governors Conference on energy policy, the Carter administration revealed that Americans expressed "widespread cynicism and skepticism regarding the nature of the energy problem," as well as "poor knowledge of how to actually save energy," despite intense White House educational efforts.[73] The White House incorporated educational items into speeches to combat that lack of knowledge, such as the idea that "lowering the temperature from 72° to 68°" actually saves energy.[74] President Carter delivered four major energy speeches and six other major addresses to the nation that targeted the energy problem.[75] By saturating presidential messages with his energy agenda, Carter was able to convince the public that there was an energy shortage by March 1979. However, the public still preferred increased production over sacrifice through conservation (58 percent to 29 percent). In 1979, Lou Harris reported to Vice President Mondale's assistant Gail Harrison that "anything we [the administration] can do to increase [oil] supplies from Alaska, Canada and Mexico would be strongly supported."[76]

In addition, as part of rhetorical content, all five administrations included public opinion data in public discourse, rather than confining it only to the development of that content. These administrations used poll data as their own representatives, by allowing public opinion to make a statement about the president or his actions with a voice that did not involve a member of the White House staff. Nixon used the results from Gallup polls (of which he had advanced notice of content), as well as other polls that he commissioned himself, to demonstrate support for his policies. After a major presidential address to the nation on Vietnam, delivered on November 3, 1969, a Gallup poll found that the "President's popularity increases 12% over last poll." The administration decided to take that approval increase and "disseminate widely and tie in with the President's Vietnam policy."[77] This tactical, if not strategic, use of poll data helped promote Nixon's Vietnam policy, requiring little administration effort. H. R. Haldeman, President Nixon's chief of staff, recommended that no references of the 12-percent increase be made by the president, but the press secretary was to refer to the poll if asked. Disseminating poll results allowed Nixon to celebrate improvement without appearing to rejoice. In a thirteen-step program, the Nixon staff took every opportunity to communicate this information to national and state elites. A memo entitled "Gallup Poll Game Plan" urged circulation of the 12-percent popularity increase and the relationship to Vietnam policy on the "Hill." The poll information was distributed to all staff and personnel, as well as to all editors, selected columnists radio and TV commentators, and executive directors of every business group or association in Washington. All GOP governors were informed and the vice president was asked to mention it. The memo recommended asking H. Ross Perot (head of United We Stand) to tie the increase to his program. Nixon and Haldeman even directed the Paris peace negotiators to "push this as a sign of unity," and the "South Vietnam Government should be asked to push this as a sign that Americans back Nixon policy." Such public opinion data sold success and confidence in a manner no official could.

Perhaps due to the aftermath of Watergate and the distrust of overt public relations, Presidents Ford, Carter, and Reagan did not disseminate their supportive poll data as blatantly as President Nixon.[78] However, some of their rhetoric was heavily seasoned with favorable poll results. During the government reorganization effort that was a centerpiece of the Carter campaign, the administration obtained poll data to derive solutions specifically from survey results that identified constituent problems. In a manner reminiscent of Nixon, Carter actively highlighted the use of the poll data, both to sell the public on reorganization solutions and to celebrate the public's input into the reorganization effort. In particular, the administration pointed to poll data bearing on "those federal activities which cause the most constituent complaint regarding inefficiency, confusion, excessive paperwork requirements and general program failure."[79] The Carter administration believed the survey gave President Carter the means to stress that he was "involved personally in an effort to make government work better for people."[80]

The Reagan administration occasionally used polling to provide rhetorical peer pressure. Interspersed with rhetoric such as "but who can deny that we face a crisis; that no more than a thin wall of wavering willpower stands between us and ruin by red ink," Reagan incorporated poll results into his speech for the kickoff rally (July 19, 1982) for his balanced-budget amendment plan.[81] Reagan's rhetoric and goal (the desire to add an amendment to the constitution) took a lofty, broad tack, artfully compelling his audience toward support. However, he suddenly abandoned his inspirational rhetoric and abruptly informed the public, "Nor should ratification be difficult. Thirty-two States have already taken a separate initiative of their own in favor of an amendment, and recent surveys show 4 of 5 Americans want a constitutional check on red-ink spending."[82] In fact, only one survey by Market Opinion Research was cited in the talking points prepared for the administration and used in the drafting of the speech.[83]

By the time of the Bush administration, public opinion rhetoric was so commonplace that even Vice President Quayle's speeches included poll data. At a speech before the Citizens for a Sound Economy Foundation, Quayle commented at length on the results of a Roper poll. The vice president concluded, "Given their broad—and accurate—understanding of the essential economic facts, it's not surprising that the American people overwhelmingly oppose tax increases as a means of ending the deficit."[84]

Where Are We Now?

Key components of successful campaigns are identifying a course of action and executing the steps to achieving one's goal. In the case of a campaign, the ultimate goal is clearly victory at the polls. Remaining on task and on target requires constant evaluation, constant measures of standing in hypothetical polls. Campaigning in office requires a similar devotion to assessment.

The Nixon, Ford, Carter, Reagan, and Bush administrations focused their thematic messages by using information about public opinion to evaluate presidential leadership efforts, and to measure the strength of those efforts. Polling also aided efforts to determine the effectiveness of public relations. With regard to thematic policy messages, the Nixon administration tested simple phrases that painted a picture of America; for example, "Positive themes which came through in the first year (for example) . . . identify with Middle America . . . orderliness and calm restored . . . ending the war honorably." Some examples of themes that didn't work were "dealing with the problems of the poor . . . the new federalism . . . [and] the streamlining of government decision-making." Sensitive to negative media and partisan views, the Nixon administration examined which negative themes resonated with the public, such as "doing the right thing for the wrong reason . . . [and] the president cannot handle Congress."[85] Thus, Nixon's staff relied on the public opinion apparatus to measure public relations successes and failures. Similarly, the Ford, Carter, Reagan, and Bush administrations tested presidential

[handwritten margin note: Good summary of using polls to campaign while in office]

[handwritten: 1]

themes using polling methods. The Reagan administration raised the bar for measuring message evaluation by asking open-ended survey questions after major addresses. Open-ended questions, such as "Tell me what some of the major points of the speech were,"[86] require real understanding by the respondent, because the respondent was not simply asked to choose among stated options, but also to remember content without prompting or specific cues. The responses to such open-ended questions, especially the responses about the "most important problem facing the nation," were tabulated and tracked for changes over time.[87]

In addition, poll data helped determine how constituencies responded to presidential messages before and after delivery. Ronald Reagan's September 24, 1981, speech on his Economic Recovery Program favorably impressed 57 percent of his audience. However, it was found that those "least likely to be impressed include: 25–34 year olds . . . Blue collar workers and retirees . . . [and] minority respondents."[88] For the Ford administration, post-speech polls revealed how the public responded to the message as well as the chosen rhetorical style. Teeter reported that the administration received a "large pay-off with men resulting from the President taking a tough stand in the area of international problems and incidents."[89]

In addition to evaluating ideas, these administrations also polled to evaluate reactions to planned and unplanned events. They firmly believed that poll results were both directly dependent on and stemmed from news events and presidential actions. The Nixon and Ford staffs designed elaborate mechanisms to identify trends in the area of presidential popularity and events. In particular, they compared "major (and non-sensitive) daily Presidential activity record of the President . . . major daily news events . . . Presidential news conferences and speech record and . . . Nielsen ratings for nationally televised Presidential news conferences and addresses."[90] Public opinion polls revealed any weak responses and positive reactions. For example, the Ford administration found that although "conventional wisdom holds that Presidential summitry should be a significant plus for the president . . . President [Ford] suffered a three-point drop in his Gallup approval ratings."[91] A memo from James Wray, director of Political Affairs, to President Bush highlights problems when attempting to track presidential efforts: "The President has launched forth a number of very positive, action oriented solutions to key domestic problems. Yet, on several of those key announcements, there have been matters occur[ing] that seem to contradict those positive actions. For example: Clean Air/Environment—Oil spill(s) [and] Crime/Ethics—HUD scandal."[92]

The Bush White House also correlated presidential poll numbers with events such as presidential travel and foreign meetings. After a trip to California, Sig Rogich, assistant to the president for public events and initiatives, informed the president that "the polling totals thru last night have Wilson [governor of California] up 50/39. More important, our numbers are 59/29 which is [a] good sign and probably [the] result of our trip."[93] Unlike the other administrations, however, the Bush White House also used the poll apparatus prior to presidential travel. In order to improve rhetorical and personal efforts while traveling, the Bush White House often informed the president of public opinion data relevant to the area to which he traveled. In July 1990, Ed Rogers, deputy chief of staff, sent the president some approval data from Texas, writing, "Since you will be in Houston this weekend, I thought you might be interested."[94]

Television coverage was an important factor in evaluating planned and unplanned events for the Nixon, Carter, Reagan, and Bush administrations. Following a dip in the August 1983 job approval ratings, David Gergen reported that "as the total percentage of coverage (measuring TV nets, major newspapers and magazines) went up for foreign policy/Central America, the president's rating went down—and vice versa . . . [due to the] tension in Central America and the possibility of greater US involvement."[95] In essence, the more television covered foreign affairs, the worse Reagan appeared to the public. Thus, the natural conclusion drawn from Gergen's memo was to keep foreign policy off the national news. The memo went on to explain how the numbers were not yet in for September, "but the experts feel that the Korean Air Lines disaster [the Soviet Union shot down Korean Air flight 007 on September 1, 1983] will be the biggest story of the year and will help the President's standing in job approval polls."[96] The "experts" were correct; by the end of 1983, Ronald Reagan's popularity figures and foreign policy job approval ratings were both over 50 percent.[97]

In the Carter and Bush administrations, television was not the strategic tool seen in the Reagan White House, at least not in regard to polling. These two administrations were aware of televised poll results; ABC News Vice President George Watson sent Press Secretary Jody Powell advance notice that ABC planned to broadcast the results of a Lou Harris poll on the president's energy program.[98] Instead, the president and his top staff were merely kept informed of televised polling data. Pollster Bob Teeter tracked televised (and print) approval ratings as well as policy attitudes for President Bush: "Current voter attitudes toward the economy will be on NBC News tonight and in the *Wall Street Journal* tomorrow as part of their on-going national polling project. A clear majority (73%) of voters think we are currently in a recession. . . . This perception of an economic recession also is modifying consumer behavior. More than half (57%) say they have been cutting down on purchases."[99]

In contrast to the Carter, Reagan, and Bush administrations' interest in the effects of media coverage, the Nixon administration used the polling apparatus to evaluate attitudes of the media. In a memo to Dwight Chapin, Charles Colson, Harry Dent, Herbert Klein, Lyn Nofziger, William Safire, and Ron Ziegler, Jeb Magruder notes that one out of ten believe the media is fair and objective all the time.[100] Moreover, Magruder urges the Nixon White House staff, "Based on the results of the latest Derge poll, continue to stress the public's awareness of the unfair treatment we receive from the press and keep up the drive for TV networks to reexamine their procedures in terms of separating news reporting from editorial commentary."[101]

Completing the Cycle

The differences illustrated at the beginning of this chapter between Paul Light and Deborah Stone centered on the notion of implementation. Light does not include implementation in the presidential process. Most likely, Light ignores implementation because, by definition, it occurs in the bureaucracy. Presidents have variable control over the day-to-day functioning of the bureaucracy. Presidents have increased their efforts to influence the implementation of policy without going through Congress by utilizing the appointment process.[102] However, there are many constraints on the president's choices for the bureaucracy, and there is uncertainty in the performance of presidential appointees.[103] The success of controlling the bureaucracy is evident in the increase of the White House staff. "Presidents are driven sooner or later toward an alternative way of imposing their will on the executive branch. Instead of trying to presidentialize the network of executive organizations over which they preside, they turn instead to the strategy of bureaucratizing the presidency."[104] Of all presidents under investigation here, President Reagan "built a set of administrative arrangements that by past standards proved coherent, well-integrated, and eminently workable."[105] However, even the Reagan administration was unable to dominate the policy implementation process in the Executive Branch.

Two concordant phenomena regarding the presidency and the bureaucracy thus combine to produce a dearth of polling in the implementation process. First, as discussed in Chapter 2, little polling data traveled outside the White House staff. Few Cabinet members ever received any polling data or exchanged any polling memoranda. Second, presidents had little control over the bureaucracy; the increased attention to polling data in the White House would not necessarily filter down the administration hierarchy. Therefore, polling did not penetrate the bureaucracy and could not penetrate the implementation or evaluation aspects of the policymaking process. I did, however, find one exception to the rule. On one issue, reorganization, and in one administration, President Carter's, I found the public's policy preferences were attended to and even relied on for the entirety of the policy process.

The Carter Exception: Reorganization

Reorganizing the government was not a wholly new idea. Nixon had reorganized the Bureau of the Budget into the Office of Management and Budget with an eye toward efficiency in 1970. In 1976, reorganization of the government became a centerpiece of the Carter campaign. His staff and supporters believed that the issue defined him. Patrick Caddell claimed, "There is no other issue with which Governor Carter is more closely identified in the public mind than the question of reorganization."[106] Early in 1977, surveys demonstrated that reorganization was a terrific policy issue. "There are no other issues the public understands less about and yet has more hope for than solving the mismanagement in the Federal government."[107] The polls suggested that Carter could "fulfill much of his reorganization promise if he can provide better service, as opposed to more difficult reductions in the budget," which served to orient the president's agenda toward achievable goals.[108] The Carter effort focused on "zero-based budgeting, sunshine provisions and declassifying materials, setting ethical standards and small deregulatory efforts." These efforts were projected to be supported by high public approval and be "quick and easy possibilities." However, they did have one major concern: "Many voters suspect that Carter may fail at government reorganization because of bureaucratic intransience or because the Congress will stop him when they see a lack of a popular support. Obviously, the second situation can be headed off by an aroused public. . . . To begin with, the President must explain to the public the purpose of reorganization and what he hopes to gain from it."[109]

The reorganization surveys of the citizenry were "aimed at identifying those areas of government causing constituents the most problems."[110] The White House asked the public to identify all levels of interaction with government officials; in particular the local caseworkers who have the most contact with average citizens. Caddell constructed surveys to identify the problem as defined by the public. In response, a majority of the public blamed each of the following: paperwork and effort duplication, a poorly organized bureaucracy, and bad management practices.[111] Correspondingly, the public preferred cost-saving solutions: "Tax dollars should be better spent, waste, frills and red tape should be cut down."[112] Additionally, Caddell's staff found that "basic restructuring is not given high priorities by most of the public."[113] The polled public overwhelmingly rejected the easy political fix: "Fewer than one-third fe[lt] reorganizing the Cabinet is the key to overall reorganization."[114] Only 22 percent felt it was important to abolish a department rather than create a Department of Energy or Department of Education.[115] The public approved zero-based budgeting and sunshine laws overwhelmingly (55 percent for the former, and 65 percent for the latter). Caddell also noted that a federal incentive system met with public approval (67 percent), but such a "system might be difficult to set up and manage."[116] Unlike most issues, the polls provided the Carter administration with clear and specific policy prescriptions that could be followed.[117]

In addition to surveying the public, Richard Pettigrew, the assistant to President Carter for reorganization, "conducted a survey of congressional offices aimed at identifying those federal activities which have caused the most constituent problems and complaints over the years."[118] Amazingly, Carter and his staff found consensus among respondents in how to "improve government's competence in serving the average citizen."[119] Focusing on "inefficiency, confusion, excessive paperwork requirements and general program failure," the survey highlighted problems with those agencies and programs that affect large numbers of people.[120] They "received some 212 [40 percent of congressional offices] responses to the casework survey, all of which have been forwarded to the affected agencies."[121]

The public saved the majority of their complaints in the casework survey for the Department of Labor, the Social Security Administration and the Immigration and Naturalization Service in the Department of Justice, and the IRS, HUD, and the Small Business Administration. The Veterans Administration was credited for its "responsiveness," as were the improvements in the Department of Labor's Occupational Safety and Health Administration (OSHA).[122] Moreover, Carter and his staff urged the government agencies to take steps to attend to the problems identified in the survey. "I am aware," Carter wrote, "that departments and agencies are already taking actions to address problems identified in the survey. Some of the problems may be beyond agencies' immediate control and have a statutory basis. Because these complaints involve the direct, day-to-day dealings of average citizens with their government, however, I would like to report to the public and the Congress as soon as possible on the steps we are taking to address them."[123] Stuart Eizenstat recommended to the president that "through such regular statements (which would range from such things as the Executive Order mandating sunset review of regulations to the elimination of unnecessary OSHA rules) you can become much more identified with government reform than you presently are. Given the country's mood, that identification should redound in the polls."[124]

As an issue, reorganization was "attractive . . . because it . . . cut across ideological, partisan and demographic lines."[125] In 1977, 54 percent had heard about the reorganization effort, and 65 percent felt that it was important.[126] After designing and implementing options recommended by the public via public opinion polls, the White House continued to employ the polling apparatus on reorganization. After 1977, the

White House employed public opinion polls to evaluate reorganization and reform efforts.[127] Nevertheless, despite the time, effort, and apparent public approval of reorganization, in the February 1979 poll, "eliminating waste and fraud" ranked fourth behind reducing inflation, creating jobs, and reducing taxes.[128] "Carter's position on reorganization appears to be fairly influential [, but] the problem the public believes the President should be working to overcome is that of inflation."[129] During more prosperous times, reorganization might have been a feather in President Carter's cap; however, any small successes were easily overshadowed by long gas lines, stagflation, and malaise.

Conclusions

The policymaking process and presidential goals merge to produce a cycle, which begins with an idea or an issue. Issues and ideas travel through this cycle and become problems with solutions, solved by legislation. Ultimately, the Executive Branch implements these legislative solutions. Do presidents approach this cycle from inside the beltway or do they employ campaigning to achieve their goals? A campaign leadership style would approach this process the same way candidates approach campaigns. Campaigns are characterized by a single endpoint in time. They depend on persuasion and are adversarial. Moreover, the public matters in campaigns, as they are the ultimate arbiters of victory—at the polls. Campaigns focus on victory, not on compromise or bargaining.

As representative of a campaign approach to governing, public opinion usage suggests that campaign leadership does indeed exist in the presidency. All five administrations employed polls during their most active legislative period. These presidents sought public input for the agenda, and to some degree for the options available as answers. Thus, as during a campaign, the presidents attempted to incorporate the public into their presidency by employing the tactics and strategies of a campaign. They used polls to plan, sell, and evaluate their identified tactics and strategies. In addition, the constituency efforts explored in Chapter 4 girded the agenda setting and persuasive opportunities, as support for publicly discussed presidential policies became an important component of core presidential supporters.

Nevertheless, what is victory? During a campaign, victory is success at the polls. Is legislative success—passage of the presidential agenda—the campaign once in office? The White House used campaign techniques primarily in years one and two—the most important, legislatively speaking, for the president. However, the use of polls across the issue environment was haphazard, although primarily staying on the president's agenda. Chapter 6 will take up this question of winning and explore the use of polls, and thus a campaign approach to governing, across the president's agenda issues, focusing on several case studies.

Do presidents campaign to govern? The assumption made by some scholars and members of the media is that the presence of campaign tools promotes an entirely new form of governing behavior. This new style of behavior rejects traditional styles of compromise, coalition building, and bargaining in favor of mass appeals to the people. In contrast, I have argued that campaigning to govern, as a theory of leadership, must incorporate more than mere campaign tools; it must employ the goals, approach, and methodology of the campaign. Campaign leadership is not simply Kernell's "going public" or Tulis' "rhetorical leadership."[1]

As evidenced in the previous chapters, campaign tools and strategies exist in the White House. Presidents and their staffs employed polls to define and connect with the presidential constituency, to prioritize and choose among agenda items and their alternatives, and to produce public relations strategies. The commonality between the permanent campaign and governing is the end goal—successful passage of the president's legislative agenda. Thus, it is the route to that goal that must define the presence of campaign leadership. Ultimately, the permanent campaign is about winning, not policymaking. As Heclo notes, "Within the confines of a campaign setting, what is true is what pleases the audience . . . campaigning is about talking to win, not to learn or to teach."[2] In exploring four legislative efforts with extensive use of public opinion polling, one each from the Carter, Reagan, Bush, and Clinton administrations, I demonstrate that using the polls does not necessarily produce campaign behavior. The White House was rarely willing to sacrifice its policy goals in order to achieve victory at all costs, with either the public or Congress.

Campaigning, Governing, or What?

Elites, members of the media, and scholars all agree that presidents use public relations. Presidents use their "bully pulpit," or their national megaphone, to set the national agenda and draw attention to issues, usually originating from their campaigns for the office. The perception underlying the theory is that "public opinion is the linchpin in securing support in Congress for presidential policy initiatives."[3] Kernell contends that in order to produce effective "going public" leadership, presidents must (1) be popular, and (2) successfully communicate with the public.[4] Once the public receives the president's message, control shifts to the citizen. Citizens must evaluate the president's proposal (along with their evaluations of the president). They must communicate their support to Congress, and then Congress must choose to follow public pressure.[5] According to Kernell, as a mode of presidential leadership, "going public is more akin to force than to bargaining" and makes compromise more difficult.[6] Moreover, it "undermines the legitimacy of other politicians. It usurps their prerogatives of office, denies their role as representatives, and questions their claim to reflect the interests of their constituents."[7]

The permanent campaign, however, goes much farther. Campaigning requires the redefinition of opposing positions as adversaries. The endpoint of the campaign is victory, but victory where?—in the polls, in Congress, or at the voting booth during the next election? Thus, the presidency can make use of campaign tools, but not in the service of a legislative agenda item campaign. The tug of war between the president and Congress, with the public as the rope, may look like a political campaign; however, the cases of energy, economic recovery, tree planting, and the balanced-budget amendment presented next suggest otherwise.

President Carter's Energy Proposal

In 1977, the goal of energy security, otherwise known as the "Moral Equivalent of War," was the focal point of President Carter's agenda. The combination of actions by OPEC and excesses in American oil usage produced a situation of oil shortages, high prices, foreign dependency, and frustration for citizens and elites. Energy was "a seemingly intractable problem . . . one that demanded a comprehensive view of many complicated and interdependent issues."[8] As Skowronek notes, the Carter approach to energy policy was a classic "going public" strategy. "By springing the package upon Congress wholesale and whipping up popular support, the President sought to overwhelm the entrenched resistance and propel a concerted drive for decisive action."[9] The "object of the president's design is not the American voter, but fellow politicians in Washington."[10] On the surface, Rafshoon and the Carter White House appear to have undertaken a classic permanent campaign strategy—convince the public and Congress, and you win on energy.

For the energy program's massive summer 1978 public campaign, Director of Communications Jerry Rafshoon sent a work plan to all relevant officials[11] claiming, "[W]e need a strategy that is appropriate to our two quite separable and different goals: 1) generation among press and public concern over energy and demand for passage of a plan; and 2) development of public support . . . targeted to specific members of the Conference Committee."[12] The Carter administration unapologetically sought public pressure on Congress in order "to hold Congress' collective feet to the fire. The success or failure of this Administration depends on Congress knowing that we can and will use public opinion effectively to make them act."[13] However, in a memo prepared for the president elect in December 1976, Caddell noted the lack of demand for energy legislation from the Carter electoral constituency. Caddell asked, "Why was Carter elected?" Answering his own question, Caddell asserted that Carter became president because of (1) personal comparisons with Ford, (2) partisan factors that favored any Democrat, and (3) social and psychological factors.[14] Moreover, in the same working paper, energy was cited as an issue but not as a constituency concern.[15]

Therefore, as early as 1976, the Carter team knew fighting for energy would be difficult. In 1976 and early 1977, during the transition, Caddell continued to argue that energy was "a vital area the president must face. He *must convince* the country not only that there is a real crisis but that the public can gain from supporting a real energy program."[16] Any effort to employ the public, via the polls, as pressure on

Congress necessitated efforts to either move public opinion to the president's preferred position or move the president's position closer to the public's position. December 1976 polls revealed that public sentiment was *not* aligned with the president's belief about the state of the country's energy crisis. Moreover, the public classified energy issues apart from larger economic and social concerns, and "doubt[ed] the need to make sacrifices."[17] The polls demonstrated how far these attitudes would have to be shifted. Finding that "two out of three people surveyed did not know that turning down the thermostat, even one or two degrees, saves energy" suggested that educating could conceivably render public support for a previously untenable program and ultimately benefit public relations attempts.[18]

Although the Carter White House accessed an extensive portrait of American attitudes on energy, the staff applied the knowledge only to the design of the public campaign. The Carter polling apparatus sought the public's opinion from questions ranging from "Have you heard about President Carter's energy program?" to highly detailed questions designed to elicit support for specific policy proposals.[19] The depth and language of the questions suggested a hunt for appropriate public relations. For example, Caddell did not ask the public, "Do you favor or oppose creation of a Federal oil reserve?" Instead, Caddell asked, "Do you favor or oppose creation of a Federal oil reserve where the U.S. would store up large amounts of oil as a protection against cut-off of foreign oil?"[20] A poll question that stopped after "reserve" required the respondent to understand the concept of the reserve. A poll question that stopped after "oil" defined the concept of the reserve but still allowed for choice. However, the addition of "as a protection" could easily serve as the definition of the search for winning language.

Beginning in 1976 and continuing through 1978, polls revealed that the public refused to believe there existed an energy crisis that required drastic household changes. The public did give high priority to national energy policy, and a majority approved of the president's handling of the energy problem by summer 1977, but the public opinion polls demonstrated no shift in policy attitudes, especially in terms of sacrifices.[21]

President Carter's rhetorical efforts during his honeymoon and first 100 days did not shift any of Caddell's indicators. "Communication with the public on energy has now stalled badly; the momentum of public support needs to be built up again. . . . People acknowledge that the threat is serious—but do not feel ready for sacrifices, resist additional gas taxes, and believe we will still be driving big cars five years from now. . . . You defined the challenge to the nation as the moral equivalent of war; but a strong call-to-arms requires vigorous follow-through, or else it quickly loses credibility . . . [and we] fear this is happening."[22] After four years and 105 presentations to the public on energy, public opinion proved surprisingly robust and resistant to direction, management, or manipulation.[23]

The White House's obsessive attention to immutable poll numbers took its toll on the message but did not influence their approach. The Carter administration continued to design messages without changing its policy solutions, all to combat the public's resistance. Rather than respond to the refusal to shift attitudes, the White House tried to link energy to what the polls revealed the public would accept. "The public will probably not be receptive to the argument that we need energy legislation because we are running out of fuel. . . . It is not surprising that Pat's figures show 'real energy shortages' running a poor third (38%) to 'the way oil companies act' (58%) and 'high fuel prices' (65%) as a cause of concern about energy. . . . Americans are most concerned about economics—particularly inflation. It is not difficult to tie energy to these concerns."[24] But energy continued its inexorable decline as a major issue on the public's agenda. By 1979, the Carter administration conceded defeat on energy with Congress and the public. "To clarify our priorities we should cease calling for victories where only defeat can be expected, e.g. the energy program."[25]

The Carter administration undertook every public opportunity imaginable to explain, educate, and manipulate the American people toward a new way of thinking about energy. However, no amount of urging, cajoling, or berating from the president altered public opinion. As the polls continually demonstrated, Americans did not want to own smaller cars, conserve energy, or otherwise change their consumptive lifestyle. Paradoxically, public opinion polls revealed support for President Carter's efforts and his ideals, in particular regarding our dependency on foreign oil. Polls even indicated that Americans approved of Carter's handling of the oil crisis. The Carter White House understood the public's attitudes on energy. The Carter White House tracked the public's attitudes on energy, but it could not alter the public's attitudes on energy, according to the polls.

President Carter was certainly out front on the issue of energy. In the 1980s, many of his ideas and proposals were adopted. Despite myriad rhetorical efforts during Carter's tenure, the public refused to follow. Oddly enough, the public's resistance to Carter's efforts reveals how the use of the polling apparatus can generate both responsiveness as well as the mere appearance of responsiveness. At no juncture did President Carter use the poll apparatus to adopt the public's attitudes on energy. He did not abandon his "Moral Equivalent of War" approach. The attention only provided the impetus for adjusting rhetoric, not policy, in order to potentially improve opportunities. However, the White House was attentive to the public's attitudes vis-à-vis the polls. The poll data ultimately provided the evidence for halting the public relations efforts. The poll apparatus clearly demonstrated the futility of continued crafted efforts. On energy, the Carter White House remained committed to leading despite the quantitative evidence of resistance. President Carter remained committed to the difficult path, but the presence of unchangeable poll numbers forced attention to those numbers. With energy, the Carter White House faced a difficult issue complicated by a muddled policy environment. The extensive energy polling information the Carter White House obtained did not provide a sufficient guide to move or manipulate the public toward the president's policies.

Reagan and Economic Recovery

Unlike President Carter, Ronald Reagan's White House targeted its legislative efforts at campaign promises: budget reductions, increased military spending, and a three-year tax cut. Reagan entered office after trouncing sitting President Jimmy Carter in what looked like a landslide. Although Reagan and his staff "treated the outcome as a mandate for his specific policy proposals . . . the 1980 outcome was more a reject of Carter than a demonstration of popular enthusiasm for Reagan or his policies."[26] However, Reagan entered office sure of what he wanted to do, albeit without the path to get there. Reagan's conservative goals did not come with clear policy prescriptions.

Initially, the Reagan White House recorded significant economic legislative victories, despite the presence of a Democratic Congress. Samuel Kernell argues that Reagan achieved his early legislative success via public appeals, occasionally accompanied by "minor, face-saving concessions or side payments to fence-sitters."[27] As with the Carter White House, the Reagan team employed the polling apparatus to design these effective public relations efforts. Also similar to the Carter White House, the design of the Reagan economic program included little public input, despite extensive polling.

During the transition and the first 100 days, the Reagan White House was a flurry of activity designing the president's economic program. Office of Management and Budget (OMB) Director David Stockman created the details of the economic plan along with his budget working group, which contained the narrowly defined, relevant Cabinet members and staff.[28] In addition, the Reagan strategy eliminated other priorities from the president's agenda. As a result, after the benchmark 100-day period, Ronald Reagan and his policies "were riding high in the polls."[29] Reagan personally averaged in the 70-percent approval rating range across several polling organizations.[30] More significantly, Reagan also received approval for his economic program. Spending cuts and tax cuts were favored and the plan was thought to be "fair and equitable." By April 28, 1981, "people said the Reagan economic program would help the economy."[31]

The administration initially limited the public's involvement to Kernell's "going public" role—pressuring Congress. According to a memo to David Gergen, Reagan's communications guru, the administration wanted to "continue to put pressure on the targeted Members of Congress by raising the public's awareness with respect to the emotional side of the Economic Program—themes such as giving the President his entire program, and trying something new for a change."[32] The problem with this strategy stemmed from the poll results themselves. Although Reagan was personally more popular than Jimmy Carter, Reagan's economic proposals were received quite similarly to Carter's energy proposals in the polls. Between February and July 1981, the more Americans learned about specifics of the Reagan economic program, the less supportive they were. The "helping or hurting the economy" responses modestly declined from a high of 78 percent to a low of 68 percent responding that it would help the economy; the number reporting that it would hurt the economy rose significantly.[33] The numbers arguing that "cutting taxes without hurting anyone was not possible" continued to climb, rising to 64 percent by July.[34] The numbers supporting "reducing both the federal budget and tax rates" as a way to "reduce inflation and increase productivity" also climbed by July.[35]

As the president's approval rating fluctuated, the administration began inviting public responses into their decision making. By June, the president's popularity dropped significantly as the public negatively responded to potential social security cuts. Edwin Meese's staff group argued that the precipitous popularity drop stemmed from a lack of public understanding of the package.[36] The White House practiced clarity through rhetoric by investigating what the public believed "should be done to avoid the crisis in the social security system." The top three responses (totaling 69 percent) were "change eligibility requirements," "increase administrative efficiency," and "no opinion."[37]

Ultimately, Reagan achieved the massive tax cut and the reduction in domestic expenditures by August 1981. Although it's not clear how much that victory could be traced to true public support, the specific pressure was effectively communicated to Congress for these two policies. Kernell argues that much of Reagan's honeymoon approval and support for his program actually waned prior to the March assassination attempt.[38] Reagan clearly benefited from the natural rally effect spurred by the incident. Richard Wirthlin, Reagan's pollster, found less resistance to the program after March. Despite the importance of the public to Reagan's strategy (and to Kernell's argument regarding going public), the battle for economic recovery, tax cuts, and spending occurred between Congress and the president during the summer months of 1981.

The remainder of the Reagan economic efforts, between fall 1981 and December 1982, employed a great deal more of the polling apparatus, evidenced by the increase in memoranda cited in Chapter 5. As the resistance among Democrats in Congress increased, the use of the public increased, as did the connections to Reagan's electoral constituency.

Connecting the president's pitch, policies, and reelection began in earnest in October 1981, as Reagan's political and policy troika, Edwin Meese, Michael Deaver, and James Baker, targeted the 1982 State of the Union Address. "Strategic Planning Memorandum #3" pressed for an electorally based campaign-like strategy. The memo credits the electoral coalitions with the president's victory, and argues, "The speech must be carefully tailored to appeal to the various individuals and groups in these coalitions."[39] The memo disaggregates the policy options and the speech's targeted goal by region, age, and other socioeconomic factors. Despite the targeted approach to the speech, the public response to the economic program remained mixed; Americans supported the economic program, but did not believe it would help them.[40]

By March 1982, "Strategic Evaluation Memorandum #13" portrayed a gloomier picture for the Reagan economic program. As Beal noted, "The economic recovery program was advanced in the face of only moderate resistance, and required only slight, short-term course adjustments."[41] The dearth of resistance allowed the Reagan White House to consider and handle the economic recovery program as a single issue. Increased resistance forced the White House to change that approach. As with energy, the polling apparatus revealed to the White House that the public supported the general efforts of the Reagan plan, but withdrew support on the specifics. Interestingly, "Strategic Evaluation Memorandum #13" noted that the president polled better on a state-by-state basis, as opposed to nationally. Overall in March 1982, the prospects were of concern to the White House: "Support for cutting domestic spending is off 10% to 16% and support for increasing defense spending is off from 23% to 31%. . . . The rapid changes . . . indicate that the public is clearly rethinking its commitment to parts of the economic recovery program."[42] Ultimately, "Strategic Evaluation Memorandum #13" recommends that the **President should contemplate some bold and sustained action to redirect the current line of thinking.**"[43] Despite the negative numbers and the deep concern for the program in Congress, the memo urges continued education and explanation of his position. The concern in the White House for the public's lack of support for the president's policies, despite his personal popularity, directly contrasts with Kernell's interpretation of Reagan's public relations strategy. Internally, the White House fretted over the vanishing supporters, at the same time publicly exhorting the public to "make your voice heard." As a result, the president "exerted far less influence over the budget in 1982—both its substance and politics—than over the one in the proceeding year."[44]

The Environmental President

"During the 1988 campaign, Bush promised an extensive domestic agenda, including initiatives and programs for education, the environment, crime control, and banking reform . . . [however,] nothing dominated the political agenda during the Bush years since the President sought only incremental changes to policies that had already been changed during the Reagan years."[45] In an incremental environment, the pervasiveness of the permanent campaign remains, but narrows to small, inconsequential issues.

Environmental leadership was a core component of the Bush presidential campaign. As the campaign heated up between Massachusetts Governor Michael Dukakis, and the vice president, the environment became part of the effective Bush media strategy. Along with the Willie Horton and revolving-door ads, and the picture of Dukakis in an army tank, George Bush's speech from a boat in Boston Harbor was a compelling component of a sophisticated campaign strategy. The Dukakis campaign ignored the stinging attacks regarding the "filthy, sewage-filled basin," and ultimately ceded the environment issue to the vice president among moderate voters.[46] After declaring himself an environmentalist during the campaign, the newly elected president sent strong signals that he was serious about environmental issues. Although his State of the Union Address ignored environmental policy specifics in favor of a "kinder and gentler nation," "three weeks later, he told Congress in his first formal message, 'I will send to you shortly legislation for a new, more effective Clean Air Act.'"[47] To substantiate the campaign focus, the Clean Air Act became a Bush priority, although it took the better part of six months to produce specific proposals and legislation.[48]

As part of its larger environmental efforts, the Bush White House created the national tree-planting program, a component of the America the Beautiful initiative. As Bush wrote to the heads of various agencies and departments, the tree-planting program "calls for public/private partnerships involving communities and volunteers throughout the Nation. Our goal is to plant and maintain in our cities and countryside an additional one billion trees per year through the year 2000. This is an ambitious goal that will significantly enhance the environment and boost economic activity."[49] The tree-planting program, and the America the

Beautiful initiative itself, were efforts to carry out the "massively mixed signals" of the Bush campaign agenda. "He would be an environmentalist . . . but he would also resist the means to pay [for new environmental programs] . . . by opposing new taxes."[50]

In his four-year tenure, President Bush made twenty-three appearances and speeches concerning tree planting across the United States. The president and his staff used these photo opportunities to stress Bush's position as the "environmental president" by showcasing his environmental efforts, such as planting trees. President Bush's rhetorical efforts regarding his tree-planting program began soon after he took office. Between April 24, 1989 and April 18, 1990, President Bush gave thirteen speeches and planted many trees in ceremonies around the country.[51] Despite being a smaller component of the president's environmental agenda, these White House rhetorical efforts reveal the effort involved in carrying the presidential electoral coalition and their goals forward.

During Bush's first year in office, there were no discussions of public opinion and tree planting, despite the various public appearances. During his second year, however, eleven separate polling discussions (via memoranda dated between May 29, 1990, and September 10, 1991) and seven more rhetorical efforts occurred regarding tree planting. In May 1990, Edward Goldstein, James Pinkerton, and Emily Mead, policy analysts in the Office of Policy Development (OPD), requested public opinion information on tree planting from Bush's pollster. Specifically, these three staffers sent Robert Teeter's polling firm, Market Opinion Research (MOR), questions that they wanted to ask the public. These questions ranged from the obvious ("Are you aware that President Bush has made tree planting by Americans an important priority of his presidency?") to the odd ("Would you care for a tree if planted in your neighborhood?").[52] From this first request for information, the Bush White House tried to identify public attitudes and the effect of Bush's rhetorical efforts. As with the Carter effort, the Bush polling apparatus factored strongly into attempts to assess the success of educationally directed rhetorical efforts.

In August 1990, the OPD staff began assessing the public's opinion about tree planting received from MOR. Ed Goldstein summarized the data for his fellow staff members and the director of OPD, Roger Porter. "The Market Opinion Research late July public opinion survey of American voters has found that public awareness of and support for the

President's tree planting initiative is significant. 48 percent of respondents said they were aware of the Presidents' support for tree planting. This contrasts with the 58 percent of the public who said they didn't know enough to comment on the Clean Air Bill in the May [1990] MOR survey."[53] White House staffers believed the president's rhetorical efforts successfully moved public opinion toward the president's preferred position. Post-tree-planting polling results revealed a dramatic swing from those reporting no knowledge to those reporting not only knowledge, but also favorable knowledge.

In addition to evaluating the success in directing public opinion, Goldstein sent a followup memo responding to a request for the detailed demographic breakdown of tree-planting poll respondents. Staffers wanted to know who specifically responded to Bush's message. Whose opinion did Bush change? "Women are more likely to be aware of and supportive of the initiative than men. Republicans/Conservatives are more supportive that Democrats/Liberals. And the initiative finds stronger backing among high income and well educated voters."[54] In addition to the demographic breakdowns of support, Goldstein highlighted aspects of the effective public relations strategy. "Awareness of and support for the tree planting initiative is significantly greater in the north central states comprised of Iowa, Kansas, Minnesota, Montana, Nebraska and North Dakota. The President planted a tree in Bismarck, North Dakota last summer."[55] The president also planted trees in Sioux Falls, South Dakota, and Helena, Montana, during the summer of 1989. Using the polling data, the Bush White House believed it could draw a clear connection between an increase of positive tree-planting feelings and presidential efforts to highlight the benefits of tree planting in 1989 and 1990. Directing opinion via rhetorical efforts worked—according to the poll results.

The positive connection between positive polling results and rhetorical efforts encouraged the OPD staff enough to distribute the information outside their own environs. The influence of presidential tree planting on public opinion was distributed to David Demarest, director of the Office of Communications, Deborah Amend, also of the Office of Communications, and David Carney, director of the Office of Political Affairs.[56] The positive tree-planting poll news continued up the White House hierarchy to the Chief of Staff's Office.

By October 1990, the White House's production of favorable public opinion moved beyond simple rhetorical efforts and into the complexities of the budget process on Capitol Hill. In a memo to Jim Cicconi, deputy chief of staff, Emily Mead of OPD drew a clear line between trees, the legislative process, and public opinion. In the memo, she cited current legislative outcomes (authorizations of $180 million to the tree-planting initiative and $25 million to the National Tree Trust) and the pending Department of the Interior appropriations bill, which fell short of White House goals. After presenting the legislation, Mead turned to public opinion. She asserted, "Polls indicate that 85% of Americans agree that the President's request for Americans to plant trees is a good idea to help the environment. 53% view his initiative to encourage voluntary tree planting an important part of his environmental program and not the political gimmick that 38% view the program." Mead concludes, "While watching the budget process unfold, please note that tree planting time has returned to our area."[57] The positive information continued up the ladder, as the president received the positive tree-planting results from Roger Porter on October 29, 1990.[58] Bush responds, scrawling "GOOD!" on the memo, and placing a check mark next to, among other points, Porter's reference to Caecilius Statius (220–169 B.C.) in De Senectute, "He plants trees to benefit another generation."[59]

By 1991, however, the political context of a declining economy limited the president's ability to direct public opinion on the environment. Emily Mead informed Roger Porter that "environmental issues are important to the American public but they do not rank among the **most important** national problems."[60] Ranking lower on the list of national agenda items does not necessarily diminish the president's ability to direct opinion, but it suggests that it might not be worth the time or presidential capital. From the public opinion surveys, the OPD staffers discovered that "the importance of the environment as a national problem is clearly driven more by events than by leadership. Environmental disasters and high profile events like Earth Day capture the public's attention. Presidential statements and actions do not seem to have the same effect."[61] Thus, the polls revealed that the White House no longer retained the ability to direct public opinion on the environment by 1991. Oddly enough, the poll data suggested that President Bush's rhetorical efforts influenced attitudes on presidential leadership rather than the issue at hand. "In

March 1991, more than half of those asked in a Gallup survey credited Bush with 'making progress' on improving the environment. On no other domestic issue, including education, was the President thought to have made as much progress as on the environment—even though two thirds of respondents thought the environment was becoming worse."[62] The public honored the president's efforts. After early successes, the president's environmental outreach efforts no longer moved public attitudes, as other attitude positions on issues such as the economy trumped public strategies on the environment.

Similar to its usage with Carter's energy initiative, or Reagan's Economic Recovery Program, the poll apparatus did not delineate the leadership strategy chosen to handle the environment. Although tree planting was a much smaller program than energy or the national budget, polls were used similarly; to vet strategies and approaches to move opinion toward the president's preferred policy position. The Bush White House was attentive to effective public relations that could be identified with the poll data. More significantly, the Bush White House demonstrated a responsiveness once the strategy was under way, similar to that of the Carter and Reagan administrations. Public opinion moderated directed public relations efforts. The polls provided evidence for halting the directed styles. On both a major and minor component of the White House agenda, the White House was mindful of the public via the poll apparatus on these significant legislative efforts.

The Ultimate Campaign

Are these efforts examples of the permanent campaign? Campaign leadership uses the public as the barometer of presidential effectiveness. The barometer is no longer mass mobilization during political campaigns. In *Politics by Other Means,* Ginsberg and Shefter assert that the president and Congress reject mobilizing the electorate as the preferred means of institutional combat in favor of media revelations, congressional investigations, and judicial proceedings.[63] However, without resorting to Ginsberg and Shefter's form of institutional combat, or requiring Kernell's level of public activity, the permanent campaign model attempts to measure mobilization without requiring any expense of citizen effort. Campaigning to govern simply asks the public to signal its support for the president, for policies, and ultimately for reelection in the polls. The poll numbers—not approval ratings, but support for policies and reelection—are the ultimate measure of success. In these four cases, the polls certainly represented the public without requiring actual mobilization, although the Reagan case, through its public relations pressuring strategy, appeared to ask for a bit more from the public.

The battle between the Clinton White House and the congressional Republicans, led by Speaker of the House Newt Gingrich, to balance the budget culminated in 1995 with a government shutdown, and encapsulates the campaign approach to presidential leadership. Balancing the budget was not a Democratic ideal. The Clinton White House began with an artificial linkage between issues and constituencies determined by the polls, added a hostile Republican party, and campaigned for victory.

Campaign-style leadership began with Dick Morris. Dick Morris used the balanced-budget issue as a mechanism to produce a presidency-centered coalition as a stepping stone to the 1996 election, to the dismay of the rest of the White House.[64] The core of the Clinton White House, especially the staffers who were a part of the Clinton campaign, were ideologically opposed to balancing the budget. Since FDR and the creation of social government spending, national budgets, for the most part, have not balanced, regardless of which party controlled the government. The idea of balancing the budget as well as a balanced-budget amendment, gathered steam during the conservatism of the Reagan administration. Ironically, the national debt tripled during the Reagan and Bush eras, through the combination of supply-side economics and increased military spending.

Morris argued that triangulation was the key to a Clinton victory in the 1996 election, and a balanced budget was a crucial component to that strategy. The budget was critical to defeating the Republicans, according to Morris, because the ideas behind their balanced budget fervor betrayed the public. "The president suspected, and I agreed, that the Republicans were not cutting Medicare, Medicaid, education, and environmental protection—areas the president cared about—in order to balance the budget. They wanted to balance the budget *in order* to cut Medicare, Medicaid, education, and environmental protection. . . . On the other hand, the Democrats were protecting these programs as an excuse *not* to balance the budget."[65] Thus, the budget was a way to beat everyone politically and at the polls—triangulation at its best.

At its heart, triangulation lacks any ideology or goal beyond victory. For Morris and Clinton, the balanced budget would be the key to Clinton's victory in 1996 because it created a link between constituencies, issues, and Clinton personally. Morris defended his approach to others inside and outside the administration: "My role in this process was to see where the budget numbers were leading him and, through polling, vet it politically. . . . I also found that voters didn't really care whether the budget was balanced in seven, eight, nine or even ten years. It didn't matter to them as long as we moved in the right direction."[66] Clinton wanted to balance the budget because the public wanted it. Moreover, how the budget would be balanced was determined with reelection in mind. The Clinton White House went to the polls early in the balanced-budget legislative battle with the primary goal of beating the Republicans.

The Clinton team used polls to design speeches, and public opinion even influenced the critical decision to shut down the government via presidential vetoes. In May 1995, Dick Morris pressed for a speech on the budget because "the key to getting that ten percent—the swing vote, the Perot vote—is to give a prime-time speech. It has to be next week, or we lose them forever."[67] "And they gave the speech on balancing the budget the following Tuesday which 'triangulated with a vengeance.'"[68] After the president's speeches on the balanced budget, the rest of the fight was played out behind the scenes—the president and Senate Majority Leader Trent Lott wanted a deal. However, the 1994 freshman Republicans in the House of Representatives did not.[69]

During the November 14–19, 1995, government shutdown, the White House polling operation went into overdrive. In *Behind the Oval Office,* Morris writes that he polled every night during the crisis. Dick Morris, George Stephanopolous, and President Clinton all started their day with "the latest polling information."[70] The polling numbers reached record approval ratings for the Clinton administration. More importantly, the public did not approve of the Republican tactics, although Morris notes that he urged a deal after the numbers began to show "impatience with the continued stalemate."[71]

President Clinton's balanced-budget program was steeped in poll data and campaign-style leadership. The bulk of the White House staff opposed balancing the budget, in accord with traditional Democratic principles. Armed with poll data supporting balancing the budget, Morris pushed for the program. President Clinton clearly had to balance not only the budget but also the competing advice he was receiving from his trusted sources. Interestingly, the balanced-budget effort was both a "repudiation and a vindication" of triangulation, as the poll numbers rewarded the line-in-the-sand approach (for example, the vetoes that shut down the government) and penalized accommodation (for example, the handshake deal with Newt Gingrich in New Hampshire).[72] Thus, the effort was classic permanent campaign strategy.

Campaigning or Crafting

As Hugh Heclo effectively articulates, there are some important differences between campaigning and governing. First and foremost, there is a clearly defined goal at the end of a campaign: victory at the polls. Moreover, to achieve victory at the polls, the audience—potential voters—must be satisfied. In business parlance, the customer is always right. Candidates who do not modify their behavior and their agenda in the face of opposition do not win. It is a rare candidate who does not have to modify his pitch to produce a winning coalition. In contrast, compromise with the opposition crystallizes the governing process. Persuasion, selling one's position, personality, and policies remain the common threads between campaigning and governing.

Of the four legislative fights, only Clinton's balanced-budget encounter with Gingrich's Republicans incorporates all aspects of a campaign. The 1995 battle over the budget epitomizes the interaction between constituency efforts, victory identification and definition, and persuasion. Clinton and Morris cast the balanced-budget policy in terms of reelection coalitions and goals, and hallmark a true permanent-campaign leadership approach. The remaining cases appeared campaign-like, but lacked a campaign approach to the legislative goal. Presidents Carter, Reagan, and Bush refused to moderate their goals in response to audience disapproval. All of them defined victory in terms of passage of their legislative agenda, and refused to compromise with the public in the face of waning coalition support simply to produce victory. Perhaps the Carter, Reagan, and Bush cases were simply ineffective campaigns. The heart of the permanent campaign theory is, not the presence of the polling tool, but that the tool guides strategy. The Carter, Reagan, and Bush cases were not campaigns, as they used the campaign polling tool to evaluate leadership strategies defined outside the polling apparatus.

Moreover, Heclo and Ornstein and Mann note that the basis of the permanent campaign stems not from simply the presence of occasional campaign behavior, but from the pervasive, nonstop application of the campaign to every decision in the White House. If campaigning to govern pervaded and penetrated the White House, then even unimportant issues or smaller agenda items would connect the president's electoral concerns to public relations campaigns. On both the big issues (Carter's energy plan and Reagan's Economic Recovery Program) and the small ones (George H. Bush's proposal for tree planting), the White House used campaign tools but not a campaign approach.

A better explanation for the behavior of presidents and the use of public opinion polls might be Jacobs and Shapiros crafted talk approach. Here, the White House employs the public after problem definition and identification, and only in persuasive efforts. The polls offer merely the means to tinker with the public strategy. The crafted talk approach seeks the same endgame—legislation—but provides a different role for the public. Jacobs and Shapiro argue that the electoral connection (the need to attract and win a majority of voters) does not trump the desire to enact preferred, but not popular, policy goals. In their conception, politicians use the public (via the polls) to create the appearance of responsiveness as cover for pursuit of their own goals.[73] To moderate the costs of ignoring the median voter, politicians design "crafted talk." Crafted talk is the art of employing public opinion polls and focus groups to choose words and phrases that resonate with the public, even when the policy does not. In contrast to the permanent campaign, a crafted talk approach asserts attentiveness to the public only during campaigns. Between campaigns, the electoral coalition and the rest of the public are managed and manipulated via poll-produced language and presentations.

The cases of energy, economic recovery, and tree planting support the concept of using the polls to manipulate public relations and language in a legislative battle. However, these cases, as well as examples presented in the previous chapters, suggest that an electoral imperative is at work between election cycles. As an approach to governing, the permanent campaign cannot explain the motivation of the White House to ignore the public and refuse to compromise. In contrast, crafted talk seemingly allows a president to have his proverbial cake and eat it too. Presidents do not have to give up their own goals, choosing manipulation over compromise and accommodation with the public. However, Jacobs and Shapiro predicate their theory on the lack of electoral attentiveness. Presidents are not abandoning their electoral connection, even as they refuse to compromise or follow opinion.

Conclusions

This chapter explored four significant legislative efforts by four different presidents in order to ascertain what it means to win the permanent campaign. Arguing that the presence of polling in the White House alters presidential behavior assumes that the findings from polls influence the White House. Chapters 2 through 4 demonstrated how and where the White House employed public opinion. This chapter, along with Chapter 5, places polling in the context of presidential leadership and policymaking.

Campaign tools are present in White House legislative efforts and they do influence those efforts. However, presidents are not abandoning traditional governing behavior in legislative battles in favor of a campaign approach. Elites are choosing to craft talk in order to deal with each other rather than a mobilized public, but not in the absence of electoral coalition and constituency management and attention. The next chapter continues this discussion, but explores crisis response rather than the president's agenda. Perhaps the permanent campaign exists only in the flight-or-fight response of a political crisis.

In media, political, and academic circles, the notion of permanent-campaign leadership thrives. Appearances suggest that presidents employ the tools and leadership styles of a campaign. However, having explored four significant presidential agenda items in the last chapter, we saw true campaign leadership existing in only one case. Presidents Carter, Reagan, and Bush entered office planning to advance the legislative efforts discussed in the previous chapter. Energy, economic recovery, and the environment were presidential campaign pledges. President Clinton's desire to balance the budget arose out of the presidential role in the budget-making process. The four cases explored in Chapter 6 are typical of the focus of a first-term president. Patterson finds that, contrary to reporters' claims, presidents typically exert considerable effort to achieve passage of their campaign promises.[1] Moreover, the annual budget battle offers significant opportunity for a president to influence national policy. In all four cases, the president was cognizant of the legislative environment; no matter how the president arrived there, the goal remained the same. The president needed a majority of the members of Congress to pass his proposal. To influence Congress, the White House used the polling apparatus, but exhibited crafted talk leadership rather than campaign approaches in three of the four agenda cases. Thus, on major campaign promises, Presidents Carter, Reagan, and Bush chose to try to influence

Congress via public appeals but did not abandon a more traditional bargaining style.

Legislative efforts are often framed as campaigns, but the constitutional necessity of political compromise rarely allows Congress and the president to engage in true campaign wars, à la the battle between Clinton and Gingrich. However, in addition to the script of a president's first term (following through on campaign promises), presidents must also respond to the unplanned and unwanted. Perhaps campaigning is not a governing tool but a form of crisis response. Ginsberg and Shefter argue that legislative efforts requiring the mobilization of the masses (Kernell's model) no longer exist.[2] Instead, first congressional Democrats and then Republicans chose institutional conflict categorized by investigation.[3] In institutional conflict, such as impeachment, there exists a clearly defined presidential goal (surviving), an endpoint (the impeachment vote), and an adversary (the opposing party). Two crises—the scandals of Watergate and Monica-gate—suggest that the permanent campaign might be more effective and more prevalent in this type of institutional battle than in a typical legislative effort.

The Nixon Crisis and Presidential Polling

Watergate began as a bungled burglary and culminated in the resignation of a president. On June 17, 1972, five men were caught breaking into the Democratic National Committee headquarters at the Watergate office building. The attempted crime was the tip of the iceberg of a president's abuse of power and obstruction of justice.

Although Watergate focused on serious legal questions, it was also a political entity in which public opinion was a key component. Richard Nixon claimed his fight against impeachment was "a race for public support" and his "last campaign . . . not for political office but for . . . political life."[4] Lang and Lang argue that there were three classifications of the role of public opinion during Watergate.[5] The first group of analysts argue that Nixon's loss of the battle for public opinion forced him to change strategies and even retreat at crucial instances. Another perspective suggests that public opinion did not hasten the end, but in fact prolonged the crisis. The third group considers public opinion irrelevant, as impeachment was a legal consideration.

During his tenure as chief of staff, until his resignation on April 30, 1973, H. R. Haldeman kept the best record of the Nixon administration via a diary. The publication of this diary offers a wonderful opportunity to see events unfold and to see how the administration handled those events. Watergate began, in Haldeman's diary, immediately following the weekend break-in at the DNC headquarters. As early as June 18, 1972, five months before Nixon's reelection, Haldeman was worried about the connection between the burglars and the Committee to Re-Elect the President. Haldeman, rather unequivocally, states that "so far the P [President Nixon] is not aware of all this, unless he read something in the paper, but he didn't mention it to me."[6] Over the life of the scandal, President Nixon and his staff interest and attentiveness to public opinion dramatically increased.

The first mention of public opinion and Watergate in Haldeman's diary arrives two months after the break-in. On Tuesday, August 29, 1972, Nixon, Haldeman, and John Ehrlichman, assistant to the president for domestic affairs, met to design a "basic strategy . . . on the release of the investigation internally of the Watergate caper."[7] Coincidentally, Haldeman notes that the Gallup organization released poll data with Nixon receiving the highest presidential approval rating they had seen (64 percent approval, 30 percent disapproval). Although public management of the scandal had begun at this point, meaningful and thus useful levels of public opinion were not in evidence. Early in the scandal, the public knew little about the Watergate incident.[8] Thus, without a significant public response, the White House embarked on scandal management, anticipating a public response.

President Nixon continued to employ his poll apparatus while Watergate swirled around him. During a Cabinet leadership breakfast meeting, Ehrlichman and Clark MacGregor, congressional liaison, discussed the polls and myriad political issues, including Watergate. The president was quite attentive to the public relations strategies and the linkage to public opinion. Nixon wanted to escalate the rhetoric and "hit hard on the issues." In response to the Watergate polls, Nixon asserted, "Not one instance in four years has there been any personal corruption of the Cabinet appointees or the White House. . . . This is an honest Administration. We will not go down on the charge of corruption."[9] For a time, the polling apparatus remained focused on the issues, existing almost in suspended animation from the crisis.

Serious concern about the polling numbers, and use of that information, did not occur until after the inauguration of Nixon's second term. According to Haldeman, in March 1973, Nixon "went into the Watergate question . . . [and] wanted to know if we had any polls on apparent reaction to whom it affects, analyzed by voter breakdowns and all."[10] The infamous Oval Office tapes show that it was Haldeman who brought to Nixon's attention the public's inattention to Watergate.[11] Haldeman notes, "[Pollster] Oliver Quayle says nobody gives a damn about the Watergate. Sindlinger [another pollster] says where it used to be during the election only about ten percent was the highest it ever got that said Watergate was a big issue, now it's two or three percent. He said we just can't find anybody who is interested." The White House continued to monitor the public for signs of concern.

In a campaign, candidates often make strategic decisions steeped in polling data: which states to visit, which issues to emphasize, and even which issues to champion. Chapters 4 and 5 demonstrated that the Nixon White House infrequently used the poll apparatus as a source of issue ideas. Nixon primarily used the polls as an evaluation of job performance. However, as the Watergate scandal grew in significance, public opinion increasingly entered the decision-making process. On April 25, 1973, Haldeman writes, "Because of the weight of public opinion, a voluntary departure is necessary," and so he and John Ehrlichman resigned.[12]

After his trusted advisors' exodus, President Nixon asked General Alexander Haig to assume Haldeman's duties. This request also included attention to public opinion. On May 8, 1973, Nixon instructed Haig to view the polling data. Nixon told Haig, "By a vote of 59 to 31, they thought the President should be given the benefit of the doubt on this matter and should be allowed to finish his term. You know, the next three and a half years. But the other interesting thing is by a vote of 77 to 13 they opposed suggestions that the President resign."[13] Public opinion data became a lifeline and a justification for the president. President Nixon took comfort in the polls and used them to bolster his desire to fight the charges. On May 8, Nixon told the General, "I didn't have to see a Harris poll to realize it, I mean apart from anything else the country doesn't want the Presidency to be destroyed."[14] The next day (May 9), Nixon is so interested in the polling data, he interrupts Press Secretary Ron Ziegler's account of a very tough press briefing:

> President Nixon: Did the Harris poll get any play, the one you mentioned?
> Ziegler: Yes it did. Oh, yes, sir. It got play on TV last night, got good play.
> President Nixon: Of course they had some negative, but did they get across that point that they didn't want the President to resign?
> Ziegler: Yes, sir. Absolutely, yes, sir.
> President Nixon: And that 59 to 31 thought that he ought to continue the work?
> Ziegler: Right.
> President Nixon: Okay.
> Ziegler: We survived, and we're going to continue to.
> President Nixon: Damn right. Okay.[15]

The public remained the final arbiter for Nixon. As long as public opinion continued to support the president, Nixon believed he could withstand the negative press barrage. On May 11, 1973, Nixon informed Secretary of State Henry Kissenger, "Hell, I'll stay here till the last Gallup polls. . . . Goddamn it. We're here to do a job and we're doing the right thing. You know it and I know it."[16] Up until the end of the taping system, June 6, 1973, public support bulwarked the president's "I will stand and fight" mentality.

Between the release of the tapes and the television coverage of the Watergate hearings, management of public opinion became difficult for the White House. Lang and Lang argue that Watergate was a "rare event," one that has the power to cause a public reaction and change opinions.[17] Nixon and the White House polling operation correctly discerned the lack of public interest in the Watergate break-in, even during the televised coverage. Moreover, until the revelation of the taping system, the polls revealed that the public believed Democrats and Republicans were equally guilty of "campaign tricks," but that the Nixon campaign "got caught at it."[18] The Nixon White House translated the cynicism and ambivalence in the polls to political strategy. As long as the polls maintained a reasonable level of public support, Nixon continued to fight hard. Over the course of 1974, Nixon pursued a strategy designed to thwart the special prosecutor and the congressional investigation. Nixon's defenders in Congress "demanded specificity—clearly documented examples of presidential abuse of power and obstruction of justice."[19] On August 5, the bottom fell out of Nixon's strategy. On August 5, 1974, Nixon complied with the Supreme Court's order to release the Oval Office conversations of June 23, 1972. These "smoking gun" tapes demonstrated that Nixon and Haldeman discussed "using the CIA to thwart the FBI investigation of the Watergate break-in."[20] Public approval of the president dropped to 20 percent and Nixon resigned.

The Clinton Crisis and Presidential Polling

Although President Nixon was not formally impeached, comparisons between Watergate and the Clinton crisis were inevitable. Lacking public memory of Andrew Johnson's 1868 impeachment, Watergate served as the backdrop for measuring Clinton's wrongdoing and the handling of the matter by Congress. The scandals were, in fact, quite different. "If Watergate was, as President Ford famously called it, a 'long national nightmare,' the Clinton scandal was more like a drug-induced hallucination."[21] According to Rozell and Wilcox, Watergate afforded the country the opportunity to consider "broad institutional and separation of powers questions."[22] Most Watergate analyses focused on the details of the break-in and cover-up from the perspective of "Nixon's personal culpability and that of his subordinates"; however, "Watergate was a transformative moment for the institution of the presidency, above and beyond its consequences for Richard Nixon."[23]

In contrast, the Clinton scandal contained few in-depth discussions of constitutional power or the power of the presidency. Parallels existed between the two cases—battles over executive privilege, the definition of impeachment, the role of the independent prosecutor, and the role of the courts.[24] Strikingly, the role played by the public for the president, via the polling apparatus, entered the context of Clinton's impeachment. President Clinton vigorously used the polls. In a continuation of the campaign leadership style, which had emerged for the balanced-budget battle, Clinton campaigned to retain his office.

The Lewinsky sex scandal broke as an international news story on January 21, 1998. News organizations reported that President Clinton had engaged in a sexual relationship with a young White House intern. The ensuing media circus covering the story continued through Clinton's testimony in August 1998 before a federal grand jury, which had originally been convened to investigate his and his wife's involvement in Whitewater (the failed Arkansas land deal, while Clinton was governor of Arkansas). The story continued with Clinton's impeachment by the House of Representatives in December 1998, and did not begin to wind down until the Senate acquitted Clinton on all impeachment charges on February 12, 1999. The media coverage of this story was overwhelming and incessant. Larry Sabato's "feeding frenzy" does not even begin to describe the coverage of this scandal.[25] The *New York Times* and the three broadcast television networks (ABC, NBC, and CBS) combined to provide over 1,300 stories. Moreover, the public was attentive to the coverage. President Clinton's admission of an inappropriate relationship and his 1998 State of the Union Address were the third- and fourth-highest watched shows of all time, behind the *M*A*S*H* and *Seinfeld* finales. Approximately 60.3 million viewers watched President Clinton's State of the Union speech in January 1998 and his mea culpa in August 1998.[26]

Given the extraordinary circumstances surrounding the scandal and the pervasiveness of public opinion in the Clinton White House, it is no surprise that the polling apparatus factored into the White House's handling of the scandal. In *All Too Human,* former Clinton advisor George Stephanopoulos reflects that the president received dichotomous advice, and chose to heed the advice that rested on the polling apparatus.[27] Advisors to the president inside and outside the White House, such as Erskine Bowles (friend and chief of staff) and Leon Panetta (former chief of staff), recommended coming clean with the country in January 1998. "But at his moment of maximum peril, the president chose to follow the pattern of his past. He called Dick Morris. Dick took a poll. The poll said lie."[28]

From the independent counsel's investigation, the world learned exactly what information Dick Morris provided the president. In his grand jury testimony, Morris indicated that his polls distinguished the depth and degree to which the president could be excused by the public.

"After the scandal broke, Morris told the grand jury, he did some polling and learned that the public was most concerned about obstruction of justice and subornation of perjury, and not whether Clinton had simply engaged in a sexual affair outside his marriage."[29] The rebuttal responses to eighty-one questions from the House of Representatives show that Morris warned the president, "The problem is they're willing to forgive you for adultery, but not for perjury or obstruction of justice or the various other things. They're even willing to forgive the conduct. They're not willing to forgive the word. In other words, if in fact you told Monica Lewinsky to lie, they can forgive that, but if you committed subornation of perjury, they won't." The rebuttal answers appear to substantiate using the polls to define a political strategy of lying, as Morris claims to have told the president that "he would lose political support by admitting to obstructing justice and suborning perjury." In true campaign fashion, the president apparently then responded, "We just have to win then."[30]

As Nixon had done, Clinton's and Morris' campaign strategy inserted the public, via the job approval ratings, as its fulcrum. As Figure 7.1 demonstrates, overall, President Clinton maintained and increased his positive approval rating during the course of the scandal, culminating

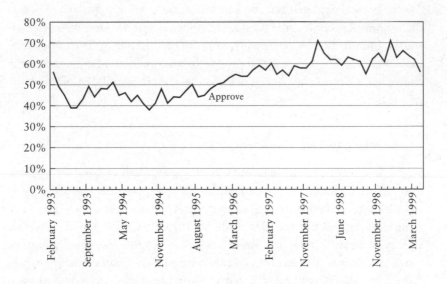

FIGURE **7.1 President Clinton's Popularity**

in the "nay" vote on removal in the Senate. In fact, Clinton's approval rating after January 1998 is higher, by about 10 percentage points, than the first three and half years of his administration. The president's approval rating initially fluctuated. Between January 21, 1998, and January 28, 1998, the first public week of the scandal, Clinton suffered as much as he was going to in the polls. After President Clinton issued his finger-wagging denial and Hilary Clinton appeared on *The Today Show* identifying a "vast right-wing conspiracy," the numbers rebounded. "That same night Clinton did what he does best, he delivered a skillful State of the Union Address to cheering crowds of Democratic supporters in Congress. With 36.5 million houses tuned in to this highly ritualized event, he reminded Americans of their current prosperity, offered them popular programs for the future, and ignored the lingering scandal."[31] Post-speech, Clinton's approval rating never dipped below 60. The stability of his approval numbers and his popularity perplexed Republicans and pundits. "The hasty release of various material—the Starr report and Clinton's videotaped testimony before the grand jury—and the push for live witnesses were all part of an effort to change public opinion, but one of the most remarkable aspects of public sentiment about Clinton, the scandal, and impeachment was its stability."[32]

Typical explanations for Clinton's unwavering popularity include the booming economy, the president's appeal on the issues, his personality, the blunders of his opponents, and the fact that at its heart, the scandal concerned sex. However, another explanation could be the use of the campaign. Clinton and Morris defined their strategy and successfully carried it out.

Polling to Save a Presidency

In contrast to the legislative battles described in Chapter 6, these two efforts contained more campaign-like components. The public was the ultimate audience for the strategy to save the presidency. Both administrations quickly and clearly defined the "enemy." The deadline or goal was survival, pure and simple. Moreover, unlike legislative battles, the polling apparatus was the critical component. Nixon's strategy would have been altered without the polls, but Clinton's strategy would have been impossible without a sophisticated polling operation.

President Nixon found comfort in public opinion. For a year into the Watergate scandal, the public supported and believed their president. As a result, the public opinion polls stiffened his resolve to stand firm. Over time, as more information was released to the public, public opinion shifted away from Nixon. As opinion shifted, Nixon's resolve to stay also shifted. When he bowed to the inevitable, public approval of the president was at an all-time low and support for his resignation was high. President Clinton's survival strategy was even more explicitly tied to public opinion. President Nixon's strategy included releasing and emphasizing favorable poll numbers. In contrast, President Clinton and his advisor Dick Morris designed a specific response strategy tailored to the poll findings. President Clinton tested the phrasing and content of his presentations to the public via public opinion. In addition, Clinton and Morris tested an approach to surviving the scandal, and ultimately impeachment. Morris tested the decision to confess to adultery, however defined, and to remain firm on perjury and obstruction of justice. The public supported those stands, but wavered in support leaning toward resignation when the legal phrases were used. A number of reasons can be identified for Clinton's choice of tactics, including his tortuous insistence he was innocent. It is significant, however, that the polling explicitly supported the conflicted and difficult strategy chosen by Clinton and Morris. Moreover, Clinton never faced a precipitous drop in approval such as that which encouraged Nixon to resign.

Both Nixon and Clinton required the public to bulwark their chosen strategy, but there was something more to Clinton's. The Nixon and Clinton impeachment scandals were qualitatively different, and as scholars have noted, there was more of a legal center to the Nixon scandal. However, both were waging a campaign for public support. Considering the depth and breadth of polling usage in the Clinton administration, it is also equally possible that the differences in scandal polling usage stemmed from the improved polling apparatus to which the Clinton administration had access.

Unlike the Nixon scandal, these exchanges regarding public opinion became significant during the impeachment investigation itself. Of the eighty-one questions submitted by the House to the president, questions 69, 70, and 71 referred to the decision to poll. These three questions asked: Did the president discuss commissioning a poll about the scandal? Did the president learn that the "American people would forgive you for adultery but not for perjury or obstruction of justice" from that poll? and Did the president respond to the poll data "we just have to win then"?[33] President Clinton claimed Morris volunteered to poll, but did not deny learning that the public was concerned with obstruction of justice or subornation of perjury. President Clinton repeated his answer three times in response to the three questions.

The Senate's investigation of and interest in the Morris scandal polling also appeared in questions submitted to the president by that body. The senators sent ten questions to the president. Question 5 concerned the poll apparatus:

> When asked why, four days after you testified under oath in the Jones proceedings, Dick Morris conducted a poll on whether the American people would forgive you for committing the crimes of perjury and obstructing justice, your attorney, Mr. Ruff, answered, 'I don't have a clue.' When asked by the House of Representatives about this poll, you answered that Dick Morris 'volunteered' to conduct this poll. Could you provide additional details as to the context in which Mr. Morris 'volunteered' and the details of any conversation you had with Mr. Morris about conducting such a poll or the results of such a poll?[34]

Of the ten questions asked by the Senate, the question concerning polling was the only "why" question asked. Only on polling did the Senate ask the president about his motivations. Moreover, it was the only question asked regarding efforts to manage the scandal arising from the Jones affidavit and testimony. Other efforts to manage the scandal (for example, telling aides he did not have an affair) were not addressed by the Senate. The remaining nine questions dealt with the veracity of the testified responses, who lied, who violated a gag order, and when the president had knowledge of what.[35]

Despite the ill fit between interest in polling and the rest of the impeachment concerns, the subjects of Morris, polling, and recommendations based on those polls continued. Representative James Rogan (R-CA) used Sydney Blumenthal's June 4 grand jury testimony about Dick Morris's suggestions to the president as evidence Morris needed to be subpoenaed as a witness. "In honing the witness list, the team split on whether to summon Dick Morris, the president's former advisor. House investigators had questioned Morris, but his own sex scandal, and his erratic testimony, gave some managers pause. Morris never made the witness list. Instead, it consisted of Lewinsky, presidential confidant Vernon E. Jordan Jr. and White House aide Sidney Blumenthal, none of whom advanced the prosecution case."[36] Without Morris, the subject of public opinion was dropped, although senators such as Gordon Smith (R-OR) used the reliance on polls as support for their impeachment trial vote:

> I struggled throughout the trial to find a way to acquit the president
> if possible on both or at least one article. But in the end, the facts, the
> stubborn facts, kept getting in my way: The stained blue dress. The
> Dick Morris poll asking whether the president could get away with
> perjur. . . . These facts and so many, many others led me to the logical,
> inescapable conclusion that what began as private indiscretions became
> public felonies.[37]

President Clinton did not poll for a strategy with which to sell a piece of legislation, but a strategy with which to survive questions of law. Is it inappropriate to use the public's attitudes under those circumstances? Part of the problem in assessing the appropriate use of polls here stems from the fissure that split the nation during the entire impeachment process: Is the process a question of law or politics? If the process is simply judicial, then polling the public for a defense is not only unacceptable but also unnecessary. As a political question, what place is there for the public in impeachment (or for that matter in any political issue)? After all, the public has few means with which to influence the process—via the polls and the polling box.[38]

However, as scholars have noted, to the disbelief of the media and the Republican leadership, the public continued to support the president professionally, albeit not personally.[39] In fact, for an entire year, the polls supported Morris' initial findings. If the president acknowledged wrongdoing, adultery but not obstruction and perjury, the public would resist impeachment and even resignation. Although it took considerable verbal gymnastics, Clinton accepted this prescription and campaigned accordingly.

Conclusions

The heart of any campaign is the fight for survival. Legislative battles between the president and Congress, particularly during periods of divided government, often look like campaigns, but actually lack the finality of losing a campaign. It is certain that a badly handled fight with Congress has the potential to influence voters and cost a president his office. However, Carter, Reagan, and Bush failed in aspects of the cases discussed in Chapter 6 and none was immediately sent home. Carter and Bush did lose their reelection bids, but those losses are rarely attributed to a public desire for energy policy or tree planting. In contrast, both Nixon and Clinton faced the possibility of being thrust out of office.

In each chapter of this book, I argue that campaign tools exist in the White House, but that the permanent campaign does not dominate decision making. This chapter and its predecessor illustrate how prevalent polls are, but also how limited in application. Did Clinton survive because of his polling acumen? Possibly. More significantly, the tenacity with which Clinton remained on the path delineated by the polls indicate how infrequently true permanent campaign behavior can occur. Only on the issue of impeachment and in the face of a government shutdown could Clinton sustain the adversarial definitions and the lack of compromise.

8 Conclusions: The Public and a Public Opinion Presidency

This book began with the premise that the presence of campaign tools in the White House naturally produced campaign leadership, and that this development was a detriment to governing. From my investigation, it is clear that campaign tools and staffers from presidential campaigns are in the White House. The administrations of Richard Nixon, Gerald Ford, Jimmy Carter, Ronald Reagan, George H. Bush, and Bill Clinton employed former campaign staff members and utilized their campaign expertise in White House decision making. The top staff and the president were attentive to public opinion, although the Cabinet and other purely policy-driven offices were not involved in the exchange of public opinion data.

Moreover, and perhaps more significantly, the poll apparatus provided the White House with more than mere evaluations of performance; the White House queried the public across agendas and issues, and not only popularity. The poll apparatus influenced message design via phrasing and speeches, and also aided event evaluation. These six White Houses used poll data to shape constituency relations. They used the information to identify, track, and employ the president's electoral coalition. The poll apparatus did not affect program design or implementation, leaving the bureaucratic phases of the policy cycle alone. The polling apparatus was predominantly present with agenda building and mapping through the legislative battles with Congress.

Polling was important and useful to six distinct White Houses. The campaign theory of leadership contends that campaigning dominates other styles of leadership and in turn shapes the governing ability of the president. However, I did not find polling and decisions produced by polling dominating White House decisions. Nor did I find a campaign mindset dominating all other approaches. The permanent campaign theorists are correct in one sense and wrong in another. Campaign tools are increasingly present in the White House and that presence has influenced White House behavior. However, there is no choice to be made between campaigning and governing. In contrast to previous work, this book clearly demonstrates that as an institution, the presidency has included a campaign style in the presidential toolbox of indirect tools. The presence of these tools has not trumped or triumphed over traditional relationships and approaches to governing.

If Not the Permanent Campaign, Then What?

In Chapter 7, I demonstrated that public opinion polls provided the White House the means to remain in office. In fighting Watergate, President Nixon longed for public support, trust, and understanding, and tried to use those attitudes as the rationale for finishing his term. Two decades later, President Clinton also used public attitudes to design a survival strategy, but moved beyond identifying support to rhetorical design. As a result, the Clinton impeachment scandal dramatized the influence of public opinion polls on presidential decisions and leadership.

Using the polls seemingly provides a desired connection between the president and the mass public. "For Bill Clinton, positive poll results are not just tools—they are vindication, ratification, and approval— whereas negative poll results are a learning process in which the pain of the rebuff to his self-image forces deep introspection. Intellectually, polls offer Clinton an insight into how people think. He uses polls to adjust not just his thinking on one issue but his frame of reference so that it is always as close to congruent with that of the country as possible."[1] Morris goes even further, arguing that the polls are a pseudo-conversation between elites and the masses. "I came to love our weekly polls of America. I saw them as a chance to chat with the country. In over a hundred polls, I got to know Americans very well."[2]

Using the poll apparatus in this manner seems like campaign leadership is present in the White House, not just the tools of the campaign. However, it is not truly campaign leadership because the behavior documented here lacks the true structure and foundation of campaign decision making. In Chapter 1, I noted that the permanent campaign contains "the merger of power-as-persuasion inside Washington with power-as-public opinion manipulation outside Washington," according to Hugh Heclo.[3] The resulting merger produces a different form (a seemingly detrimental form) of behavior because campaigning is inherently different than governing. Campaigning depends on persuasive efforts, but also "is geared to one unambiguous decision point in time . . . [and] is necessarily adversarial."[4] Conceivably, then, the more the behavior of a campaign penetrates the process, the more the values of a campaign perspective will overrule governing.[5]

The poll apparatus does encourage adversarial definition and approach. However, candidates do not typically compromise with their opponents in the battle for electoral victory. Outcomes, once in the White House, are not as cleanly defined or achieved. Presidents are rarely able to refuse to compromise and refuse to work with their identified adversaries. Moreover, once in the White House, presidents work for four years without the fixed endpoint of losing and going home. As the framers of the Constitution designed, the four-year time span allows for time to ignore the whims and wishes of public input, even while remaining aware of them via the polling apparatus.

The presence of campaign tools injects the campaign into aspects of the presidential leadership process—but not the entirety of it. Rather than relying on approval ratings as the basis for public relations, the polling apparatus enables a more sophisticated approach to public evaluation. In contrast to the crafted talk theory of leadership, the White House is not ignoring the public between elections—although it clearly is not as attentive as during a run for reelection. The polling apparatus enables the presidency to pursue both an inside and outside strategy, often simultaneously, seemingly limited only by the skill of the White House in concocting such a plan. However, the polls themselves constrain White House activities. During campaigns, and in the White House, polls highlight which issues to stress and not the particular policy stand to adopt.

How did a particular issue achieve a place on a presidential survey? As discussed in Chapters 2 and 4, the presidential pollster designed most of the poll questions. Consequently, the pollster set the policy focus of the survey. All four administrations moderated pollster control by inserting questions into these surveys. The Domestic Policy Staff and the individuals controlling the public opinion apparatus dominated White House additions to surveys. Prior presidential issues or upcoming legislative actions provided the impetus for question insertion from both the White House staff and the pollster. Therefore, relatively few new issues or policy problems appeared on presidential polls. As occurs in campaigns, using polls can cause the president to "miss crucial opportunities to convert voters on wholly new issues."[6]

The presidential polls provide another powerful public constraint on presidential avenues for action, via the "most important problem facing the country today" (MIP) question. Presidents do not often veer from MIP directives. Using MIP and non–open-ended policy poll questions enables the White House to "know exactly what people are thinking in terms of where the President is strongest on each particular issue, where we are weak, and what issues are most important to the people . . . this can be helpful in our selection of themes."[7] As discussed in Chapter 6, the presidential selection of themes, as Dwight Chapin suggests, is the key to the presidential agenda. Not only are themes the agenda item; themes also include the presidential response to the issue. Utilizing MIP questions to determine what the presidential focus should be, and then using policy-based questions to determine support, limits the scope of presidential action. President Nixon claimed the purpose of utilizing polls "will not be to help us work out our policy but let us know what obstacles we confront in attempting to sell a policy."[8]

As Chapter 6 delineates, presidents often do not use polls to select policy options or design programs. After policy decisions are made, however, if poll data reveal limited public support, then presidents have difficult choices to make. Lack of support for a policy suggests three options: de-emphasize the issue; abandon the issue; or undertake an intense public education effort. De-emphasizing and abandoning an issue obviously remove public relations as a potential leadership strategy. An intense public education effort, such as the effort undertaken for energy by President Carter, depletes presidential capital with uncertain outcomes.

Using polls to create a model of presidential constituents and their wants and desires also provides public constraints on the presidential agenda. Polls also reveal who will not approve or support a particular policy. On any given issue, all traditional Democratic or Republican groups might not support the president. By segmenting the population into $25,000–35,000 income earners, religious affiliates, or twenty-five-to thirty-five-year-olds, presidents find a very detailed picture of which supporters they will lose, which they can gain, and which will not care about particular policy options. Thus, polling for policy issues provides a president with a range of acceptable action within which his presidential coalition will continue to offer support and legitimacy for both his presidency and particular issues.

The president's artificially created continuum of support lacks cohesiveness between individuals and creates conflict when a single individual falls into different poll-produced categories. In 1973, Bob Teeter noted that "the economy is the one issue that could smash the New Majority apart. It touches the ethnic, the worker, the laborer, etc. It could drive the various elements of the New Majority back to the Democratic party."[9] Attempting to appeal to such narrow slivers of the American pie and to broad-based groups simultaneously promotes ideological confusion. Table 4.1 revealed how constituent identification factors overlap, not within categories but between them, and thus across individuals. One individual who was between thirty-five and fifty-four years old, a blue-collar worker, a union member, of an ethnic background, and high school educated, crisscrosses all three levels of Reagan support. One individual could simultaneously be strongly supportive, a mixed supporter, or offer low support. Ideological confusion occurs from trying to select the characteristic or personal affiliation that is most important: Which characteristic promotes support of Reagan and his policies? And how do strategists target a single characteristic in one person without alienating other factors? Does the dominant characteristic change as the issue changes, and how is that evident? Socioeconomic status and party philosophy data may appear to widen the presidential leadership net by offering a variety of sectors to target. Narrowcasting issues and narrowing appeals actually limit the capacity for a universal message and eradicate the potential for large-scale change.

The Permanent Campaign After Clinton

In his acceptance speech at the Republican National Convention, George W. Bush passionately distanced himself from Clinton's polling presidency: "I believe great decisions are made with care, made with conviction, not made with polls," said Bush, "I do not need to take your pulse before I know my own mind." Publicly, Bush rejected the permanent campaign stylings of the Clinton era. However, Kathryn Tenpas and Stephen Hess of the Brookings Institution argue that once in office, the forty-third president "out-Clintoned Clinton" by instituting an Office of Strategic Initiatives (OSI). OSI exists to expand Bush's electoral coalition and monitor the Republican base.[10]

As was the case with Gerald Ford, Bush entered office with a problematic electoral coalition. Although the controversy in Florida dramatically marked the 2000 presidential election, the electoral college victory without a popular victory plagued the Bush White House. The 2000 battle between Vice President Al Gore and then-Governor George W. Bush was fascinating to observers for its lack of change in the trial-heat polls. From September 2000 to Election Day 2000, the polls revealed remarkably similar results. Approximately 45 percent of eligible voters were prepared to vote for Bush and approximately 45 percent of eligible voters planned to vote for Gore. The remaining 10 to 15 percent, depending on the poll of the day, were unsure. The split between the candidates reflected the distribution of Republicans, Democrats, and Independents across the country. As Wilson McWilliams argues, "Both parties attempted to reach beyond their traditional bases, and both pretty much failed."[11]

Thus, Bush entered office with an electoral coalition reflecting the complexities of the 2000 campaign. Bush earned office primarily via the votes of white men and married white women. He made some gains with Catholics and Hispanics.[12] "African Americans, Jews, about two-thirds of Hispanics, and a majority of Asians . . . union members and unmarried women" voted for Gore.[13] A geographic split matched the dramatic demographic split. Bush won the South, the Prairie states, and the Mountain

West states, and Gore won the big cites and the coasts. The geographic disparity produced a striking blue-edged and red-middled United States electoral map. Consequently, Bush entered office with a poorly constructed electoral coalition that posed myriad problems for governing.

Lacking a mandate and a large base of support, the Bush White House entered office forced to undertake delicate coalition building while continuing publicly to reject the need to use the polling apparatus to do so. The first nine months of the president's tenure mirrored the divisions established in the campaign. The president's public statements began reflecting the difficulty in leading without a large percentage of committed supporters. On March 20, 2001, Bush claimed, "We set out a set of principles and stand by them. . . . We don't use polls and focus groups to figure out where to head."[14] By the end of April, Bush noted that "you read these polls. They're saying, you know, 'Do you want to take away somebody's Social Security check, or do you want to have tax relief?' But that's not the choice."[15] Bush's early statements and decisive shifts in policy, particularly on the environment and energy, cost him in the polls. The first few months of the Bush presidency were reminiscent of two boxers weaving about the ring, testing each other's stances. The Bush White House initially tossed out positions such as scaling back limitations on arsenic and scrapping a promise to curb carbon dioxide emissions, but quickly reversed them or shifted to appear environmental. The White House proposed, the public reacted, and the administration adjusted. Clearly, the White House was attentive to both supporters and critics.

The Bush team spent much of its first nine months dancing around the efforts to employ public opinion and tried to distance itself from the Clinton poll-driven presidency. Andrew Card, Bush's chief of staff, informed reporters that the Bush White House was not concerned with polls, but rather with *marketing*. Therefore, "if a policy goes amok, it may not be the policy that is at fault, Card suggested, but flawed marketing."[16] Repeatedly, the White House insisted that Bush would not use the polls as Clinton did. "He still won't govern by polls, says White House press secretary Ari Fleischer. He's aware of them, but he doesn't lead by the polls. He leads by what he thinks is right for America."[17] However, Stephen Hess contends that Bush "does seem to be tacking back to where the polls are. . . . It's as if we've watched the first George W. Bush presidency yield to the second."[18]

In his first months in office, Bush "failed to ease the partisan divisions in the country . . . frustrating administration efforts to enlarge his fragile political base and prompting advisers to look for ways to redefine his presidency."[19] To expand the coalition, Bush desperately needed independents. As was Clinton, Bush was sharply polarizing; he was immensely popular with his own party and despised by Democrats. Karl Rove and OSI planned a fall 2001 offensive "aimed at carving out a different kind of orthodoxy for the party."[20] Rove's plans sound very similar to Patrick Caddell's and Dick Morris's efforts to assemble presidency-centered coalitions for Jimmy Carter and Bill Clinton, respectively.[21] If not for the terrorist attacks on September 11, 2001, the Bush White House likely would have undertaken a permanent campaign approach to governing.

In the wake of September 11, working with the public paradoxically eased for the Bush administration. The president now had a war to fight and a nation to calm. After the worst attack on the United States since Pearl Harbor, the public surged behind its president. In classic rally-around-the-flag response, the public offered President Bush stratospheric approval ratings. Terror easily muted much of the debate about the public and its mixed support for the president. By the midterm of his administration, Bush's popularity fell, approximately 20 percentage points to the 70-percent range. In July 2001, Matthew Dowd, the Republican National Committee's director of polling, claimed that a "sharply polarized electorate . . . means that the president will rarely have approval ratings above 60 percent and that about one-third of the country will say they disapprove of how he is doing his job."[22] Thus, terrorism accomplished what the White House marketing team could not: bringing together the country behind the president and his proscribed course of action.

False Responsiveness

So what does this mean for the public? What kind of representation does the public receive from a polling president? To borrow terms, where does a poll-oriented presidency fit into typical trustee-delegate models of representation? "The 'trustee' model advocates low responsiveness and decisive, independent leadership, while the 'delegate' paradigm champions minimal leadership and strong responsiveness."[23]

Arguing that the choice between responsiveness or direction is a false one, Jacobs and Shapiro present a model of responsive leadership.[24] "In contrast to the delegate and trustee models, responsive leadership incorporates popular sovereignty and political leadership that facilitates reasoned public discussion. . . . The case for government responsiveness to informed public opinion rests not only on a normative commitment but also on its practical necessity for inducing the consent and trust of the mass public and maintaining the stable operation of government."[25]

The manner in which presidents are currently incorporating public opinion into presidential decision making does not speak to Jacobs and Shapiro's enlightened theoretical leadership—which they acknowledge. From their empirical findings in the case of health care, Jacobs and Shapiro argue that crafting presentations "corrupts public communications and the public debate by making manipulation and deception the currency of political discourse."[26] Jacobs and Shapiro contend that the very efforts to direct and mold opinion sour not only the public's view of elites but also the process by inviting misdirection and manipulation. My investigation of six administrations suggests a more sanguine view of the use of public opinion by the president.

Jacobs and Shapiro focus on the use of public opinion to design public relations strategies—what they term "crafted talk." However, crafted talk is only part of the presidential polling story, albeit a substantial one. As discussed in Chapters 3 and 4, presidents and their staffs also devote considerable attention to their public from what I deemed a constituency perspective (averaging over 20 percent of the polling apparatus). Here, presidents use the polling apparatus to monitor support—the ebb and flow based on issues and circumstances arising throughout the president's tenure. In addition, albeit to a lesser degree, the White House also connects the public's attitudes to specific policy options and solutions. Manipulation loses saliency as an argument if the polling apparatus is taken as a whole. Instead, presidents appear to be operating under a modified central-mean theorem. Presidents are functioning within boundaries. The poll apparatus quickly and painlessly instructs the White House with regard to the limits the public will move and be moved. Rather than only the manipulation of crafted talk, the entirety of presidential use of the poll apparatus offers some hope of achieving responsiveness. The overriding check on manipulation is the need to achieve a presidency-centered perspective that will survive incumbency and a reelection campaign.

Nevertheless, poll results seemingly reveal a public begging for ideological coherence. From polling, presidential strategists determine that the public seeks unifying leadership with a direction and an inspirational vision to follow. Polls tell strategists that the public wants to know why a president is calling for the programs on his agenda. During the Nixon administration there was constant debate over the need for a thematic umbrella under which all policies could be linked for the public. Initially, the "New Federalism" was the unifying doctrine the administration tried, but it was "poorly understood by the general public."[27] Nixon rejected the idea that this leadership problem stemmed from issues and programs. He firmly believed that the intangibles and personal qualities drove leadership acceptance.[28] The Nixon administration, despite incorporating polls into presidential leadership, was a hybrid, linking old leadership beliefs to new technology. As pollsters and political strategists moved away from popularity and image as the driving force behind public support, they also moved away from leadership based on public prestige. Without the parties and without the trust in government that existed before Vietnam and Watergate, the direction and vision of the presidential agenda are not easily articulated. In 1975, Foster Chanock of the Ford administration discovered a "critical need for a major Presidential statement—of vision and philosophy—which will unify."[29] By December 1976, Patrick Caddell called for newly elected President Carter to create a "fundamentally new ideology." Based on poll data, Caddell argued that voters were less ideological. He wanted to produce "a context that is neither traditionally liberal nor traditionally conservative, one that cuts across traditional ideology."[30] Caddell believed the issues had changed. Polls in the mid-seventies revealed that "quality of life" issues were increasingly important. But using the poll data provided a backward approach to leadership. Finding mixed signals from the public, Caddell wanted Carter to create a mixed ideology that was the ideological equivalent of a Chinese menu: Select one from column A and two from column B. Instead of offering a compelling vision, Caddell recommended creating a tapestry of ideological threads that would appeal to various segments of society. Thus, relying on public opinion polls for anything presidential potentially yields mixed messages.

Regardless of what Dick Morris likes to project, the president and the public are not truly having a conversation via the poll apparatus. No one is satisfied in a conversation in which one side controls the questions and the range of answers available. However, the poll apparatus does provide some semblance of the public's voice for an institution distanced from its audience. The combination of the polling apparatus and election imperatives moderates fears of direction and followership and produces a modicum of responsiveness for the public.

Notes

Preface

1. Bert A. Rockman, *The Leadership Question: The Presidency and the American System* (New York: Praeger, 1984), p. 20.

2. Dom Bonafede, "Carter and the Polls—If You Live By Them, You May Die By Them," *National Journal* 10, no. 33 (August 19, 1978): 1312–15.

3. George Edwards, III, *At the Margins: Presidential Leadership of Congress* (New Haven, CT: Yale University Press, 1989).

4. Bonafede, "Carter and the Polls," p. 1314.

5. Dom Bonafede, "A Pollster to the President, Wirthlin Is Where the Action Is," *National Journal* 13, no. 50 (December 12, 1981): 2184–88.

6. James Barnes, "Clinton's Horse-Race Presidency," *National Journal* 25, no. 22 (May 29, 1993): 1308–12.

7. Ibid.

8. Diane J. Heith, "Presidential Polling and the Potential for Leadership," in *Presidential Power: Forging the Presidency for the 21st Century,* eds. L. Jacobs, M. Kumar, and R. Shapiro (New York: Columbia University Press, 2000), pp. 380–407.

9. These articles appeared in *Public Opinion Quarterly* 62 (Summer 1998): 165–89, and *Presidential Studies Quarterly* 30, no. 4 (December 2000): 783–90 respectively.

Chapter 1

1. Elmer E. Cornwell, Jr., *Presidential Leadership of Public Opinion* (Bloomington, IN: Indiana University Press, 1965), p. 248.

2. Dom Bonafede, "Carter and the Polls—If You Live By Them, You May Die By Them," *National Journal* 10, no. 33 (August 19, 1978): 1312–15.

3. Richard, Morris, *Behind the Oval Office: Getting Reelected Against All Odds* (Los Angeles: Renaissance, 1999), p. 9.

4. Lawrence Jacobs, "The Recoil Effect: Public Opinion and Policymaking in the U.S. and Britain," *Comparative Politics* (January 1992): 199–217.

5. Robert Eisinger, "Gauging Public Opinion in the Hoover White House: Understanding the Roots of Presidential Polling," *Presidential Studies Quarterly* 30, no. 4 (2000): 643–61.

6. Ibid.

7. Jacobs, "Recoil Effect."

8. Robert Eisinger and Jeremy Brown, "Polling as a Means Toward Presidential Autonomy: Emil Hurja, Hadley Cantril and the Roosevelt Administration," *International Journal of Public Opinion Research* 10 (1998): 237–56.

9. Eisinger and Brown, "Polling as a Means Toward Presidential Autonomy," p. 253.

10. Ibid.

11. Benjamin Ginsberg, *The Captive Public: How Mass Opinion Promotes State Power* (New York: Basic Books, 1986), p. 70.

12. Eisinger and Brown, "Polling as a Means Toward Presidential Autonomy."

13. Cornwell, *Presidential Leadership*; Eisinger and Brown, "Polling as a Means Toward Presidential Autonomy"; Ginsburg, *Captive Public*; Jacobs, "Recoil Effect," p. 209.

14. Jacobs, "Recoil Effect."

15. Lawrence Jacobs and Robert Shapiro, "The Rise of Presidential Polling: The Nixon White House in Historical Perspective," *Public Opinion Quarterly* 59 (Summer 1995): 163–95.

16. Lawrence Jacobs and Robert Shapiro, "Public Decisions, Private Polls: John F. Kennedy's Presidency," prepared for the Annual Meeting of the Midwest Political Science Association, April 9–11, Chicago, 1992; Lawrence Jacobs and Robert Shapiro "Issues, Candidate Image and Priming: The Use of Private Polls in Kennedy's 1960 Presidential Campaign," *American Political Science Review* 88 (September 1994); Jacobs and Shapiro, "Rise of Presidential Polling."

17. Jacobs and Shapiro, "Public Decisions, Private Polls"; "Issues, Candidate Image and Priming"; "Rise of Presidential Polling."

18. Richard E. Neustadt, *Presidential Power and the Modern Presidents: The Politics of Leadership from Roosevelt to Reagan,* rev. ed. (New York: Free Press, 1990), p. 73.

19. Approval ratings are simple measures of presidential popularity, produced by asking the question "What do you think of the job the president is doing?"

20. Cornwell, *Presidential Leadership of Public Opinion.*

21. Ibid., p. 303.

22. Neustadt, *Presidential Power;* Cornwell, *Presidential Leadership of Public Opinion.*

23. Cornwell, *Presidential Leadership of Public Opinion,* p. 300.

24. Samuel Kernell, *Going Public: New Strategies of Presidential Leadership,* 3rd ed. (Washington, DC: CQ Press, 1997), p. 6.

25. Jon Bond and Richard Fleisher, *The President in the Legislative Arena* (Chicago: University of Chicago Press, 1990), p. 29.

26. Mark Peterson, *Legislating Together: The White House and Capitol Hill from Eisenhower to Reagan* (Cambridge, MA: Harvard University Press, 1990).

27. George Edwards, III, *At the Margins: Presidential Leadership of Congress* (New Haven, CT: Yale University Press, 1989).

28. Paul Brace and Barbara Hinckley, *Follow the Leader: Opinion Polls and Modern Presidents* (New York: Basic Books, 1992).

29. Brace and Hinckley, *Follow the Leader.*

30. Ibid.

31. Richard Brody, *Assessing the President: The Media, Elite Opinion and Public Support* (Palo Alto, CA: Stanford University Press, 1991), p. 3.

32. Theodore J. Lowi, *The Personal President: Power Invested, Promise Unfulfilled* (Ithaca, NY: Cornell University Press, 1985); Jeffrey Tulis, *The Rhetorical Presidency* (Princeton, NJ: Princeton University Press, 1987).

33. Kernell, *Going Public,* p. 30.

34. Ibid., p. 31.

35. The Center of Responsive Politics, "All Presidential Candidates: Total Raised and Spent," www.opensecrets.org, 2001.

36. Richard Fenno, *Home Style: House Members in Their Districts* (Boston: Little, Brown, 1978); David Mayhew, *Congress: The Electoral Connection* (New Haven, CT: Yale University Press, 1974). There are discussions of the importance of reelection for the first-term president, but few categorize it as an imperative. See Kathryn Dunn Tenpas, *Presidents as Candidates: Inside the White House for the Presidential Campaign* (New York: Garland, 1997).

37. George Edwards, III and Stephen J. Wayne, *Presidential Leadership: Politics and Policy Making*, 5th ed. (New York: St. Martin's Press, 1999).

38. Lester Seligman and Cary Covington, *The Coalitional Presidency* (Chicago: Dorsey Press, 1989).

39. Seligman and Covington, *Coalitional Presidency*.

40. James R. Beniger and Robert Guiffra, Jr., "Public Opinion Polling: Command and Control in Presidential Campaigns," in *Presidential Selection*, eds. Alexander Heard and Michael Nelson (Durham, NC: Duke University Press, 1987).

41. Hugh Heclo, "Campaigning and Governing: A Conspectus," in *The Permanent Campaign and Its Future*, eds. Norman Ornstein and Thomas Mann (Washington, DC: Brookings Institution Press, 2000), p. 26.

42. Heclo, "Campaigning and Governing," p. 29.

43. Ibid., p. 12.

44. Ibid., p. 15.

45. Susan Herbst, *Numbered Voices: How Opinion Polling Has Shaped American Politics* (Chicago: University of Chicago Press, 1995), p. 153.

46. Herbst, *Numbered Voices*, p. 29.

47. Ibid., p. 30.

48. Ibid.

49. Amy Fried, *Muffled Echoes: Oliver North and the Politics of Public Opinion* (New York: Columbia University Press, 1997).

50. Lawrence Jacobs and Robert Shapiro, *Politicians Don't Pander: Political Manipulation and the Loss of Democratic Responsiveness* (Chicago: University of Chicago Press, 2000), p. xvi.

51. Heclo, "Campaigning and Governing," pp. 25–26.

52. Martha Kumar, "Presidential Libraries: Gold Mine, Booby Trap or Both," in *Studying the Presidency*, eds. George Edwards, III and Stephen Wayne (Knoxville, TN: University of Tennessee Press, 1983), p. 206.

53. Kumar, "Presidential Libraries," p. 211.

54. David Horrocks, e-mail to author, November 13, 2000.

55. Ibid.

56. To include only relevant memos, the memos were first screened for germaneness. To be considered a "polling memo," a memorandum had to include a reference to poll data. Poll references came in a variety of forms. For example, poll memos could refer to a public poll, cite recent popularity figures, incorporate poll data into an argument, instruct others to use poll data for policymaking, or discuss creating poll questions. To be considered a "White House memo," the memoranda had to have been sent or received either by a member of the White House staff, the president or vice president, or the pollster. Memoranda between

members of the White House staff, the President or Vice President, the pollster, and staffers of the National Committees were included, but memoranda between only National Committee staffers were excluded (which removed a statistically insignificant portion of the sample).

57. Shoon Kathleen Murray and Peter Howard, "Variation in White House Polling Operations: Carter to Clinton," *Public Opinion Quarterly* 66 (2002): 527–58; Philip Powlick, "Public Opinion in the Foreign Policy Process: An Attitudinal and Institutional Comparison of the Reagan and Clinton Administrations," prepared for the Annual Meeting of the American Political Science Association, Chicago, September 1–4, 1995; Ronald Hinckley, *People, Polls and Policymakers: American Public Opinion and National Security* (New York: Lexington Books, 1992).

58. This project only discusses polling usage in the domestic arena. Ronald Hinckley, in *People, Polls and Policymakers,* notes that there "are fundamental attitudinal factors . . . believed to underlie American opinion about foreign policy matters" (p. 10). There are two cleavage lines (involvement in affairs abroad and isolation from abroad) that produce three orientations (unilateralism, multilateralism, and isolationism). Additionally, on foreign policy issues, the Executive Branch has a monopoly on information and expertise, and uses that monopoly to affect outcomes. Therefore, as long as presidents account for the attitudinal factors of particular constituencies, they have the ability to move public opinion, as they control the information the public uses to apply their attitudinal factors to a particular instance. On domestic issues, the public lacks clear-cut attitudinal factors (although Piazza and Sniderman, and Carmines and Stimson, argue race is such a cleavage), and the White House lacks a monopoly on either expertise or information. Edwards, in *The Public Presidency,* claims that "foreign policy is more distant from the lives of most Americans . . . people tend to defer more to the president on these issues than on domestic issues that they can directly relate to their own experiences" (1983, p. 42). Thus, permanent campaign behavior is much more likely on the domestic front than on the foreign policy side of the arena.

Chapter 2

1. The Center for Responsive Politics, "All Presidential Candidates: Total Raised and Spent," www.opensecrets.org, 2001.

2. Lawrence Jacobs and Robert Shapiro, "The Rise of Presidential Polling: The Nixon White House in Historical Perspective," *Public Opinion Quarterly* 59 (Summer 1995): 163–95.

3. Dom Bonafede, "A Pollster to the President, Wirthlin Is Where the Action Is," *National Journal* 13, no. 50 (December 12, 1981): 2184; Shoon Kath-

leen Murray and Peter Howard, "Variation in White House Polling Operations: Carter to Clinton," *Public Opinion Quarterly* 66 (2002): 527–58.

4. Bonafede, "A Pollster to the President"; Federal Election Commission, Party disclosure documents.

5. Memo to Wray from Matalin, 8/4/89, in PR 13-8, 062870-06609SS, George Bush Library.

6. Murray and Howard, "Variation in White House Polling Operations."

7. Bonafede, "A Pollster to the President," p. 2186 (not adjusted for inflation).

8. Benjamin Ginsberg, *The Captive Public* (New York: Basic Books, 1986).

9. James Morone, *The Democratic Wish: Popular Participation and the Limits of American Government* (New York: Basic Books, 1990), p. 9.

10. Ibid., p. 11.

11. Robert Dahl, "A Democratic Dilemma: System Effectiveness versus Citizen Participation," *Political Science Quarterly* 109, no. 1 (Spring 1994): 23–34.

12. Philip E. Converse, "The Nature of Belief Systems in Mass Publics," in *Ideology and Discontent,* ed. David Apter (New York: Free Press, 1964), pp. 206–61; Christopher Achen, "Social Psychology, Demographic Variables, and Linear Regression: Breaking the Iron Triangle in Voting Research," *Political Behavior* 14 (1992):195–211; Samuel Popkin, *The Reasoning Voter* (Chicago: University of Chicago Press, 1991).

13. Walter Lippmann, *Public Opinion* (New York: Harcourt Brace and Co., 1922).

14. Lawrence Jacobs and Robert Shapiro, *Politicians Don't Pander: Political Manipulation and the Loss of Democratic Responsiveness* (Chicago: University of Chicago Press, 2000), p. 303.

15. Patricia Witherspoon, *Within These Walls: A Study of Communication Between Presidents and Senior Staffs* (New York: Praeger, 1991); John Burke, *The Institutional Presidency* (Baltimore: Johns Hopkins University Press, 1992).

16. Bob Woodward, *The Agenda: Inside the Clinton White House* (New York: Simon and Schuster, 1995), p. 11.

17. Richard Morris, *Behind the Oval Office: Getting Reelected Against All Odds* (Los Angeles: Renaissance, 1999).

18. Ibid., p. 143.

19. Burke, *Institutional Presidency.*

20. Paul Light, *The President's Agenda: Domestic Policy Choice From Kennedy to Reagan* (Baltimore: Johns Hopkins University Press, 1999).

21. Benjamin Ginsberg, Theodore Lowi, and Margaret Weir, *We the People: An Introduction to American Politics,* 2nd ed. (New York: Norton, 1999), p. 510.

22. John Burke, "The Institutionalized Presidency," in *The Presidency and the Political System,* 5th ed., ed. Michael Nelson (Washington, DC: CQ Press, 1999).

23. Richard Tanner Johnson, *Managing the White House: An Intimate Study of the President* (New York: Harper and Row, 1974).

24. Ibid.

25. Jacobs and Shapiro, "Rise of Presidential Polling," p. 181.

26. Ibid.

27. Memo to Ehrlichman from Nixon, 3/10/73, in WHSF Ehrlichman box 18, Nixon Presidential Materials.

28. However, the prevention of fellow Republicans from utilizing the poll data is not surprising considering Nixon's hostility towards some fellow Republicans (see H. R. Haldeman, *The Haldeman Diaries: Inside the Nixon White House* [New York: Berkeley Books, 1995, p. 35] for examples of this antipathy).

29. Memo to Dick Howard from Kathleen Baldson, 5/5/72, WHSF, in Colson box 102, Nixon Presidential Materials.

30. Memo to Baroody from Garrish, 5/29/75, in Baroody box 22 Hartmann, R (2), Gerald R. Ford Library.

31. Handwriting File, Office of the Staff Secretary, 3/4/77, in box 11, Jimmy Carter Library.

32. No change occurred in the distribution of poll information after a chief of staff was added to the unworkable, collegial Carter staff arrangement.

33. Memo for E. Meese from E. Harper, 10/18/82, WHORM doc. #098069, in PR 15 091000-0984466, Ronald Reagan Library.

34. John H. Kessel, "The Structures of the Reagan White House," *American Journal of Political Science* 28 (1984): 231–58.

35. Memo to Carney from Barron, 9/22/89; Memo to OPA Staff from Carney, 9/22/89; Memo to Card, Demarest, Fitzwater, Kristol, Porter, Rogich from Rogers, 10/24/89, in Sig Rogich, David Hansen, Kathryn Moran files, George Bush Library.

36. Only the Ford polling apparatus does not represent a microcosm of the larger White House structure. I would argue this stems from Ford's hybrid design. Many of the sublevels of the Ford White House hierarchy remained from the Nixon White House. Only the top layer was truly redesigned in the "spokes-of-the-wheel" system.

37. Sydney Milkis, "The Presidency and the Political Parties," in *The Presidency and the Political System,* 5th ed., ed. Michael Nelson (Washington DC: CQ Press, 1998), p. 376.

38. Ibid., p. 379.

39. James Davis, *The President as Party Leader* (New York: Praeger, 1992).

40. Thomas Weko, *The Politicizing Presidency: The White House Personnel Office: 1948–1994* (Lawrence, KS: University Press of Kansas, 1995), p. 14.

41. Weko, *Politicizing Presidency.*

42. Harold Bass, "President and National Party Organizations," in *Presidents and Their Parties: Leadership or Neglect?*, ed. Robert Harmel (New York: Praeger, 1984).

43. Richard Pious, *The Presidency* (Boston: Allyn and Bacon, 1996); Thomas Cronin and Michael Genovese, *The Paradoxes of the American Presidency* (New York: Oxford University Press, 1998).

44. Milkis, "Presidency and the Political Parties."

45. Terry Moe, "The Politicized Presidency," in *The New Direction in American Politics*, eds. John Chubb and Paul E. Peterson (Washington, DC: Brookings Institution Press, 1985).

46. Charles Jones, *Passages to the Presidency: From Campaigning to Governing* (Washington DC: Brookings Institution Press, 1998), p. 193.

47. Cronin and Genovese, *Paradoxes*, p. 214.

48. Jacobs and Shapiro, "The Rise of Presidential Polling."

49. Memo to Jones from Slight, 1/6/74, in Chanock box 2 Polls, General Gerald R. Ford Library.

50. Ibid.

51. I found no DNC memos to confirm or deny receipt of information from the White House. Analysis of Recent Polls I in Public Communication, Relations and Appearances CF O/A 34, in Eizenstat box 264, Jimmy Carter Library.

52. Susan Herbst, *Numbered Voices: How Opinion Polling Has Shaped American Politics* (Chicago: University of Chicago Press, 1995); Lawrence Jacobs and Robert Shapiro, "The Politicization of Public Opinion: The Fight for the Pulpit," in *The Social Divide: Political Parties and the Future of Activist Government*, ed. Margaret Weir (Washington, DC: Brookings Institution Press, 1998).

53. Jacobs and Shapiro, *Politicians Don't Pander*. Not until the revolutionary Republican leadership of Newt Gingrich did the leadership make a concerted effort to utilize public opinion poll data in strategizing (Jacobs and Shapiro, "Politicization of Public Opinion"; Lawrence Jacobs, Eric D. Lawrence, Robert Shapiro, and Steven Smith, "Congressional Leadership of Public Opinion," *Political Science Quarterly* 113, no. 1 (1998): 21–41). "Republican leaders in 1995–96 pursue a political strategy that paralleled the Clinton White House's strategy of crafted talk . . . of using polls and focus groups to pinpoint the words, arguments, and symbols to move centrist opinion to support their desired policies" (Jacobs and Shapiro, *Politicians Don't Pander*).

54. Jacobs and Shapiro, "Politicization of Public Opinion."

55. Memo to Carter from Caddell in Cabinet Selection Political Problems, 11/76–1/77, in box 1 Handwriting File, 12/7/76.

56. Memo to Carter from Caddell in Caddell, Patrick 12/76–1/77, in box 1 Handwriting File, 1/10/77.

57. Milkis, "Presidency and the Political Parties," p. 379.

58. Davis, *President as Party Leader.*

59. Richard Neustadt, "Foreword," in *Chief of Staff: Twenty-Five Years of Managing the Presidency,* eds. Samuel Kernell and Samuel Popkin (Berkeley, CA: University of California Press, 1986), p. 4.

60. Ibid., p. 2.

61. Carter's collegial arrangement originally did not include a chief of staff. Bowing to organizational stresses, Carter eventually appointed Hamilton Jordan to the position. As Table 2.1 demonstrates, Jordan was also actively involved in the polling apparatus.

62. Kernell and Popkin, eds., *Chief of Staff,* p. 208.

63. For clarity, I call this office the Domestic Policy Office, as it was known as the Domestic Counsel under Nixon, the Domestic Policy Staff (DPS) under Carter, and both the Office of Policy Development (OPD) and Office of Planning and Evaluation (OPE) under Reagan.

64. John H. Kessel, *The Domestic Presidency: Decision Making in the White House* (North Scituate, MA: Duxbury Press, 1975), p. 19.

65. Jon Bond and Richard Fleisher, *The President in the Legislative Arena* (Chicago: University of Chicago Press, 1990); Mark Peterson, *Legislating Together: The White House and Capitol Hill from Eisenhower to Reagan* (Cambridge, MA: Harvard University Press, 1990). Jacobs, Lawrence, Shapiro, and Smith, "Congressional Leadership."

66. Jacobs and Shapiro, *Politicizing the Presidency;* Jacobs, Lawrence, Shapiro, and Smith, "Congressional Leadership."

67. President Ford declared "no new starts" of domestic programs, thereby minimizing the role of all policy specialists (Peterson, *Legislating Together*).

68. This study only includes domestic policy memos; secretaries of state in the Nixon, Ford, and Carter administrations did receive and exchange polling data.

69. William Lammers and Michael Genovese, *The Presidency and Domestic Policy: Comparing Leadership Styles from FDR to Clinton* (Washington DC: CQ Press, 2000).

70. Ibid. p. 4; Stephen Skowronek, *The Politics Presidents Make: Leadership from John Adams to George Bush* (Cambridge, MA: Harvard University Press, 1993).

71. Lammers and Genovese, *Presidency and Domestic Policy,* p. 4.

72. Lawrence Jacobs and Robert Shapiro, "Issues, Candidate Image and Priming: The Use of Private Polls in Kennedy's 1960 Presidential Campaign," *American Political Science Review* 88 (September 1994): 527–40; Jacobs and Shapiro, "The Rise of Presidential Polling."

73. Jacobs and Shapiro, "The Rise of Presidential Polling," p. 176.

74. WHSF Haldeman box 334, 4/3/71, Nixon Presidential Materials.

75. By 1972 the Nixon administration had replaced Derge with Teeter, who also worked for Presidents Ford and Bush. While working for the Ford administration, Teeter subcontracted regional polls to Wirthlin's firm, Decision Management Information (DMI). In a memo from Jerry Jones to Fed Slight, dated 1/6/74, Jones indicated that the Republican National Committee relied primarily on Teeter and Market Opinion Research (MOR), but was considering Wirthlin and his firm, in Chanock box 2, Polls, General, Gerald R. Ford Library. On 1/27/75, Wirthlin had detailed a proposal and received a contract for the purchase of poll data and analysis. The Ford White House continued to discuss the possibility of hiring Wirthlin's firm and continued to purchase polls and analysis until 9/17/75. In a memo to Donald Rumsfeld and Richard Cheney, Jerry Jones informed his superiors that Wirthlin agreed to poll for Ronald Reagan from 9/75 to 1/76 to determine the viability of a run for the Republican nomination, in Cheney box 17 Polling, Gerald R. Ford Library. Naturally, the Ford White House ended contact with Wirthlin and his polling firm.

76. "Presidential Survey Research Proposal," in Hartmann box 34, Gerald R. Ford Library.

77. "Public Relations Public Opinion Polls" memo to Dick Cheney from Dave Gergen, 3/2/76, PR 15, box 42, Gerald R. Ford Library.

78. For an example of the Wirthlin charts, 12/3/81, in PR 015, box 1 056001–063000, Ronald Reagan Library.

79. George Edwards, III, "Frustration and Folly: Bill Clinton and the Public Presidency," in *The Clinton Presidency: First Appraisals,* eds. Colin Campbell and Bert Rockman (Chatham, NJ: Chatham House, 1996); Morris, *Behind the Oval Office;* George Stephanopoulos, *All Too Human: A Political Education* (Boston: Little, Brown, 1999).

80. Stephanopoulos, *All Too Human,* p. 335.

81. Morris, *Behind the Oval Office,* p. 41.

82. Stephanopoulos, *All Too Human,* p. 335.

83. Charles Jones, *Passages to the Presidency: From Campaigning to Governing* (Washington, DC: Brookings Institution Press, 1998).

84. David Gergen is the exception, although he entered the Clinton administration in year two. Gergen worked in the Nixon, Ford, and Reagan

administrations before working for President Clinton. Woodward notes that former campaign staffers reacted strongly and negatively to the hiring of Gergen. Not
only was Gergen the "engineer and the spokesman for what Clinton ran against,"
but Gergen also appeared to be stepping on and over the popular George
Stephanopoulos (Bob Woodward, *The Agenda*; Stephanopoulos, *All Too Human*).

85. Woodward, *The Agenda*; Morris, *Behind the Oval Office*;
Stephanopoulos, *All Too Human*.

86. Morris, *Behind the Oval Office*, p. 348.

87. Woodward, *The Agenda*; Morris, *Behind the Oval Office*;
Stephanopoulos, *All Too Human*.

88. Haldeman and Ehrlichman, as well as Strachan, Higby, Colson, and
Chapin, contacted Derge and Teeter directly in the Nixon administration. In the
Ford White House, the list was even narrower, as only Hartmann, Cheney,
Rumsfeld, and Chanock had direct pollster access.

89. Jacobs and Shapiro, "Rise of Presidential Polling."

90. Ibid., p. 173.

91. Memo to Campbell and Granquist from Simmons, 11/27/78, in PR
15 Jimmy Carter Library (emphasis added).

92. Memo to President Carter from Caddell, 1/17/79, in CF o/a box 1
Eizenstat, Jimmy Carter Library.

93. Ibid.

94. Robert Strong, "Recapturing Leadership: The Carter Administration
and the Crisis of Confidence," *Presidential Studies Quarterly* 16 (Fall 1986): 640.

95. Ibid.

96. Ibid., p. 647.

97. Ibid.

98. Series of memos, 3/24/77, in Eizenstat box 264 Pollster's Reports
Public Opinion 2, Jimmy Carter Library. The Republican administrations often
received Harris, Gallup, and Roper poll digests before they went to press, and
often purchased the poll data as well.

99. Memo to Harper from Bauer, 3/29/82, in PR 013 093915, Ronald
Reagan Library.

Chapter 3

1. Burdett Loomis, "The Never Ending Story: Campaigns Without Elections," in *The Permanent Campaign and Its Future,* eds. Norman Ornstein and
Thomas Mann (Washington, DC: Brookings Institution Press, 2000).

2. Samuel Kernell, *Going Public: New Strategies of Presidential Leadership,* 3rd ed. (Washington, DC: CQ Press, 1997).

3. Charles O. Jones, "Preparing for 2001: Lessons from the Clinton Presidency," in *The Permanent Campaign and Its Future,* eds. Norman Ornstein and Thomas Mann (Washington, DC: Brookings Institution Press, 2000), p. 187.

4. This analysis does not include the Clinton administration because the Clinton universe of memoranda is not currently available.

5. For coding purposes, I ignored the larger poll books or replications of entire surveys provided by presidential pollsters because I had no evidence that the staff used the data in that format.

6. The method of issue coding was adopted from Lori Cox Han, *Governing from Center Stage: White House Communication Strategies During the Television Age of Politics* (Cresskill, NJ: Hampton Press, 2001); and Lori Cox NyBlom, "Presidential Rhetoric and Media Agenda Setting: The Presidential Honeymoons of Kennedy, Nixon, Reagan and Clinton," presented at the Annual Meeting of the Midwest Political Science Association, April 10–12, 1997.

7. NyBlom, "Presidential Rhetoric and Media Agenda Setting," p. 13.

8. Ibid. In addition to NyBlom's categories, the category Economic Affairs was added to capture references to "how the president was handling the economy," a typical opinion reference. Clearly this opinion information lacks specificity, but remains relevant to the president and his agenda.

9. Of course, my analysis does not account for any additional verbal discussions of Popularity. However, given the limited amount of written discussions, it is unlikely that there would be enough verbal linking of popularity with decisions to challenge these findings.

10. The frequency of references comes from my sentence-level coding analysis. It could be argued that the increase in Policy references over Popularity references comes from the additional verbiage and additional questions it would take to cite Policy opinion in contrast to Popularity opinion. However the staff members who are referencing data are choosing to cite the material; it is the *choice* that my analysis seeks to capture. These administrations have a multitude of data in the polling books and materials described in Chapter 2; it is the decision to exchange this particular information that is central to my analysis. Thus, more than one reference to Policy data indicates greater attention by the staff.

11. Figure 3.1 reflects the fact that Table 3.3 sums across and not down; poll question usage is specific to each presidency. All values within a category are independent of each other, and all data within a presidency are related. Figure 3.1 visually demonstrates the appearance of trends in question type usage over time. The percentage totals of question type, listed in Table 3.2, are not nearly as useful a measure because they provide no trend data. Figure 3.1 demonstrates how presidential usage of opinion data changed over time, for each question type.

12. Mann-Kendall test for trends: $S = \Sigma \, \Sigma \, sgn(x_j - x_k)$, where S is the test statistic. See Richard Gilbert, *Statistical Methods for Environmental Pollution Monitoring* (New York: Van Nostrand, Reinhold, 1987), for a complete description of the test.

13. The observed probability levels (p) are as follows: for Policy, $p = .01$; for Popularity, $p = .04$; for Personal, $p = .59$. Thus, only the Personal category contains a probability level greater than alpha, which was set at .05. However, within the 99-percent confidence interval, only Policy has a significant trend (upward) with $p = .01$.

14. For this discussion it is enough that the White House is using poll data, and thus believes that poll data can account for the complexities of the political system.

15. Richard Brody, *Assessing the President: The Media, Elite Opinion and Public Support* (Palo Alto, CA: Stanford University Press, 1991), p. 4.

16. Paul Brace and Barbara Hinckley, *Follow the Leader: Opinion Polls and Modern Presidents* (New York: Basic Books, 1992), p. 163.

17. Kernell, *Going Public,* p. 189.

18. George Edwards, III, *At the Margins: Presidential Leadership of Congress* (New Haven, CT: Yale University Press, 1989); Jon Bond and Richard Fleisher, *The President in the Legislative Arena* (Chicago: University of Chicago Press, 1990), p. 29.

19. Mark Peterson, *Legislating Together: The White House and Capitol Hill from Eisenhower to Reagan* (Cambridge, MA: Harvard University Press, 1990).

20. Kernell, *Going Public;* George Edwards, III, *The Public Presidency: The Pursuit of Popular Support* (New York: St. Martin's Press, 1983); Edwards, *At the Margins.*

21. Paul Light, *The President's Agenda: Domestic Policy Choice From Kennedy to Reagan* (Baltimore: Johns Hopkins University Press, 1999); John Kingdon, *Agendas, Alternatives and Public Policies* (Boston: Little, Brown, 1984).

22. Hugh Heclo, "Campaigning and Governing: A Conspectus," in *The Permanent Campaign and Its Future,* eds. Norman Ornstein and Thomas Mann (Washington, DC: Brookings Institution Press, 2000), p. 15.

23. Light, *President's Agenda,* p. 19.

24. Memo to Bush from Teeter, 8/29/91, in Chief of Staff John Sununu Files, Polling (2 of 3), 1991 [1 of 3], CF00473, George Bush Library.

25. Memo to Neustadt, Onek, and Lemle from Steichen, 1/13/78, in box 59, Government Reform—Neustadt, Jimmy Carter Library.

26. Kernell, *Going Public.*

27. Environment Memo, in White House Central Files, box 4 Anderson, Nixon Presidential Materials.

28. Public Relations $p = .04$; Constituency Building $p = .24$; Information Gathering $p = .18$; Program Development $p = .24$. When alpha is set at .05 for a 95-percent confidence test, however, the Public Relations category exhibits a trend (downward), with $p = .04$. With the Bush data removed, at the 95-percent confidence interval, the Public Relations category, as with the other three categories, exhibits no trends either upward or downward.

29. Marija Norusis, *SPSS for Windows: Base System User's Guide Release 6.0* (Chicago: SPSS Inc., 1993), p. 213.

30. Ibid.

Chapter 4

1. Hugh Heclo, "Campaigning and Governing: A Conspectus," in *The Permanent Campaign and Its Future,* eds. Norman Ornstein and Thomas Mann (Washington, DC: Brookings Institution Press, 2000).

2. Ibid. p. 11.

3. John H. Kessel, *Presidential Campaign Politics: Coalition Strategies and Citizen Response,* 3rd ed. (Chicago: Dorsey Press, 1988).

4. Kessel, *Presidential Campaign Politics,* p. 141.

5. Martin Wattenberg, *The Rise of Candidate-Centered Politics: Presidential Elections of the 1980s* (Cambridge, MA: Harvard University Press, 1991), p. 162.

6. Memo to Higby from Strachan, 6/8/71, in WHSF Haldeman box 334, Nixon Presidential Materials.

7. Memo to Haldeman from Moore, 12/20/70, in WHSF Haldeman box 141, Nixon Presidential Materials.

8. Memo to Ehrlichman from Butterfield, 7/15/69, in Polls, Nixon Presidential Materials.

9. Memo to Higby from Haldeman, 7/31/70, in WHSF Haldeman box 403, Derge Poll File, Nixon Presidential Materials.

10. Memo to Rumsfeld, Cheney from Goldwin, 9/30/75, in Robert Goldman Papers box 26, Norman Nie, Gerald R. Ford Library.

11. Ibid.

12. Memo to Dent from Fisher, 11/1/69, in WHSF Dent box 8, Middle America, Nixon Presidential Materials. Joel Fisher summarized Scammon's comments from a meeting earlier that day in this memorandum to Harry Dent.

13. Memo to Cashen from Nathan, 11/3/69, in WHSF Dent box 8, Nixon Presidential Materials.

14. Memo to Ehrlichman from Nixon, 3/10/73, in WHSF Ehrlichman box 18, Nixon Presidential Materials.

15. Presidential Survey Research Proposal, in Hartmann Papers box 34 (2), Gerald R. Ford Library.

16. Memo to Cheney from Teeter, 11/12/75, in Hartmann Papers box 163 Public Opinion Polling, General (1), Gerald R. Ford Library.

17. Ibid.

18. "Responses to Cynicism Items," 2/75, in Teeter box 51, U.S. National, Forward and Overview, Gerald R. Ford Library.

19. Memo to Carter from Caddell, 12/7/76, Cabinet Selection, Political Problems, in 11/76–1/77, box 1 Handwriting File, p. 11, Jimmy Carter Library.

20. Ibid., p. 13.

21. Ibid., p. 15.

22. Herbert B. Asher, *Presidential Elections and American Politics: Voters, Candidates, and Campaigns Since 1952*, 5th ed. (Pacific Grove, CA: Brooks Cole, 1992), p. 168.

23. Cambridge Report, First Quarter 1977, in Pat Caddell Energy Material, 2 in Rafshoon box 24, Jimmy Carter Library.

24. Ibid.

25. Lester Seligman and Cary Covington, *The Coalitional Presidency* (Chicago: Dorsey Press, 1989), p. 13.

26. Memo to the Senior Staff from Beal, 12/21/81, in PR 15 050001–56000 doc. #0533818, Ronald Reagan Library.

27. Memo for File from Harper, 6/24/82, Pr 15 068001–073000, doc. #072629, Ronald Reagan Library.

28. Memo to Wirthlin from Burgess, 7/22/81, in PR 15, doc. #034283, Ronald Reagan Library.

29. Ibid.

30. Memo to Harper from Bauer, 3/29/82, in PR 15, doc. #093915, Ronald Reagan Library.

31. Memo to Meese, Baker, Deaver from Beal, 10/2/81, in SP 230, doc. #580230, Ronald Reagan Library.

32. Ibid.

33. Ibid.

34. Memo to Meese, Baker, Deaver, Clark from Beal, 3/12/82, in Strategic Evaluation Memorandum #13, Ronald Reagan Library.

35. Memo to Meese, Baker, Deaver from Wirthlin, 2/2/82, in PR 15, doc. #061990, Ronald Reagan Library.

36. Memo to Sununu from Demarest, in Sununu box 3, Persian Gulf Working Groups, OA/ID, CF 00472, George Bush Library.

37. 1988 Presidential Election Thematic Components, in Sununu box 13, 1990 Polling, OA/ID, CF 00153 1 of 3, p. 6, George Bush Library.

38. Ibid., p. 9.

39. Memo to Porter from Goldstein, 9/28/90, in Ed Goldstein Files Public Opinion, 1991, OA/ID 06681 2 of 2, George Bush Library.

40. Memo to Card, Demarest, Fitzwater, Kristol, Porter, and Rogich from Rogers, 10/24/89, in Sig Rogich Files, Campaign Polls, OA/ID 04732 1 of 2, George Bush Library; memo to Darman from Scully, 4/26/91, in Sununu polling 2 of 3, p. 199, George Bush Library.

41. Stephen Wayne, *The Road to the White House 1996: The Politics of Presidential Elections* (New York: St Martin's Press, 2000); George Edwards, "Frustration and Folly: Bill Clinton and the Public Presidency," in *The Clinton Presidency: First Appraisals*, eds. Colin Campbell and Bert Rockman (Chatham, NJ: Chatham House, 1996).

42. Edwards, "Frustration and Folly," p. 236.

43. Wayne, *Road to the White House.*

44. Ibid.

45. Craig Allen Smith, "Redefining the Rhetorical Presidency," in *The Clinton Presidency: Images, Issues and Communication Strategies,* eds. Robert E. Denton and Rachel Holloway (Westport, CT: Praeger, 1996), p. 228; Richard Cohen, *Changing Course in Washington: Clinton and the New Congress* (New York: Macmillan, 1994).

46. Richard Morris, *Behind the Oval Office: Getting Reelected Against All Odds* (Los Angeles: Renaissance, 1999), p. 409. The Nixon, Ford, and Carter administrations did not utilize focus groups at all. Reagan and Bush appeared to have employed focus groups in their campaigns, but I did not find more than occasional references to them in the White House memoranda.

47. Morris, *Behind the Oval Office,* p. 361.

48. Ibid., p. 363.

49. George Stephanopoulos, *All Too Human: A Political Education* (Boston: Little, Brown, 1999), p. 334.

50. Thomas Edsall, "Confrontation Is the Key to Clinton's Popularity; Adviser Morris's Strategy Proves Inconsistent," *Washington Post,* 24 December 1995, sec A, p. 6.

51. Morris, *Behind the Oval Office,* p. 208.

52. Edsall, "Confrontation Is the Key."

53. Gary King and Lyn Ragsdale, *The Elusive Executive: Discovering Statistical Patterns in the Presidency* (Washington, DC: CQ Press, 1988).

54. Ibid.

55. President Ford had only slightly more appearances in front of common and constituent audiences than total appearances before partisan audiences.

56. King and Ragsdale, *Elusive Executive,* p. 274; Lyn Ragsdale, *Vital Statistics on the Presidency* (Washington, DC: CQ Press, 1996).

Chapter 5

1. Deborah Stone, *The Policy Paradox* (New York: HarperCollins, 1997), p. 7.

2. Ibid. p. 11.

3. Paul Light, *The President's Agenda: Domestic Policy Choice From Kennedy to Reagan,* rev. ed. (Baltimore: Johns Hopkins University Press, 1999), p. 3.

4. William Lammers and Michael Genovese, *The Presidency and Domestic Policy: Comparing Leadership Styles From FDR to Clinton* (Washington, DC: CQ Press, 2000).

5. Sidney Blumenthal, "Marketing the President," *New York Times Magazine,* 13 September 1981, p. 43.

6. Light, *President's Agenda,* pp. 41–43; see also James Pfiffner, *The Strategic Presidency: Hitting the Ground Running* (Chicago: Dorsey Press, 1988).

7. The Clinton administration is not included in this assessment, as the memos from that administration are not currently available. The curves do not begin at zero because the totals of polling usage represent year-end totals.

8. Light, *The President's Agenda.*

9. Ibid., p. 41.

10. Although Nixon staff usage peaks in the third year, I contend that the delay stems from having to establish polling as an institutional feature. Polling was a new governing tool in 1969, and innovation takes time. Contrarily, the following three administrations began their tenure with poll familiarity (Ford inherited what was left of Nixon's staff and poll apparatus; Carter and Reagan retained their extensive campaign poll organizations into the governing period).

11. Diane J. Heith, "Polling for Policy: Public Opinion and Presidential Leadership" (Ph.D. diss., Brown University, 1997). I base my assessment of campaign polls on polls done during the years 1971, 1972, 1975, 1976, 1979, 1980, 1983, and 1984. Data sources: Nixon Presidential Materials; Gerald R. Ford Library; Jimmy Carter Library; Ronald Reagan Library.

12. Kathryn Dunn Tenpas, *Presidents as Candidates: Inside the White House for the Presidential Campaign* (New York: Garland, 1997).

13. Federal Election Commission, party disclosure documents, 1980–2000.

14. Pfiffner, *Strategic Presidency;* Charles Jones, *Passages to the Presidency: From Campaigning to Governing* (Washington, DC: Brookings Institution Press, 1998).

15. White House Communications Director George Stephanopoulos quoted in Thomas Friedman and Maureen Sown, "Amid Setbacks, Clinton Team Seeks to Shake Off the Blues," *New York Times,* 25 April 1993, sec. A, p. 12.

16. Light, *President's Agenda;* John Kingdon, *Agendas, Alternatives and Public Policies* (Boston: Little, Brown, 1984).

17. Light, *President's Agenda,* p. 93.

18. This was not the case with Bush and the entitlement issue; only 40 percent of the questions were alternative.

19. Light, *President's Agenda,* p. 18.

20. Memo to Wexler from Hartley, 12/4/78, in PR 15, Jimmy Carter Library.

21. Anonymously quoted in Light, *President's Agenda,* p. 93.

22. Memo to Holiday from Bush, 8/5/91, in PR 15 box 157, 26668855–2999372, George Bush Library.

23. Aaron Wildavsky, *Speaking Truth to Power* (Boston: Little, Brown, 1979), p. 42.

24. Light, *President's Agenda,* p. 105.

25. Memo to Erhlichman, Harlow, Kissinger, Klein, and Ziegler from Haldeman, 12/18/69, in WHSF Haldeman box 141, Nixon Presidential Materials.

26. Anonymous memo, 2/74, in Hartmann box 34, Presidential Survey Research (2), Gerald R. Ford Library.

27. Jeffrey E. Cohen, "Presidential Rhetoric and the Public Agenda," *American Journal of Political Science* 39 (1995): 87–107; Jeffrey Cohen and John Hamman, "Beyond Popularity: Presidential Ideology and the Public Mood, 1956–1989," prepared for the Annual Meeting of the American Political Science Association, September 1–4, 1996; Jeffrey E. Cohen, *Presidential Responsiveness and Public Policy Making* (Ann Arbor, MI: University of Michigan Press, 1997).

28. Memo to Cheney from Teeter, 12/24/75, in Chanock box 4, Teeter Memos (2), Gerald R. Ford Library.

29. White paper on the environment, in White House Central Files box 4 Anderson, Nixon Presidential Materials.

30. Ibid.

31. Memo to Ehrlichman from Nixon, in WHSF box 18 Ehrlichman, 12/28/72, Nixon Presidential Materials.

32. Memo to Valis from Knauer, 4/7/76, in Wayne Valis Files box 12, Gerald R. Ford Library.

33. Ibid.

34. Memo to Meese, Baker, Deaver, and Clark from Beal, 3/12/82, in PR 15, Ronald Reagan Library.

35. Memo to senior staff from Ursomarso, 4/28/81, in PR 15, doc. #081907, Ronald Reagan Library.

36. Memo to the president from Hutcheson, 6/10/77, in PR 15, Jimmy Carter Library.

37. Anonymous memo, in Hartmann box 34, Presidential Survey Research (2), Gerald R. Ford Library.

38. Light, *President's Agenda;* Jimmy Carter, *Keeping Faith: Memoirs of a President* (New York: Bantam Books, 1982).

39. The People's Program was part of the Domestic Policy Staff, run by Richard Neustadt, Jr. The program was designed to eliminate the insulation between the president and his constituents. In addition to traditional forms of contact, this program sought different ways, including polling and the town hall meeting, to routinely connect the president to public wants and desires. The goal was to provide a legitimate interaction between leader and followers.

40. Memo to Eizenstat from Caddell, 8/9/77, in CF O/A 743, box 1 Eizenstat, Jimmy Carter Library.

41. Ibid.

42. Memo to Darman from Clarkson, 11/17/82, in doc. #098467SS, Ronald Reagan Library.

43. Memo from Steeper, 1/9/91, in Sununu Polling 1 of 3, 1991, OAID CF 00473, 1 of 4, George Bush Library.

44. "Energy: Shortages of Supplies and Credibility," in Pat Caddell Energy material 2, box 24 Rafshoon, p. 168, Jimmy Carter Library.

45. Daniel Yankelovich, *Coming to Public Judgment: Making Democracy Work in a Complex World* (Syracuse, NY: Syracuse University Press, 1991).

46. Ibid. p. 5.

47. Memo to Darman from Clarkson, 11/17/82, in doc. #098467SS, Ronald Reagan Library.

48. Ibid.

49. Samuel Kernell, *Going Public: New Strategies of Presidential Leadership,* 3rd ed. (Washington, DC: CQ Press, 1997), p. 148.

50. Kernell, *Going Public;* Blumenthal, "Marketing the President." The goal, of course, is different—the goal is winning. This will be discussed in Chapter 6.

51. Blumenthal, "Marketing the President," p. 43.

52. Pfiffner, *Strategic Presidency.*

53. Ibid., p. 158.

54. Light, *President's Agenda,* p. 155.

55. "The Public Appraises the Nixon Administration and Key Issues," from Derge, 5/70, in Polls, Nixon Presidential Materials.

56. "Government Spending," 12/72, in White House Special Files, Haldeman box 170, Nixon Presidential Materials.

57. Memo to Bush from Wray, 8/3/89, in PR 13 062870–0609SS, George Bush Library.

58. "Public Supports Nixon on No New Taxes, Holding Down Spending," 3/21/73, in White House Special Files, Haldeman box 170, Nixon Presidential Materials.

59. Memo to Richard Richards from Wirthlin, 10/7/81, in PR 15, box 1 044601–050000, doc. #045132, Ronald Reagan Library.

60. Memo to Cheney from Chanock, 11/26/75, in Chanock box 2, Polls, General (2), Gerald R. Ford Library.

61. Memo to Cheney from Teeter, 12/24/75, in Chanock box 4, Teeter Memo Public Opinion Data (2), Gerald R. Ford Library; Gerald Ford, *Papers of the President,* 1976.

62. Jeffrey Tulis, *The Rhetorical Presidency* (Princeton, NJ: Princeton University Press, 1987).

63. Memo to Cheney from Teeter, 12/24/75, in Chanock box 4, Teeter Memo Public Opinion Data (2), Gerald R. Ford Library.

64. Caddell originally pitched his tale of woe to President Carter in a January memo. Receiving no presidential response, Caddell related his information to sympathizers with the President's ear, in April 1979 (Robert Strong, "Recapturing Leadership: The Carter Administration and the Crisis of Confidence," *Presidential Studies Quarterly* 16 [Fall 1986]: 636–650).

65. Memo to Carter from Caddell, 1/1/7/79, in CF O/A 743 box 1 Eizenstat, Jimmy Carter Library.

66. Memo for Distribution from Rafshoon in Public Support for the President's Energy Plan in box 44 Rafshoon, Jimmy Carter Library.

67. Ibid.

68. Memo to the president from Hutcheson, 6/10/77, in PR 15, Jimmy Carter Library.

69. Briefing Book, White House Governors Conference on Energy, July 8–9, 1977, in Rafshoon box 43, Jimmy Carter Library.

70. Memo to Ferrara from Harper, 11/18/82, in PR 15 doc. #105906, Ronald Reagan Library.

71. Memo to Sununu from Rogers, 6/25/90, in Sununu box 3, 1990 Polling OA/ID CF 00153, 2 of 3, George Bush Library.

72. Memo to Nixon from Dent, 1/9/70, in WHSF Haldeman box 403, Nixon Presidential Materials. This poll was of Minnesota voters and not the nation.

73. Briefing Book, White House Governors Conference on Energy, July 8–9, 1977, in Rafshoon box 43, Jimmy Carter Library.

74. Ibid.

75. Gary King and Lyn Ragsdale, *The Elusive Executive: Discovering Statistical Patterns in the Presidency* (Washington, DC: CQ Press, 1988). See Table 5.3.

76. Memo to Mondale from Harrison, 3/17/79, in PR 15, Jimmy Carter Library.

77. Gallup Poll Game Plan, in WHSF Chapin box 22, Nixon Presidential Materials. This memo has no date provided. However, based on Haldeman's notes, the memo was written soon after the "Silent Majority" Speech (address to the nation on the war in Vietnam, November 3, 1969), most likely as soon as these Gallup figures were known.

78. The blatant distribution of positive poll data was also found in the Johnson administration. Jacobs and Shapiro note that "Johnson suspended his links" to his pollster due to overexposure (Lawrence Jacobs and Robert Shapiro, "The Rise of Presidential Polling: The Nixon White House in Historical Perspective," *Public Opinion Quarterly* 59 [Summer 1995], p. 183). Haldeman noted in his diary, February 3, 1969, that Nixon wanted to avoid LBJ's boasting of positive poll results (H. R. Haldeman, *The Haldeman Diaries: Inside the Nixon White House* [New York: Berkeley Books, 1995], p. 35). The concern for poor publicity apparently faded nine months later when the Nixon administration worked so diligently to release its own positive popularity figures.

79. Survey of Congressional Case Work Fact Sheet, 10/77, in PR 15, Jimmy Carter Library.

80. Memo to Powell from Pettigrew, 10/6/77, in PR 15, Jimmy Carter Library.

81. Memo to Senior Staff from Darman, 7/15/82, in SP 644 doc. #085240PD, Ronald Reagan Library.

82. Ibid.

83. Ibid.

84. Letter to Gray from Gable, 1/30/89, in PR 14 box 156, 003204–069838SS, George Bush Library.

85. Memo to HR Haldeman from Safire, in WHSF Haldeman box 141, Nixon Presidential Materials.

86. Memo to Richards from Wirthlin, 10/7/81, in box 1 PR 15, doc. #045132, Ronald Reagan Library.

87. Initial Aggregate Results, Eagle IX, 7/81, in box 1 PR 15 doc. #044601–05000, Ronald Reagan Library.

88. Memo to Richards from Wirthlin, 10/7/81, in box 1 PR 15, 044601–50000 doc. #045132, Ronald Reagan Library.

89. Memo to Calloway from Teeter, 12/5/75, in Chanock box 4, Teeter Memoranda (3), Gerald R. Ford Library.

90. Memo to Jerry Jones from Slight, 1/28/75, in Chanock box 2, Polls, General, Gerald R. Ford Library.

91. Memo to Cheney from Gergen, 6/21/76, in PR 15 box 42, Public Relations Public Opinion Polls, Ronald Reagan Library.

92. Memo to President Bush, Card from Wray, 8/6/89, in PR 13, 062870–06609SS, George Bush Library.

93. Memo to Bush from Rogich, 10/30/90, in Sig Rogich files, Campaign Polls, OA/ID 04732 1 of 2, George Bush Library.

94. Memo to Bush from Rogich, 7/3/90, in PR 15, 14880255–187932SSS, George Bush Library.

95. Memo to Baker, Deaver, Duberstein, Darman, and Fuller from Gergen, 9/12/83, doc. #171615, Ronald Reagan Library.

96. Ibid.

97. James W. Ceaser, "The Reagan Presidency and American Public Opinion," in *The Reagan Legacy: Promise and Performance,* ed. Charles O. Jones (Chatham, NJ: Chatham House, 1988).

98. Letter to Powell from Watson, 4/22/77, in PR 15 box 76, Jimmy Carter Library.

99. Memo to Bush from Teeter, 12/13/90, in Sununu box 13, 1990 polling OA/ID CF 00153, 1 of 3, George Bush Library.

100. Memo to Chapin, Colson, Dent, Keogh, Klein, Nofziger, Safire, and Ron Ziegler from Magruder, in White House Special Files Chapin box 22, Nixon Presidential Materials.

101. Ibid.

102. Francis Rourke, "Presidentializing the Bureaucracy: From Kennedy to Reagan," in *The Managerial Presidency,* ed. James Pfiffner (Pacific Grove, CA: Brooks/Cole, 1991), pp. 123–34; Richard Harris and Sidney Milkis, *The Politics of Regulatory Change: A Tale of Two Agencies* (New York: Oxford University Press, 1989).

103. Rourke, "Presidentializing the Bureaucracy."

104. Ibid., p. 131.

105. Terry Moe, "The Politicized Presidency," in *The Managerial Presidency,* ed. James Pfiffner (Pacific Grove, CA: Brooks/Cole, 1991), pp. 135–57.

106. Ibid.

107. Patrick Caddell, "Initial Working Paper on Political Strategy," 12/76, in Memoranda Pat Caddell CF O/A 590, Jimmy Carter Library, pp. 42–44.

108. Patrick Caddell, *An Analysis of Political Attitudes in the United States of America,* Vols. I, II, III (Cambridge, MA: Cambridge Research Survey), Jimmy Carter Library, p. 263.

109. Caddell, "Initial Working Paper," pp. 42–44.

110. Memo to all heads from president, 10/28/77, in FG 31, Jimmy Carter Library.

111. Memo re: Survey Information on Government Reorganization in Caddell, Patrick 2, box 33, Chief of Staff Jordan, p. 2, Jimmy Carter Library.

112. Ibid., p. 3.

113. Ibid., p. 6.

114. Ibid., p. 7.

115. Ibid., p. 8.

116. Caddell, *Analysis of Political Attitudes,* p. 269.

117. See Yankelovich, *Coming to Public Judgment,* for a discussion of the difficulties of using polls for issue discussions.

118. Survey of Congressional Casework Fact Sheet, 10/77, in PR 15, Jimmy Carter Library.

119. Memo to all heads from president, 10/28/77, in FG 31, Jimmy Carter Library.

120. Survey of Congressional Casework Fact Sheet, 10/77, in PR 15, Jimmy Carter Library.

121. Letter to Congressman Myers from Pettigrew, 12/16/77, in PR 15, Jimmy Carter Library.

122. Survey of Congressional Casework Fact Sheet, 10/77, in PR 15, Jimmy Carter Library.

123. Memo to all heads from president, 10/28/77, in FG 31, Jimmy Carter Library.

124. Memo to Carter from Eizenstat, 2/21/78, in box 254, Eizenstat Pollster Reports Public Opinion, Jimmy Carter Library.

125. Memo to Carter from Eizenstat, 2/21/78, in box 254, Eizenstat Pollster Reports Public Opinion, p. 43, Jimmy Carter Library.

126. Caddell Poll, 9/77, in box 68, Rafshoon Office of Communication, Jimmy Carter Library.

127. "Survey Questions" memo to Campbell and Granquist from Simmons, 11/27/78, in PR 15, Jimmy Carter Library.

128. Caddell Poll, 9/77, in box 68 Rafshoon Office of Communication, Jimmy Carter Library, p. 13.

129. Survey information on government reorganization, in Caddell, Patrick 2, box 33, Chief of Staff, Jordan, Jimmy Carter Library.

Chapter 6

1. Samuel Kernell, *Going Public: New Strategies of Presidential Leadership,* 3rd ed. (Washington, DC: CQ Press, 1997); Jeffrey Tulis, *The Rhetorical Presidency* (Princeton, NJ: Princeton University Press, 1987).

2. Hugh Heclo, "Campaigning and Governing: A Conspectus," in *The Permanent Campaign and Its Future,* eds. Norman Ornstein and Thomas Mann (Washington, DC: Brookings Institution Press, 2000), p. 13.

3. Kathleen McGraw, "Manipulating Public Opinion," in *Understanding Public Opinion,* 2nd ed., eds. Clyde Wilcox and Barbara Norrander (Washington, DC: CQ Press, 2002), p. 267.

4. Kernell, *Going Public.*

5. Ibid.

6. Ibid., p. 3.

7. Ibid., p. 4. Because less than half the eligible voting population typically exercises their right to participate in the constitutionally mandated role for the public, the need to inspire the gumption in citizens to expend the effort to contact their representatives is a herculean task for the president. Thus, as an activity, public relations efforts are an expected form of presidential behavior. As a leadership model, Kernell's "going public" leaves a lot to chance for a strategically minded political actor.

8. Stephen Skowronek, *The Politics Presidents Make: Leadership from John Adams to George Bush* (Cambridge, MA: Harvard University Press, 1993), p. 389.

9. Ibid. p. 390.

10. Kernell, *Going Public,* p. viii.

11. These relevant officials were the vice president, Robert Lipshutz, Hamilton Jordan, Stuart Eizenstat, Anne Wexler, Frank Moore, Jack Watson, Jody Powell, Tim Kraft, Zbigniew Brzezinski, Scott Burnett, Landon Butler, Les Francis, Betty Rainwater, David Rubenstein, Kitty Schirmer, Steve Selig, and Walt Wurfel.

12. Public Support for the President's Energy Plan, in box 44, Rafshoon Office of Communications, Jimmy Carter Library, p. 4.

13. Ibid., p. 3.

14. Memo to Carter from Caddell, "Initial Working Paper on Political Strategy," in 12/10/76–12/21/76 CF O/A, box 4, Staff Office, Powell, Jimmy Carter Library.

15. Ibid.

16. Patrick Caddell, *Initial Working Paper on Political Strategy,* December 1976, in Memoranda Pat Caddell CF O/A 590, p. 46, Jimmy Carter Library (emphasis added).

17. Ibid. (emphasis added).

18. Energy briefing book Governor's Conference on Energy, in box 43 Rafshoon, Jimmy Carter Library.

19. Caddell Poll, 9/77, in box 68, Rafshoon Office of Communications, Jimmy Carter Library; Caddell, Patrick 2, box 33, Chief of Staff Jordan, Jimmy Carter Library.

20. Pat Caddell Energy Material, in Caddell, Patrick 2, box 24, Rafshoon Office of Communication, Jimmy Carter Library.

21. Memo to Copper and Katz from H. Carter, Memo on Energy Plan, 7/15/77, in box 44, Rafshoon Office of Communication, Jimmy Carter Library.

22. Memo to Carter from Watson, Hutcheson, 6/10/77, in PR 15, Jimmy Carter Library.

23. There were twelve major speeches, forty-five interviews and public appearances, and forty-eight news conferences on energy during Jimmy Carter's four years in office. *The Public Papers of the Presidents of the United States: Jimmy Carter, 1977–1980* (Washington, DC: U.S. Government Printing Office, 1979–1981).

24. Public Support for the President's Energy Plan, in box 44, Office of Communication Rafshoon, p. 4, Jimmy Carter Library.

25. Memo to Eizenstat from Stern, 7/11/78, in Eizenstat, box 254, Pollster Reports Public Opinion, Jimmy Carter Library.

26. Fred Greenstein, "The Need for An Early Appraisal of the Reagan Presidency," in *The Reagan Presidency: An Early Assessment,* ed. Fred Greenstein (Baltimore: Johns Hopkins University Press, 1983), p. 15.

27. Kernell, *Going Public,* p. 167.

28. William Greider, "The Education of David Stockman," *Atlantic Monthly,* December 1981, 27.

29. Memo to Bush, Meese, Deaver, Stockamn, Allen, Dole, Fielding, Friersdorf, Garrick, Gergen, Harper, James, Murphy, Nofziger, Weidenbaum, Canzeri, Fuller, Hickey, Hodsoll, McCoy, and Williamson, from Ursomarso, 4/4/81, in PR 15, doc. #081907, Ronald Reagan Library.

30. Ibid., p. 2.

31. Ibid., p. 2.

32. Memo to Gergen from Russo, 5/21/81, in PR 15, Ronald Reagan Library.

33. Initial Aggregate Results Eagle IX, 7/81, in PR 15, 045438, Ronald Reagan Library.

34. Ibid.

35. Ibid.

36. Conference Report, from EM Staff Group Meeting, 6/22/81, in CF 045410, Ronald Reagan Library.

37. Initial Aggregate Results Eagle IX, 7/81, in PR 15, 045438, Ronald Reagan Library.

38. Kernell, *Going Public.*

39. Memo to Meese, Deaver, Baker from Beal, 10/2/81, in SP 230, #580230, Ronald Reagan Library.

40. Memo to Richards from Wirthlin in PR 15, 0611990, Ronald Reagan Library.

41. Memo to Meese, Baker, Deaver, and Clark from Beal, 3/12/82, in Ronald Reagan Library.

42. Ibid., p. 4.

43. Ibid., p. 5 (boldface in original).

44. Kernell, *Going Public*, p. 159.

45. Lori Cox Han, *Governing from Center Stage: White House Communication Strategies During the Television Age of Politics* (Cresskill, NJ: Hampton Press, 2001), p. 211.

46. Richard Cohen, *Washington at Work: Back Rooms and Clean Air* (Needham Heights, MA: Allyn and Bacon, 1995), pp. 54–55.

47. Ibid. p. 51.

48. Paul Quirk, "Divided Government and Cooperative Presidential Leadership," in *The Bush Presidency: First Appraisal*, eds. Colin Campbell and Bert Rockman (Chatham, NJ: Chatham House, 1991); Cohen, *Washington at Work*.

49. Memorandum on the President's Tree Planting Initiative, 7/23/92, *The Public Papers of the Presidents of the United States: George H. Bush, 1989–1992* (Washington, DC: U.S. Government Printing Office, 1990–1993).

50. Bert A. Rockman, "The Leadership Style of George Bush," in *The Bush Presidency: First Appraisals*, eds. Colin Campbell and Bert Rockman (Chatham, NJ: Chatham House, 1991).

51. *Public Papers of the Presidents: George H. Bush*.

52. These are not the questions actually asked by the pollster, just the framework provided by the Bush people. Letter to Jan Lohuizen (MOR) from Goldstein, 5/29/90, in Emily Mead Polls OA/ID 075974, George Bush Library.

53. Memo to Porter, Gorman, Pinkerton, and Mead from Goldstein, 8/7/90, in PR 14 box 156, 194820, George Bush Library.

54. Ibid.

55. Ibid.

56. Memo to Pinkerton from Mead in Emily Mead Files, 10/15/90, Polls OA/ID 07594, George Bush Library.

57. Memo to Cicconi from Mead, 10/10/90, in PR 14 box 19, 194826, George Bush Library. Mead also included a cute Ziggy cartoon on tree planting.

58. Memo to Bush from Porter, 10/29/90, PR 14 box 156, 186526SS, George Bush Library.

59. Ibid.

60. Memo to Porter from Mead, 9/8/91, in Emily Mead Polls OA/ID 07594, George Bush Library (boldface in original).

61. Memo to Porter from Mead, 9/8/91, in Emily Mead Polls OA/ID 07594, George Bush Library (underline in original).

62. Ibid.

63. Benjamin Ginsberg and Martin Shefter, *Politics by Other Means: Politicians, Prosecutors and the Press from Watergate to Whitewater,* rev. ed. (New York: W. W. Norton, 1999).

64. Morris does note, however, that Erskine Bowles, Bill Curry, Don Baer, and Bruce Reed were supportive of a balanced budget (Richard Morris, *Behind the Oval Office: Getting Reelected Against All Odds* [Los Angeles: Renaissance, 1999]).

65. Morris, *Behind the Oval Office,* p. 161 (italics in original).

66. Ibid., p. 165.

67. George Stephanopoulos, *All Too Human: A Political Education* (Boston: Little, Brown, 1999), p. 350.

68. Ibid., p. 358.

69. An excellent discussion of the Republican stand can be found in Linda Killian, *The Freshman: What Happened to the Republican Revolution* (Boulder, CO: Westview Press, 1998).

70. Morris, *Behind the Oval Office,* p. 183.

71. Ibid., p. 185.

72. Thomas Edsall, "Confrontation Is the Key to Clinton's Popularity; Adviser Morris's Strategy Proves Inconsistent," *Washington Post,* 24 December 1995, sec. A, p. 6.

73. Lawrence Jacobs and Robert Shapiro, *Politicians Don't Pander: Political Manipulation and the Loss of Democratic Responsiveness* (Chicago: University of Chicago Press, 2000).

Chapter 7

1. Thomas Patterson, *Out of Order* (New York: Vintage, 1994).

2. Benjamin Ginsberg and Martin Shefter, *Politics by Other Means: Politicians, Prosecutors and the Press from Watergate to Whitewater,* rev. ed. (New York: W. W. Norton, 1999).

3. Ibid.

4. Richard Nixon, *RN: The Memoirs of Richard Nixon* (New York: Grosset and Dunlap, 1978), pp. 971–72.

5. Gladys Engel Lang and Kurt Lang, *The Battle for Public Opinion* (New York: Columbia University Press, 1983).

6. H. R. Haldeman, *The Haldeman Diaries: Inside the Nixon White House* (New York: Berkeley Books, 1995) p. 574.

7. Ibid., p. 608.

8. Moreover, Haldeman argues that all the subsequent attempts to re-spond to the incident were in fact reactions to negative public relations and not efforts at a "planned, conscious cover-up operation" (Ibid., p. 575).

9. Ibid., p. 625.

10. Ibid., pp. 715–16.

11. Stanley Kutler, ed., *Abuse of Power: The New Nixon Tapes* (New York: Simon and Schuster, 1997), pp. 275–76.

12. Haldeman, *Haldeman Diaries,* p. 803.

13. Kutler, *Abuse of Power,* p. 407.

14. Ibid., p. 409.

15. Ibid., pp. 425–26.

16. Ibid., p. 460.

17. Kurt Lang and Gladys Lang, "Televised Hearings: The Impact Out There," in *Watergate and the American Political Process,* ed. Ronald E. Pynn (New York: Praeger, 1975), p. 71.

18. Lang and Lang, "Televised Hearings," p. 75.

19. Kutler, *Abuse of Power,* p. xv.

20. Ibid.

21. Mark Rozell and Clyde Wilcox, "The Clinton Presidency and the Politics of Scandal," in *The Clinton Scandal and the Future of American Government,* ed. Mark Rozell and Clyde Wilcox (Washington, DC: Georgetown University Press, 2000), p. 3.

22. Ibid.

23. Ibid., pp. 3–4.

24. Ibid., p. 4.

25. Larry Sabato, *Feeding Frenzy: How Attack Journalism Has Trans-formed American Politics* (New York: Free Press, 1991).

26. Richard Berke, "Testing of a President: The Reaction; Split Between Commentators and People May Help Clinton," *New York Times,* 20 August 1998, sec. A, p. 20.

27. By January 1998, Stephanopoulos was a Columbia University pro-fessor and a commentator for ABC News.

28. George Stephanopoulos, *All Too Human: A Political Education* (Boston: Little, Brown, 1999), p. 436.

29. Richard Serrano and Marc Lacey, "Clinton Tells House Panel He Did Not Lie, Obstruct Law Inquiry: Replying in Writing to 81 Questions from GOP Members, President Says He Misled Others But Committed No Crime to Hide Tryst. His Responses Contain No Surprises," *Los Angeles Times,* 28 November 1998, sec. A, p. 1.

30. U.S. House Committee on the Judiciary, Impeachment of William Jefferson Clinton President of the United States Report, 105th Cong., 2d sess., 1998, H. Rept. 105–830, p. 257.

31. Molly Andolina and Clyde Wilcox, "Public Opinion: The Paradoxes of Clinton's Popularity," in *The Clinton Scandal and the Future of American Government,* ed. Mark Rozell and Clyde Wilcox (Washington, DC: Georgetown University Press, 2000), p. 174.

32. Ibid., p. 172.

33. U.S. House Committee on the Judiciary, 1998.

34. Associated Press, "The President's Trial: The 10 Questions Sent to the President From Senate Republicans," *New York Times,* 26 November 1999, sec. A, p. 16.

35. Richard Posner, *An Affair of State: The Investigation, Impeachment, and Trial of President Clinton* (Cambridge, MA: Harvard University Press, 1999).

36. Marc Lacey, "For Managers a Tough Loss to Stomach," *Los Angeles Times,* 11 February 1999, sec. A, p. 1.

37. "Trial of the President; Excerpts of Debate Comments; Be Clinton a Villain or Victim, Most Jurors Toeing the Party Line," *Los Angeles Times,* 12 February 1999, sec A, p. 17.

38. Rozell and Wilcox, "Clinton Presidency."

39. John Zaller, "Monica Lewinsky's Contribution to Political Science," *PS: Political Science and Politics* 31, no. 2 (June 1998): 182–89; Arthur Miller, "Sex, Politics, and Public Opinion: What Political Scientists Really Learned from the Clinton-Lewinsky Scandal," *PS: Political Science and Politics* 32, no. 4 (December 1999): 721–29; Andolina and Wilcox, "Public Opinion."

Chapter 8

1. Richard Morris, *Behind the Oval Office: Getting Reelected Against All Odds* (Los Angeles: Renaissance, 1999), p. 11.

2. Ibid., p. 233.

3. Hugh Heclo, "Campaigning and Governing: A Conspectus," in *The Permanent Campaign and Its Future,* eds. Norman Ornstein and Thomas Mann (Washington, DC: Brookings Institution Press, 2000), p. 29.

4. Ibid., p. 12.

5. Ibid., p. 15.

6. James R. Beniger and Robert Guiffra, Jr., "Public Opinion Polling: Command and Control in Presidential Campaigns," in *Presidential Selection,* eds. Alexander Heard and Michael Nelson (Durham, NC: Duke University Press, 1987), p. 203.

7. Memo to Colson from Chapin, 1/17/72, in WHSF Colson box 99, Nixon Presidential Materials.

8. Memo to Haldeman from Nixon, 12/30/69, in WHSF Haldeman box 403, Nixon Presidential Materials.

9. Memo to Haldeman from Higby, 3/13/73, in WHSF Haldeman box 170, Nixon Presidential Materials.

10. Kathryn Tenpas and Stephen Hess, "Bush's A Team: Just Like Clinton's, But More So," *Washington Post,* 27 January 2002, sec. B, p. 5.

11. Wilson Carey McWilliams, "The Meaning of the Election," in *The Election of 2000,* ed. Gerald M. Pomper (Chatham, NJ: Chatham House, 2001), pp. 171–201.

12. Ibid., p. 184.

13. Ibid., pp. 184–185.

14. Alexis Simendinger, "In His Own (Mixed) Words," *National Journal* (28 April 2001); p. 1249.

15. Ibid.

16. Bill McAllister, "Bush Polls Apart From Clinton in Use of Marketing," *Denver Post,* 17 June 2001, sec. A, p. 14.

17. Sara Fritz, "As Bush Sinks in Polls, He Tries New Directions," *St. Petersburg Times,* 2 July 2002, sec. A, p. 1.

18. Ibid.

19. Dan Balz, "Partisan Divisions Bedevil Bush; Advisors Seek Ways to Redefine Presidency as Popularity Slips," *Washington Post,* 1 July 2001, sec. A, p. 1.

20. Ibid.

21. See Diane J. Heith, *Polling for Policy: Public Opinion and Presidential Leadership* (Ph.D. diss., Brown University, 1997) for a discussion of Caddell's plans.

22. Balz, "Partisan Divisions Bedevil Bush."

23. Lawrence Jacobs and Robert Shapiro, *Politicians Don't Pander: Political Manipulation and the Loss of Democratic Responsiveness* (Chicago: University of Chicago Press, 2000), p. 298.

24. Ibid.

25. Ibid., p. 312.

26. Ibid., p. 321.

27. Memo to Magruder from Khachigian, 12/22/70, in WHSF Khachigian box 12, Nixon Presidential Materials.

28. Memo to Haldeman from Nixon, 1/1/71, in WHSF Haldeman box 141, Nixon Presidential Materials.

29. Memo to Cheney from Chanock, 11/26/74, in Chanock box 2, Polls, General (2)—Gerald R. Ford Library.

30. Memo to Carter from Caddell, 12/7/76, Cabinet Selection, Political Problems, in 11/76–1/77, box 1 Handwriting File, p. 19, Jimmy Carter Library.

Bibliography

Achen, Christopher. "Social Psychology, Demographic Variables, and Linear Regression: Breaking the Iron Triangle in Voting Research." *Political Behavior* 14 (1992): 195–211.

Andolina, Molly, and Clyde Wilcox. "Public Opinion: The Paradoxes of Clinton's Popularity." In *The Clinton Scandal and the Future of American Government,* edited by Mark Rozell and Clyde Wilcox. Washington, DC: Georgetown University Press, 2000.

Asher, Herbert B. *Presidential Elections and American Politics: Voters, Candidates, and Campaigns Since 1952.* 5th ed. Pacific Grove, CA: Brooks Cole, 1992.

Associated Press. "The President's Trial: The 10 Questions Sent to the President From Senate Republicans." *New York Times,* 26 November 1999, sec. A, p. 16.

Balz, Dan. "Partisan Divisions Bedevil Bush; Advisors Seek Ways to Redefine Presidency Slips." *Washington Post,* 1 July 2001, sec. A, p. 1.

Barnes, James. "Clinton's Horse-Race Presidency." *National Journal* 25, no. 22 (May, 29, 1993): pp 1308–12.

Bass, Harold. "President and National Party Organizations." In *Presidents and Their Parties: Leadership or Neglect?,* edited by Robert Harmel. New York: Praeger, 1984.

"Be Clinton a Villain or Victim, Most Jurors Toeing the Party Line." *Los Angeles Times,* 12 February 1999, sec. A, p. 17.

Beniger, James R., and Robert Guiffra, Jr. "Public Opinion Polling: Command and Control in Presidential Campaigns." In *Presidential Selection,* edited by

Alexander Heard and Michael Nelson. Durham, NC: Duke University Press, 1987.

Berke, Richard. "Testing of a President: The Reaction; Split Between Commentators and People May Help Clinton." *New York Times,* 20 August 1998, sec. A, p. 20.

Blumenthal, Sidney. "Marketing the President." *New York Times Magazine,* 13 September 1981, p. 43.

Bonafede, Dom. "Carter and the Polls—If You Live By Them, You May Die By Them." *National Journal* 10, no. 33 (August 19, 1978): 1312.

———. "A Pollster to the President, Wirthlin is Where the Action is." *National Journal* 13, no. 50 (December 12, 1981): 2184.

Bond, Jon, and Richard Fleisher. *The President in the Legislative Arena.* Chicago: University of Chicago Press, 1990.

Brace, Paul, and Barbara Hinckley. *Follow the Leader: Opinion Polls and Modern Presidents.* New York: Basic Books, 1992.

Brody, Richard. *Assessing the President: The Media, Elite Opinion and Public Support.* Palo Alto, CA: Stanford University Press, 1991.

Burke, John. *The Institutional Presidency.* Baltimore: Johns Hopkins University Press, 1992.

———. "The Institutionalized Presidency." In *The Presidency and the Political System.* 5th ed., edited by Michael Nelson. Washington, DC: CQ Press, 1999.

Carter, Jimmy. *Keeping Faith: Memoirs of a President.* New York: Bantam Books, 1982.

Ceaser, James W. "The Reagan Presidency and American Public Opinion." In *The Reagan Legacy: Promise and Performance,* edited by Charles O. Jones. Chatham, NJ: Chatham House, 1988.

Center of Responsive Politics. "All Presidential Candidates: Total Raised and-Spent." Retrieved n.d. from http://www.opensecrets.org

Cohen, Jeffrey E. "Presidential Rhetoric and the Public Agenda." *American Journal of Political Science* 39 (1995): 87–107.

———. *Presidential Responsiveness and Public Policy Making.* Ann Arbor, MI: University of Michigan Press, 1997.

Cohen, Jeffrey, and John Hamman. "Beyond Popularity: Presidential Ideology and the Public Mood, 1956–1989." Prepared for the Annual Meeting of the American Political Science Association, September 1–4, San Francisco, 1996.

Cohen, Richard. *Changing Course in Washington: Clinton and the New Congress.* New York: Macmillan, 1994.

———. *Washington at Work: Back Rooms and Clean Air.* Needham Heights, MA: Allyn and Bacon, 1995.

Converse, Philip E. "The Nature of Belief Systems in Mass Publics." In *Ideology and Discontent,* edited by David Apter, pp. 206–61. New York: Free Press, 1964.

Cornwell, Elmer E., Jr. *Presidential Leadership of Public Opinion.* Bloomington, IN: Indiana University Press, 1965.

Cronin, Thomas, and Michael Genovese. *The Paradoxes of the American Presidency.* New York: Oxford University Press, 1998.

Dahl, Robert. "A Democratic Dilemma: System Effectiveness versus Citizen Participation," *Political Science Quarterly* 109, no. 1 (Spring 1994): 23–34.

Davis, James. *The President as Party Leader.* New York: Praeger, 1992.

Edsall, Thomas. "Confrontation Is the Key to Clinton's Popularity; Advisor Morris's Strategy Proves Inconsistent." *Washington Post,* 24 December 1995, sec. A., p. 6.

Edwards, George, III. *The Public Presidency: The Pursuit of Popular Support.* New York: St. Martin's Press, 1983.

———. *At The Margins: Presidential Leadership of Congress.* New Haven, CT: Yale University Press, 1989.

———. "Frustration and Folly: Bill Clinton and the Public Presidency." In *The Clinton Presidency: First Appraisals,* edited by Colin Campbell and Bert Rockman. Chatham, NJ: Chatham House, 1996.

Edwards, George, III, and Stephen J. Wayne. *Presidential Leadership: Politics and Policy Making.* 5th ed. New York: St. Martin's Press, 1999.

Eisinger, Robert. "Gauging Public Opinion in the Hoover White House: Understanding the Roots of Presidential Polling." *Presidential Studies Quarterly* 30, no. 4 (2000): 643–61.

Eisinger, Robert and Jeremy Brown. "Polling as a Means Toward Presidential Autonomy: Emil Hurja, Hadley Cantril and the Roosevelt Administration." *International Journal of Public Opinion Research* 10 (1998): 237–56.

Federal Election Commission. Party disclosure documents, 1980–2000.

Fenno, Richard. *Home Style: House Members in Their Districts.* Boston: Little, Brown, 1978.

Fried, Amy. *Muffled Echoes: Oliver North and the Politics of Public Opinion.* New York: Columbia University Press, 1997.

Friedman, Thomas, and Maureen Sown. "Amid Setbacks, Clinton Team Seeks to Shake Off the Blues." *New York Times,* 25 April 1993, sec. A, p. 12.

Fritz, Sara. "As Bush Sinks in Polls, He Tries New Directions." *St. Petersburg Times,* 2 July 2002, sec. A., p. 1.

Gilbert, Richard. *Statistical Methods for Environmental Pollution Monitoring.* New York: Van Nostrand, Reinhold, 1987.

Ginsberg, Benjamin. *The Captive Public: How Mass Opinion Promotes State Power.* New York: Basic Books, 1986.

Ginsberg, Benjamin, Theodore Lowi, and Margaret Weir. *We the People: An Introduction to American Politics.* 2nd ed. New York: W. W. Norton, 1999.

Ginsberg, Benjamin, and Martin Shefter. *Politics by Other Means: Politicians, Prosecutors and the Press from Watergate to Whitewater.* Rev. ed. New York: W. W. Norton, 1999.

Greenstein, Fred. "The Need for an Early Appraisal of the Reagan Presidency." In *The Reagan Presidency: An Early Assessment,* edited by Fred Greenstein. Baltimore: Johns Hopkins University Press, 1983.

Greider, William. "The Education of David Stockman," *Atlantic Monthly,* December 1981, 105–128.

Haldeman, H. R. *The Haldeman Diaries: Inside the Nixon White House.* New York: Berkeley Books, 1995.

Han, Lori Cox. *Governing from Center Stage: White House Communication Strategies During the Television Age of Politics.* Cresskill, NJ: Hampton Press, 2001.

Harris, Richard and Sidney Milkis. *The Politics of Regulatory Change: A Tale of Two Agencies.* New York: Oxford University Press, 1989.

Heclo, Hugh. "Campaigning and Governing: A Conspectus." In *The Permanent Campaign and Its Future,* edited by Norman Ornstein and Thomas Mann. Washington, DC: Brookings Institution Press, 2000.

Heith, Diane J. "Polling for Policy: Public Opinion and Presidential Leadership." Ph.D. diss., Brown University, 1997.

———. "Presidential Polling and the Potential for Leadership." In *Presidential Power: Forging the Presidency for the 21st Century,* edited by Lawrence Jacobs, Marth Kumar, and Robert Shapiro. New York: Columbia University Press, 2000.

Herbst, Susan. *Numbered Voices: How Opinion Polling Has Shaped American Politics.* Chicago: University of Chicago Press, 1995.

Hinckley, Ronald. *People, Polls and Policymakers: American Public Opinion and National Security.* New York: Lexington Books, 1992.

Jacobs, Lawrence. "The Recoil Effect: Public Opinion and Policymaking in the U.S. and Britain," *Comparative Politics* (January 1992): 199–217.

Jacobs, Lawrence, Eric D. Lawrence, Robert Shapiro, and Steven Smith. "Congressional Leadership of Public Opinion." *Political Science Quarterly* 113, no. 1 (1998): 21–41.

Jacobs, Lawrence, and Robert Shapiro. "Public Decisions, Private Polls: John F. Kennedy's Presidency." Prepared for the Annual Meeting of the Midwest Political Science Association, Chicago, April 9–11, 1992.

————. "Issues, Candidate Image and Priming: The Use of Private Polls in Kennedy's 1960 Presidential Campaign." *American Political Science Review* 88 (September 1994): 527–40.

————. "The Rise of Presidential Polling: The Nixon White House in Historical Perspective." *Public Opinion Quarterly* 59 (Summer 1995): 163–95.

————. "The Politicization of Public Opinion: The Fight for the Pulpit." In *The Social Divide: Political Parties and the Future of Activist Government,* edited by Margaret Weir. Washington, DC: Brookings Institution Press, 1998.

————. *Politicians Don't Pander: Political Manipulation and the Loss of Democratic Responsiveness.* Chicago: University of Chicago Press, 2000.

Johnson, Richard Tanner. *Managing the White House: An Intimate Study of the President.* New York: Harper and Row, 1974.

Jones, Charles O. "Preparing for 2001: Lessons from the Clinton Presidency." In *The Permanent Campaign and Its Future,* edited by Norman Ornstein and Thomas Mann. Washington, DC: Brookings Institution Press, 2000.

Jones, Charles. *Passages to the Presidency: From Campaigning to Governing.* Washington, DC: Brookings Institution Press, 1998.

Kernell, Samuel. *Going Public: New Strategies of Presidential Leadership.* 3rd ed. Washington, DC: CQ Press, 1997.

Kessel, John H. *The Domestic Presidency: Decision Making in the White House.* North Scituate, MA: Duxbury Press, 1975.

————. "The Structures of the Reagan White House." *American Journal of Political Science* 28 (1984): 231–58.

————. *Presidential Campaign Politics: Coalition Strategies and Citizen Response.* 3rd ed. Chicago: Dorsey Press, 1988.

Killian, Linda. *The Freshman: What Happened to the Republican Revolution.* Boulder, CO: Westview Press, 1998.

King, Gary, and Lyn Ragsdale. *The Elusive Executive: Discovering Statistical Patterns in the Presidency.* Washington, DC: CQ Press, 1988.

Kingdon, John. *Agendas, Alternatives and Public Policies.* Boston: Little, Brown, 1984.

Kumar, Martha. "Presidential Libraries: Gold Mine, Booby Trap or Both." In *Studying the Presidency,* edited by George Edwards and Stephen Wayne. Knoxville, TN: University of Tennessee Press, 1983.

Kutler, Stanley, ed. *Abuse of Power: The New Nixon Tapes.* New York: Simon and Schuster, 1997.

Lacey, Marc. "For Managers a Tough Loss to Stomach." *Los Angeles Times,* 11 February 1999, sec. A, p. 1.

Lammers, William, and Michael Genovese. *The Presidency and Domestic Policy: Comparing Leadership Styles From FDR to Clinton*. Washington, DC: CQ Press, 2000.

Lang, Gladys Engel, and Kurt Lang. *The Battle for Public Opinion*. New York: Columbia University Press, 1983.

Lang, Kurt, and Gladys Lang. "Televised Hearings: The Impact Out There." In *Watergate and the American Political Process*, edited by Ronald E. Pynn. New York: Praeger, 1975.

Light, Paul. *The President's Agenda: Domestic Policy Choice From Kennedy to Reagan*, rev. ed. Baltimore: Johns Hopkins University Press, 1999.

Lippmann, Walter. *Public Opinion*. New York: Harcourt Brace and Co., 1922.

Loomis, Burdett. "The Never Ending Story: Campaigns Without Elections." In *The Permanent Campaign and Its Future*, edited by Norman Ornstein and Thomas Mann. Washington, DC: Brookings Institution Press, 2000.

Lowi, Theodore J. *The Personal President: Power Invested, Promise Unfulfilled*. Ithaca, NY: Cornell University Press, 1985.

Mayhew, David. *Congress: The Electoral Connection*. New Haven, CT: Yale University Press, 1974.

McAllister, Bill. "Bush Polls Apart From Clinton in Use of Marketing." *Denver Post*, 17 June 2001, sec. A, p. 14.

McGraw, Kathleen. "Manipulating Public Opinion." In *Understanding Public Opinion*, 2nd ed., edited by Clyde Wilcox and Barbara Norrander. Washington, DC: CQ Press, 2002.

McWilliams, Wilson Carey. "The Meaning of the Election." In *The Election of 2000*, edited by Gerald M. Pomper. New York: Chatham House, 2001.

Milkis, Sydney. "The Presidency and the Political Parties." In *The Presidency and the Political System*, 5th ed, edited by Michael Nelson. Washington, DC: CQ Press, 1998.

Miller, Arthur. "Sex, Politics, and Public Opinion: What Political Scientists Really Learned from the Clinton-Lewinsky Scandal." *PS: Political Science and Politics* 32, no. 4 (December 1999): 721–29.

Moe, Terry. "The Politicized Presidency." In *The New Direction in American Politics*, edited by John Chubb and Paul E. Peterson. Washington, DC: Brookings, 1985.

———. "The Politicized Presidency." In *The Managerial Presidency*, edited by James Pfiffner. Pacific Grove, CA: Brooks/Cole, 1991.

Morone, James. *The Democratic Wish: Popular Participation and the Limits of American Government*. New York: Basic Books, 1990.

Morris, Richard. *Behind the Oval Office: Getting Reelected Against All Odds.* Los Angeles: Renaissance, 1999.

Murray, Shoon Kathleen, and Peter Howard. "Variation in White House Polling Operations: Carter to Clinton." *Public Opinion Quarterly* 66 (2000): 527–58.

Neustadt, Richard E. "Foreword." In *Chief of Staff: Twenty-Five Years of Managing the Presidency,* edited by Samuel Kernell and Samuel Popkin. Berkeley, CA: University of California Press, 1986.

———. *Presidential Power and the Modern Presidents: The Politics of Leadership from Roosevelt to Reagan.* Rev. ed. New York: Free Press, 1990.

Nixon, Richard. *RN: The Memoirs of Richard Nixon.* New York: Grosset and Dunlap, 1978.

Norusis, Marija. *SPSS for Windows: Base System User's Guide Release 6.0.* Chicago: SPSS Inc., 1993.

NyBlom, Lori Cox. "Presidential Rhetoric and Media Agenda Setting: The Presidential Honeymoons of Kennedy, Nixon, Reagan, and Clinton." Presented at the Annual Meeting of the Midwest Political Science Association, April 10–12, Chicago, 1997.

Patterson, Thomas. *Out of Order.* New York: Vintage, 1994.

Peterson, Mark. *Legislating Together: The White House and Capitol Hill from Eisenhower to Reagan.* Cambridge, MA: Harvard University Press, 1990.

Pfiffner, James. *The Strategic Presidency: Hitting the Ground Running.* Chicago: Dorsey Press, 1988.

Pious, Richard. *The Presidency.* Boston: Allyn and Bacon, 1996.

Popkin, Samuel. *The Reasoning Voter.* Chicago: University of Chicago Press, 1991.

Posner, Richard. *An Affair of State: The Investigation, Impeachment, and Trial of President Clinton.* Cambridge, MA: Harvard University Press, 1999.

Powlick, Philip. "Public Opinion in the Foreign Policy Process: An Attitudinal and Institutional Comparison of the Reagan and Clinton Administrations." Prepared for the Annual Meeting of the American Political Science Association, Chicago, September 1–4, 1995.

Public Papers of the Presidents of the United States: George H. Bush, 1989–1992 (Washington, DC: Government Printing Office, 1990–1993).

Public Papers of the Presidents of the United States: Jimmy Carter, 1977–1980 (Washington, DC: Government Printing Office, 1979–1981).

Quirk, Paul. "Divided Government and Cooperative Presidential Leadership." In *The Bush Presidency: First Appraisal,* edited by Colin Campbell and Bert Rockman. Chatham, NJ: Chatham House, 1991.

Ragsdale, Lyn. *Vital Statistics on the Presidency.* Washington, DC: CQ Press, 1996.

Rockman, Bert A. *The Leadership Question: The Presidency and the American System.* New York: Praeger, 1984.

———. "The Leadership Style of George Bush." In *The Bush Presidency: First Appraisals,* edited by Colin Campbell and Bert Rockman. Chatham, NJ: Chatham House, 1991.

Rourke, Francis. "Presidentializing the Bureaucracy: From Kennedy to Reagan." In *The Managerial Presidency,* edited by James Pfiffner. Pacific Grove, CA: Brooks/Cole, 1991.

Rozell, Mark, and Clyde Wilcox. "The Clinton Presidency and the Politics of Scandal." In *The Clinton Scandal and the Future of American Government,* edited by Mark Rozell and Clyde Wilcox. Washington, DC: Georgetown University Press, 2000.

Sabato, Larry. *Feeding Frenzy: How Attack Journalism Has Transformed American Politics.* New York: Free Press, 1991.

Seligman, Lester, and Cary Covington. *The Coalitional Presidency.* Chicago: Dorsey Press, 1989.

Simendinger, Alexis. "In His Own (Mixed) Words" *National Journal* (28 April 2001): 1249.

Skowronek, Stephen. *The Politics Presidents Make: Leadership from John Adams to George Bush.* Cambridge, MA: Harvard University Press, 1993.

Smith, Craig Allen. "Redefining the Rhetorical Presidency." In *The Clinton Presidency: Images, Issues and Communication Strategies,* edited by Robert E. Denton and Rachel Holloway. Westport, CT: Praeger, 1996.

Stephanopoulos, George. *All Too Human: A Political Education.* Boston: Little, Brown, 1999.

Stone, Deborah. *The Policy Paradox.* New York: Harper Collins, 1997.

Strong, Robert. "Recapturing Leadership: The Carter Administration and the Crisis of Confidence." *Presidential Studies Quarterly* 16 (Fall 1986): 636–50.

Tenpas, Kathryn Dunn. *Presidents as Candidates: Inside the White House for the Presidential Campaign.* New York: Garland, 1997.

Tenpas, Kathryn, and Stephen Hess. "Bush's A Team: Just Like Clinton's, But More So." *Washington Post,* 27 January 2002, sec. B, p. 5.

Tulis, Jeffrey. *The Rhetorical Presidency.* Princeton, NJ: Princeton University Press, 1987.

U.S. House Committee on the Judiciary. Impeachment of William Jefferson Clinton President of the United States Report, 105th Cong., 2d sess., 1998, H. Rept. 105–830, pp. 1–263.

Wattenberg, Martin. *The Rise of Candidate-Centered Politics: Presidential Elections of the 1980s*. Cambridge, MA: Harvard University Press, 1991.

Wayne, Stephen. *The Road to the White House 1996: The Politics of Presidential Elections*. New York: St Martin's Press, 2000.

Weko, Thomas. *The Politicizing Presidency: The White House Personnel Office: 1948–1994*. Lawrence, KS: University Press of Kansas, 1995.

Wildavsky, Aaron. *Speaking Truth to Power*. Boston: Little, Brown, 1979.

Witherspoon, Patricia. *Within These Walls: A Study of Communication Between Presidents and Senior Staffs*. New York: Praeger, 1991.

Woodward, Bob. *The Agenda: Inside the Clinton White House*. New York: Simon and Schuster, 1995.

Yankelovich, Daniel. *Coming to Public Judgment: Making Democracy Work in a Complex World*. Syracuse, NY: Syracuse University Press, 1991.

Zaller, John. "Monica Lewinsky's Contribution to Political Science." *PS: Political Science and Politics* 31, no. 2 (June 1998): 182–89.

Index